בס"ד

Dear Shirley,

שתחי'

For an Esther Chayil who has spent a lifetime devoted to increasing the knowledge of generations of Jewish children. It has been such a priviledge to have gotten to know you this year.

With Best wishes,

Shira Hochheimer
June 2019

Eishes Chayil

ANCIENT WISDOM FOR WOMEN OF TODAY

Eishes Chayil

ANCIENT WISDOM FOR WOMEN OF TODAY

SHIRA HOCHHEIMER

Mosaica Press, Inc.
© 2017 by Shira Hochheimer
Cover Design: Rayzel Broyde
Typesetting: Brocha Mirel Strizower

ISBN-10: 1-946351-06-7
ISBN-13: 978-1-946351-06-7

All rights reserved. No part of this book may be used or reproduced or transmitted in any form or by any means, electronic or mechanical, including photocopying, recording, or by any information storage and retrieval system, without written permission from the publisher.

Published and distributed by:
Mosaica Press, Inc.
www.mosaicapress.com
info@mosaicapress.com

בס"ד

Rabbi Zev Leff
Rabbi of Moshav Matityahu
Rosh HaYeshiva—Yeshiva Gedola Matityahu

הרב זאב לף

מרא דאתרא מושב מתתיהו
ראש הישיבה—ישיבה גדולה מתתיהו

D.N. Modiin 71917   Tel: 08-976-1138 טל'   Fax: 08-976-5326 פקס'   ד.נ. מודיעין 71917

Dear Friends,

I have seen portions of the manuscript "Becoming an Eishes Chayil – A positive journey of growth for all women" by Rebbitzen Shira Hochheimer. The authoress presents a commentary on the verses of Eishes Chayil found in the last chapter of Proverbs. The commentary is culled from traditional sources. She also relates the verses to specific women in history based on a medrash. The authoress presents this information in a manner that is fluent, interesting and informative. She masterfully takes all this theoretical information and relates it to real life situations and provides practical, down to earth sage advice in how to implement these ideas into one's everyday life. She also provides concise questions at the end of each chapter to enable one to ponder how they can successfully use these lessons for personal growth, for marital harmony and how to convey these ideas to one's daughters so they can integrate them as they develop into wives and mothers.

I am truly impressed with the masterful manner that Rebbitzen Hochheimer has woven together this magnificent tapestry and am sure that countless women will benefit greatly from studying this work.

I highly recommend this work as a true Torah perspective on the essence of the true Eishes Chayil and an effective guide to all those who wish to put in the effort to embody these traits to the best of their ability.

May Hashem bless the authoress and her family with life, health and the wherewithal to continue to merit the community in many and varied ways.

Sincerely,
With Torah blessings

Rabbi Zev Leff

From the Desk of
RABBI AHRON LOPIANSKY
Rosh HaYeshiva

בס"ד

21/Sivan/5776

Eishes Chayil is a book bringing together a unique blend of a keen reading of the sources, and a most practical application of it to the realities of life. This is reinforced by the fact that almost all of the illustrations therein are taken from the author's own life and her personal challenges. This book is perhaps a paradigm for the highly accomplished and educated modern woman, who seeks to lead a life with the heart and neshama of our mothers and grandmothers, whilst making use of the opportunities that Hashem has given our generation. She realizes this in a way that brings out the qualities that are uniquely a woman's, rather than a knee jerk imitations of man's religious activities.

It is a book that is strong in its Torah analysis of the sources, teasing out the fuller meaning of the verse and its source; and it is thoroughly grounded in the realities of life. In our generation, when so many Orthodox women are struggling to define their role in the religious community, this will serve both an intellectual and practical guide.

אל יגיע שכם וגו׳.
Ahron Shraga Lopiansky

YESHIVA OF GREATER WASHINGTON – TIFERES GEDALIAH
1216 ARCOLA AVENUE, SILVER SPRING, MD 20902 ■ 301-649-7077 ■ WWW.YESHIVA.EDU

Table of Contents

Dedication 9
Acknowledgments 13
The Text of Eishes Chayil 16
The Midrash on Eishes Chayil 18
Introduction 26
Chapter 1: First Impressions 31
Chapter 2: The Midrash 37
Chapter 3: A Woman of Valor — A Partnership 44
Chapter 4: Trust 64
Chapter 5: Consistent Kindness 81
Chapter 6: Initiative 95
Chapter 7: Effort 109
Chapter 8: Preparation 130
Chapter 9: Vision 146
Chapter 10: Strength 158
Chapter 11: Self-Actualization 170
Chapter 12: Creative Femininity 187
Chapter 13: As a Charitable Woman (Kindness) 203
Chapter 14: As a Homemaker (Preparation/Responsibility) 218
Chapter 15: As an Individual (Self-Respect) 233
Chapter 16: As a Wife (Supportiveness) 244
Chapter 17: As a Professional (Self-Sacrifice) 260

Chapter 18: As a G-d-Fearing Woman (Priorities) 274
Chapter 19: As a Woman of Intelligence (Communication) 286
Chapter 20: As a Mother (Involvement) 306
Chapter 21: Results: Recognition 319
Chapter 22: Results: Excellence. 329
Chapter 23: Results: True Beauty and True Rewards. 339
Conclusion. 356
Appendix A: Glossary of Jewish Names and Terms. 357
Appendix B: Personalities and Sources 364
Appendix C: The Eishes Chayil Chaburah 369

Dedication

With tremendous gratitude to my parents, Hillel and Regina Markowitz, who have sponsored this book, I am dedicating this book on *Eishes Chayil* in memory of my grandmothers: Grandma Hannah Markowitz, חנה בת יעקב משה, and Bubby Sabina Kohane, שיינדל רחל בת אהרן יהודה.

To outside observers, my grandmothers looked like typical Jewish women; to me, they were larger-than-life influences who shaped who I am and everything I have accomplished. Their stories have given me strength and guided my life decisions over the years.

My Grandma, Hannah Markowitz, was a cheerful woman who lived each day to its fullest. When I was growing up, I thought she was a normal, nice Grandma who was cheerful, patient, and kind to all. I never realized how much strength of character it takes to be just that. Only as I reached my teen and adult years did I realize what gifts Grandma had bequeathed me.

When Grandma was in her late sixties, my Grandpa was diagnosed with terminal cancer. Their marriage had been one of deep respect and love, and I expected Grandma to lose her vitality and enthusiasm for life with his death. But Grandpa didn't want that to happen. Grandpa knew that Grandma had never driven and would be ineligible to get her license after her sixty-ninth birthday, leaving her at the mercy of others' good will. Grandpa made Grandma promise that she would learn to drive, get a license, and continue living life to its fullest.

After Grandpa died, Grandma took driving lessons and got that license. Soon after, she babysat for us for two weeks during a snowy winter and insisted on taking the car out every day so she wouldn't lose her nerve and quit driving. I remember sitting beside her as she slowly backed our brown station wagon out of the driveway, peering over the steering wheel to take us on our daily trip to the supermarket. I also remember praying that we survive the trip. Grandma kept at it and kept going strong.

Her life without my Grandpa continued. In her seventies, Grandma went to volunteer in the Israeli army for a few months. In her eighties, when the membership in her small synagogue dwindled, Grandma became the Hebrew tutor for the children and started taking on more roles to keep the synagogue open. When I got engaged, I went to Grandma and asked her for any advice for a happy life. She told me words that I continue to live by: "Reinvent yourself every decade."

> My Grandma's advice for a happy life: Reinvent yourself every decade.

My Grandma's advice has allowed me to raise my family, write this book, change careers, and bravely make new friends and explore new vistas. I learned from her that I am never stuck in who I am and that I should not let my fear or the judgment of others hold me back. I can always create a different tomorrow as long as I am open to the possibility.

My Grandma would be proud of this book, and I hope her warmth and strength shines through my writing.

My Bubby, Sabina Kohane, was a heroine who looked trauma in the eye and persevered. Bubby was a survivor of Bergen-Belsen, originally hailing from Poland.

Bubby did not leave our education to chance. She was infused with a passion for Judaism and Torah and felt it her life's mission to share with her children and grandchildren the values of the world in which she had been raised.

We would spend Pesach and other holidays with my Bubby and Zaidy. I would sit on a high-backed bench and listen to Bubby share stories of her childhood while she cooked and baked for Zaidy and the family. She would tell me how her father was taken away by the Nazis as he taught *Daf Yomi*. She would recount her pride at being a Bais Yaakov girl who met Sara Schenirer and was taught by one of her students. She told stories of the *Bnos* convention after the war and how she married my grandfather — who was from her hometown — because of his family's commitment to Torah learning and living. She would repeat the important stories over and over so that the messages became infused into my outlook.

For a number of summers, I spent a week or two at Bubby's home, and I joined her for her daily activities. We shopped for groceries, cooked dinners, and played Rummikub. She taught me how to make roast chicken and delicious stuffed cabbage. We chatted and we walked. She was in her element.

While doing these household chores with Bubby, I learned not to underestimate the power of a Jewish woman or the importance of being a homemaker. Bubby's vision and conviction came through in each of her chosen activities. When we shopped and cooked for a Shabbos dinner, we weren't just shopping and cooking: we were celebrating Shabbos, honoring my Zaidy, and supporting a Jewish business.

Over the years, Bubby followed our accomplishments and choices with a keen interest. Her proudest moments came when she saw we were perpetuating the life she had known as a child that had been so utterly destroyed.

> Bubby taught me that being an *eishes chayil* is a life calling. Building a Jewish home is the most valuable job in the world.

When I think of my Bubby, I think of her love and the smell of her chicken soup, as well as her will of steel to rebuild her Jewish family. Nothing and nobody could threaten that dream. There have been times when I have been faced with making decisions that would strengthen my Jewish home — decisions that require determination — and I wondered where I would find the strength necessary to do so. That strength has always been there because my Bubby's commitment lives within me, as she knew it would.

Bubby lived to be a Jew. She did not take the role lightly, and she often reminded us of our responsibility to the Jewish People and to Hashem's Torah. From her I learned that there is no more valuable job in the world than building a Jewish home and raising children to be G-d-fearing Jews. I learned that being an *eishes chayil* is a life calling and requires articulating the stories and values of our heritage to the next generation. It is my hope that I can continue to pass along her passion, determination, and commitment to a life of Torah through these pages.

Acknowledgments

There are so many people I'd like to thank for their support and encouragement in helping me write this book.

Abba and Mommy — Hillel and Regina Markowitz — have generously sponsored this work in memory of their mothers, Hannah Markowitz and Sabina Kohane. My parents have always taken pride in my learning and accomplishments and encouraged me to be the best I can be. Their own devotion to learning Torah and their constant search for more *shiurim* and opportunities to learn has served as a model of how to bring Torah into every day of my life. May the *zechus* of this book give them many years of health, happiness, and opportunities to continue to learn and practice the Torah. May they have *nachas* from their children and grandchildren following in their footsteps.

Mom and Dad — Frank and Beverly Hochheimer — have been a constant source of love and support to my husband and me throughout our marriage. They have encouraged us and helped us devote ourselves to build a beautiful family and help others. I cannot sufficiently express my thanks and love for everything they have done. May they have tremendous joy and *nachas* from all of us.

My siblings, Rachel and Michael Harris, Chaim and Rochel Leah Markowitz, Benjy and Chavi Markowitz, Dovid and Dvorah Markowitz, and their children have been there as true friends. They have always been just a phone call away with support and help in more ways than I can count. Their care has been a source of strength, joy, and encouragement.

I am very grateful to Mosaica Press for their confidence in this book. Their professionalism and clear guidance has helped me move this book from a manuscript on my computer to a finished product. Rabbi Kornbluth's editorial guidance has greatly enhanced this work, and the staff of Mosaica Press has been a pleasure to work with.

It would have been impossible to write a book for women without being surrounded by inspirational women who have been my friends, sounding boards, and role models. Thank you to the women of Rochester and to my friends from over the years who have helped me continue to learn and grow at each stage of life.

My mentors and teachers have given me a foundation of Torah upon which to build. They continue to provide wisdom and guidance to help me navigate my changing roles as my children grow.

Thank you to my sons, Avraham Yeshaya, Yitzchok Simcha, Chaim Shlomo, and Michoel Shmuel Yaakov. You have made me a mother and given me the gifts of boundless joy and love. Each of you is so precious to me. You cheer me on and are thoughtful and generous whenever I need help. You have given advice on many aspects of the book, which I have incorporated. I am so blessed and fortunate to have such caring and loving sons.

I would also like to thank my wonderful, sweet daughter, Chana Nechama. Although you are but a newborn, you have been the motivation to learn *Eishes Chayil* and write this book. Raising a daughter in today's world is complex, and I want to be the best mother I can be to you; I want to help you find your voice as a strong woman who carries on the traditions of the women who came before you. I am so grateful that Hashem has given me such a beautiful daughter.

To my dear husband, Mordechai. You have made me want to be an *eishes chayil* so that I can give you the love and encouragement that you have given me. You have been my biggest cheerleader and the force behind this book. You had confidence in my abilities even when I didn't, and you pushed me to develop my skills so I could write, learn, and teach other women. When you heard that I wanted to write this book, you surprised me with *sefarim* from Israel and filled up the shelves of our library with *sefarim* you knew would make the difference. You have also lived through my creative, moody phases when I had writer's block, knowing your wife would come back at the other end, and juggled responsibilities that should have been shared so that I could meet deadlines and fulfill my dreams. May we continue, with the help of Hashem, to build a home filled with warmth, love, Torah, and lots of humor for many, many years.

Finally, I must thank Hashem who has lovingly given me a wonderful life filled with abundant blessings.

The Text of Eishes Chayil

A woman of valor who can find?	אֵשֶׁת חַיִל מִי יִמְצָא
For she is more valuable than pearls.	וְרָחֹק מִפְּנִינִים מִכְרָהּ:
The heart of her husband trusts in her,	בָּטַח בָּהּ לֵב בַּעְלָהּ
and he lacks no wealth.	וְשָׁלָל לֹא יֶחְסָר:
She does him good and not evil	גְּמָלַתְהוּ טוֹב וְלֹא רָע
all the days of her life.	כֹּל יְמֵי חַיֶּיהָ:
She seeks wool and flax	דָּרְשָׁה צֶמֶר וּפִשְׁתִּים
and works willingly with her palms (hands).	וַתַּעַשׂ בְּחֵפֶץ כַּפֶּיהָ:
She is like the merchant ships;	הָיְתָה כָּאֳנִיּוֹת סוֹחֵר
she brings her bread from afar.	מִמֶּרְחָק תָּבִיא לַחְמָהּ:
She rises while it is still night	וַתָּקָם בְּעוֹד לַיְלָה
and gives food to her household,	וַתִּתֵּן טֶרֶף לְבֵיתָהּ
and a portion to her maidens.	וְחֹק לְנַעֲרֹתֶיהָ:
She considers a field and takes it;	זָמְמָה שָׂדֶה וַתִּקָּחֵהוּ
with the fruit of her palms	מִפְּרִי כַפֶּיהָ
she plants a vineyard.	נָטְעָה כָּרֶם:
She girds her loins with strength	חָגְרָה בְעוֹז מָתְנֶיהָ
and makes strong her arms.	וַתְּאַמֵּץ זְרוֹעֹתֶיהָ:
She perceives that her merchandise is good;	טָעֲמָה כִּי טוֹב סַחְרָהּ
her candle is not extinguished at night.	לֹא יִכְבֶּה בַלַּיְלָה נֵרָהּ:

She lays her hands to the distaff,	יָדֶיהָ שִׁלְּחָה בַכִּישׁוֹר
and her palms hold the spindle.	וְכַפֶּיהָ תָּמְכוּ פָלֶךְ:
She stretches out her hand to the poor;	כַּפָּהּ פָּרְשָׂה לֶעָנִי
she reaches forth her hands to the needy.	וְיָדֶיהָ שִׁלְּחָה לָאֶבְיוֹן:
She is not afraid of the snow for her household,	לֹא תִירָא לְבֵיתָהּ מִשָּׁלֶג
for all her household are clothed with scarlet.	כִּי כָל בֵּיתָהּ לָבֻשׁ שָׁנִים:
She makes for herself linens;	מַרְבַדִּים עָשְׂתָה לָּהּ
her clothes are fine linen and purple.	שֵׁשׁ וְאַרְגָּמָן לְבוּשָׁהּ:
Her husband is known in the gates	נוֹדָע בַּשְּׁעָרִים בַּעְלָהּ
when he sits among the elders of the land.	בְּשִׁבְתּוֹ עִם זִקְנֵי אָרֶץ:
She makes linen garments and sells them	סָדִין עָשְׂתָה וַתִּמְכֹּר
and delivers belts to the merchant.	וַחֲגוֹר נָתְנָה לַכְּנַעֲנִי:
Strength and dignity are her clothing,	עוֹז וְהָדָר לְבוּשָׁהּ
and she laughs at the last day.	וַתִּשְׂחַק לְיוֹם אַחֲרוֹן:
She opens her mouth with wisdom,	פִּיהָ פָּתְחָה בְחָכְמָה
and the law of kindness is on her tongue.	וְתוֹרַת חֶסֶד עַל לְשׁוֹנָהּ:
She monitors the ways of her household	צוֹפִיָּה הֲלִיכוֹת בֵּיתָהּ
and does not eat the bread of laziness.	וְלֶחֶם עַצְלוּת לֹא תֹאכֵל:
Her children rise up and praise her;	קָמוּ בָנֶיהָ וַיְאַשְּׁרוּהָ
her husband also, and he extols her.	בַּעְלָהּ וַיְהַלְלָהּ:
Many girls have done valiantly,	רַבּוֹת בָּנוֹת עָשׂוּ חָיִל
but you excelled above them all.	וְאַתְּ עָלִית עַל כֻּלָּנָה:
Grace is deceitful, and beauty is vain,	שֶׁקֶר הַחֵן וְהֶבֶל הַיֹּפִי
but a woman who fears Hashem,	אִשָּׁה יִרְאַת ה'
she shall be praised.	הִיא תִתְהַלָּל:
Give her of the fruit of her hands,	תְּנוּ לָהּ מִפְּרִי יָדֶיהָ
and let her be praised	וִיהַלְלוּהָ
in the gates by her deeds.	בַשְּׁעָרִים מַעֲשֶׂיהָ:

The Midrash on Eishes Chayil

"אֵשֶׁת חַיִל מִי יִמְצָא" זֶהוּ שֶׁאָמַר הַכָּתוּב עוֹד יְנוּבוּן בְּשֵׂיבָה וְגוֹ' (תהילים צב, טו) כְּנֶגֶד אַבְרָהָם וְשָׂרָה, שֶׁהָיוּ שְׁקוּלִים כְּאֶחָד בִּצְדָקָה וּבִגְמִילַת חֲסָדִים וְהָיוּ סִימָן טוֹב לָעוֹלָם, כָּךְ אֵין מוֹנֵעַ מִן הַצַּדִּיקִים נָשִׁים כְּשֵׁרוֹת שֶׁהוּא מְזַוֵּג לָהֶם, שֶׁכֵּן מָצִינוּ בְּאִשְׁתּוֹ שֶׁל נֹחַ שֶׁהָיוּ שְׁקוּלִין מַעֲשֶׂיהָ בְּמַעֲשָׂיו, לְפִיכָךְ זָכְתָה עִמּוֹ וְנִצְּלָה מִמֵּי הַמַּבּוּל.

"A woman of valor who can find;" this is as it says, "They shall still bring forth fruit in old age" (*Tehillim* 92:15). [This verse] parallels Avrohom and Sarah who were equivalent as one in charity and good deeds. And it was a good sign for the world. So too, G-d does not prevent righteous men from marrying proper women that He matched to them, as we found with the wife of Noach — that her deeds were equal to his deeds. Therefore, she merited to be saved with him from the waters of the Great Flood.

"בָּטַח בָּהּ לֵב בַּעְלָהּ" — זוֹ שָׂרָה אִמֵּנוּ, שֶׁהֶעֱשִׁיר אַבְרָהָם בִּשְׁבִילָהּ שֶׁנֶּאֱמַר "וּלְאַבְרָם הֵיטִיב בַּעֲבוּרָהּ" (בראשית יב, טז).

"The heart of her husband trusts in her." This is Sarah, our matriarch, on whose behalf Avrohom became wealthy, as it is written, "And to Avrohom he was good on her behalf" (*Bereishis* 12:16).

"גְּמָלַתְהוּ טוֹב וְלֹא רָע" — זוֹ רִבְקָה אִמֵּנוּ, שֶׁגָּמְלָה לְיִצְחָק בְּשָׁעָה שֶׁמֵּתָה שָׂרָה אִמּוֹ.

"She does him good and not evil." This is Rivkah, our matriarch, who did kindness to Yitzchok when his mother, Sarah, died.

"דָּרְשָׁה צֶמֶר וּפִשְׁתִּים" — זוֹ לֵאָה אִמֵּנוּ, שֶׁקִּבְּלָה לְיַעֲקֹב בְּסֵבֶר פָּנִים יָפוֹת דִּכְתִיב "וַיָּבֹא יַעֲקֹב מִן-הַשָּׂדֶה, בָּעֶרֶב, וַתֵּצֵא לֵאָה לִקְרָאתוֹ וַתֹּאמֶר אֵלַי תָּבוֹא, כִּי שָׂכֹר שְׂכַרְתִּיךָ וְגו'" (שם כט, טז) לְפִיכָךְ זָכְתָה וְיָצְאוּ מִמֶּנָּה מְלָכִים וּנְבִיאִים.

"She seeks wool and flax." This is Leah, our matriarch, who accepted Yaakov with a pleasant countenance, as it is written, "And Yaakov came home from the field in the evening, and Leah went out to greet him, and she said to him, 'You should come to me because I paid for you.'" Therefore, she merited to have kings and prophets come from her.

"הָיְתָה כָּאֳנִיּוֹת סוֹחֵר" — זוֹ רָחֵל אִמֵּנוּ, שֶׁהָיְתָה מִתְבַּיֶּשֶׁת עַל הַבָּנִים בְּכָל יוֹם, לְפִיכָךְ זָכְתָה וְיָצְאָה מִמֶּנָּה בֵּן, שֶׁהוּא דוֹמֶה לַסְּפִינָה, שֶׁהִיא מְלֵאָה כָּל טוֹב שֶׁבָּעוֹלָם כָּךְ יוֹסֵף מִתְקַיֵּם כָּל הָעוֹלָם בִּזְכוּתוֹ, וְכִלְכֵּל אֶת הָעוֹלָם בִּשְׁנֵי רְעָבוֹן.

"She is like the merchant ships." This is Rochel, our matriarch, who was embarrassed regarding the children every day. Accordingly, she merited to have a son come from her who resembled a ship that is filled with all the best of the world; Yosef upheld all of the world in his merit and sustained the world in the years of famine.

"וַתָּקָם בְּעוֹד לַיְלָה" — זוֹ בִּתְיָה בַת פַּרְעֹה, גּוּיָה הָיְתָה וְנַעֲשְׂתָה יְהוּדִיָּה, וְהִזְכִּירוּ שְׁמָהּ בֵּין הַכְּשֵׁרוֹת, בִּשְׁבִיל שֶׁעָסְקָה בְּמֹשֶׁה, לְפִיכָךְ זָכְתָה וְנִכְנְסָה בְּחַיֶּיהָ לְגַן עֵדֶן.

"She rises while it is still night." This is Basya, daughter of Pharaoh. She was a non-Jew who became a Jew. And her name is mentioned among the righteous ones: Since she dealt with Moshe, she accordingly merited to enter into paradise in her life.

"זָמְמָה שָׂדֶה וַתִּקָּחֵהוּ" — זוֹ הִיא יוֹכֶבֶד, שֶׁיָּצָא מִמֶּנָּה מֹשֶׁה, שֶׁהוּא שָׁקוּל כְּנֶגֶד כָּל יִשְׂרָאֵל, שֶׁנִּקְרְאוּ כֶרֶם שֶׁנֶּאֱמַר "כִּי כֶרֶם ה' צְבָאוֹת בֵּית יִשְׂרָאֵל" (ישעיה ה, ז).

"She considers a field and takes it." This is Yocheved, from whom came Moshe who was equivalent to all of Yisroel, who are called a vineyard. As it says, "Because a vineyard of Hashem is the House of Yisroel" *(Yeshayah 5:7).*

"חָגְרָה בְעוֹז מָתְנֶיהָ" — זוֹ מִרְיָם שֶׁקֹּדֶם שֶׁנּוֹלַד מֹשֶׁה אָמְרָה עֲתִידָה אִמִּי שֶׁתֵּלֵד בֵּן שֶׁמּוֹשִׁיעַ אֶת יִשְׂרָאֵל, כֵּיוָן שֶׁנּוֹלַד וְכָבֵד עֲלֵיהֶם עֹל מַלְכוּת, עָמַד אָבִיהָ וְטָפְחָה עַל רֹאשָׁהּ, אָמַר לָהּ הֵיכָן נְבוּאָתֵיךְ, וְעָמַד וְיָרַק בְּפָנֶיהָ, וְעִם כָּל זֹאת הִיא מִתְאַמֶּצֶת בִּנְבוּאָתָהּ, דִּכְתִיב "וַתֵּתַצַּב אֲחוֹתוֹ מֵרָחֹק" (שמות ב, ד).

"She girds her loins with strength." This is Miriam, who, before Moshe was born, said, "In the future my mother will bear a son who will save Yisroel." When he was born, and the tyranny of the government intensified for them, her father stood and struck her on her head. He told her, "Where are your predictions?" And he stood and spit in her face. And with all that, she maintained her prophecy, as it is written, "And his sister guarded from afar" *(Shemos 2:4).*

"טָעֲמָה כִּי טוֹב סַחְרָהּ" — זוֹ חַנָּה שֶׁטָּעֲמָה טַעַם תְּפִלָּה, שֶׁנֶּאֱמַר: "וַתִּתְפַּלֵּל חַנָּה, וַתֹּאמַר, עָלַץ לִבִּי בַּה'" (ש"א ב, א) לְפִיכָךְ זָכְתָה וְיָצָא מִמֶּנָּה בֵּן שֶׁהָיָה בֶן זוּג לְמֹשֶׁה וְאַהֲרֹן, שֶׁהָיוּ מְאִירִין לְיִשְׂרָאֵל כְּנֵרוֹת, דִּכְתִיב "מֹשֶׁה וְאַהֲרֹן בְּכֹהֲנָיו, וּשְׁמוּאֵל, בְּקֹרְאֵי שְׁמוֹ" (תהלים צט, ו), וּכְתִיב בֵּיהּ בִּשְׁמוּאֵל " וְנֵר אֱלֹהִים טֶרֶם יִכְבֶּה, וּשְׁמוּאֵל שֹׁכֵב, בְּהֵיכַל ה'" (ש"א ג, ג).

"She perceives that her merchandise is good." This is Channah, who understood the meaning of prayer. As it says: "And Channah prayed, and she said, 'My soul rejoiced with Hashem' " *(I Shmuel* 2:1). Accordingly, she merited a son from her who was a match to Moshe and Aharon [in] that they lit up Yisroel like candles, as it is written, "Moshe and Aharon among His priests, and Shmuel among them that call upon His name" *(Tehillim* 99:7), and it is written about Shmuel, "And the lamp of G-d

had not yet gone out, and Shmuel laid down to sleep in the temple of Hashem" (*I Shmuel* 3:3).

"יָדֶיהָ שִׁלְּחָה בַכִּישׁוֹר" — זוֹ יָעֵל שֶׁלֹּא הָרְגָה אֶת סִיסְרָא בִּכְלִי זַיִן, אֶלָּא בְיָתֵד בְּכֹחַ יָדֶיהָ, וּמִפְּנֵי מַה לֹּא הֲרָגַתּוּ בִּכְלִי זַיִן, לְקַיֵּם מַה שֶּׁנֶּאֱמַר: "לֹא יִהְיֶה כְלִי גֶבֶר עַל אִשָּׁה" (דברים כב, ה).

"**She lays her hands to the distaff.**" This is Yael who did not kill Sisera with a weapon, but with a peg, through the force of her hands. And why did she not kill him with a weapon? To fulfill that which is written, "A woman shall not wear the clothing of a man" (*Devarim* 22:5).

"כַּפָּהּ פָּרְשָׂה לֶעָנִי" — זוֹ אִשָּׁה אַלְמָנָה הַצָּרְפִית, שֶׁכִּלְכְּלָה לְאֵלִיָּהוּ בְּלֶחֶם וּבְמַיִם.

"**She stretches out her hand to the poor.**" This is the woman who was the widow of Tzarfas, who supported Eliyahu with bread and water.

"לֹא תִירָא לְבֵיתָהּ מִשָּׁלֶג כִּי כָל בֵּיתָהּ לָבֻשׁ שָׁנִים" — זוֹ רָחָב הַזּוֹנָה, בְּשָׁעָה שֶׁבָּאוּ יִשְׂרָאֵל לְהַחֲרִיב יְרִיחוֹ, לֹא נִתְיָרְאָה מֵהֶם, מִפְּנֵי שֶׁנָּתְנוּ לָהּ סִימָן "אֶת תִּקְוַת חוּט הַשָּׁנִי" (יהושע ב, יח).

"**She is not afraid of the snow for her household, for all her household are clothed with scarlet.**" This is Rachav, the harlot. When Yisroel came to destroy Yericho, she wasn't afraid of them because they gave her a sign, "This line of scarlet thread" (*Yehoshua* 2:18).

"מַרְבַדִּים עָשְׂתָה לָּהּ" — זוֹ בַּת שֶׁבַע, שֶׁיָּצָא מִמֶּנָּה שְׁלֹמֹה, שֶׁהָיָה מְרֻקָּם בְּשֵׁשׁ וְאַרְגָּמָן, וּמָלַךְ מִסּוֹף הָעוֹלָם וְעַד סוֹפוֹ.

"**She makes for herself linens.**" This is BasSheva, who had Shlomo come from her, who was clothed in linen and purple wool and ruled the world from end to end.

"נוֹדָע בַּשְּׁעָרִים בַּעְלָהּ" — זוֹ מִיכַל שֶׁהִצִּילָה דָוִד מִן הַמִּיתָה.

"**Her husband is known in the gates.**" This is Michal, who saved Dovid from death.

"סָדִין עָשְׂתָה וַתִּמְכֹּר" — זוֹ אִמּוֹ שֶׁל שִׁמְשׁוֹן
שֶׁנּוֹשְׁעוּ יִשְׂרָאֵל עַל יָדוֹ.

"She makes linen garments and sells them." This is the mother of Shimshon through whom Yisroel was saved.

"עֹז וְהָדָר לְבוּשָׁהּ" — זוֹ אֱלִישֶׁבַע בַּת עַמִּינָדָב שֶׁרָאֲתָה אַרְבַּע שְׂמָחוֹת [בְּיוֹם אֶחָד], אָחִיהָ נָשִׂיא, וּבַעְלָהּ כֹּהֵן גָּדוֹל, וְאָחִי בַּעְלָהּ מֶלֶךְ, וּשְׁנֵי בָנֶיהָ פִּרְחֵי כְהֻנָּה.

"Strength and dignity are her clothing." This is Elisheva, the daughter of Aminadav, who saw four celebrations [in one day]: her brother the prince, her husband the high priest, her husband's brother the king, and two of her sons young priests.

"פִּיהָ פָּתְחָה בְחָכְמָה" — זוֹ אִשָּׁה חֲכָמָה, שֶׁאָמְרָה
"שִׁמְעוּ שִׁמְעוּ, אִמְרוּ נָא אֶל-יוֹאָב, קְרַב עַד-הֵנָּה,
וַאֲדַבְּרָה אֵלֶיךָ" (ש״ב כ:טז). שֶׁהִצִּילָה אֶת הָעִיר בְּחָכְמָתָהּ
וְזוֹ הָיְתָה סֶרַח בַּת אָשֵׁר.

"She opens her mouth with wisdom." This is the woman of intelligence, who said, "Listen, listen, please say to Yoav, come here and I will speak to you." She saved the city with her intelligence. This was Serach, the daughter of Asher.

"צוֹפִיָּה הֲלִיכוֹת בֵּיתָהּ" — זוֹ אִשְׁתּוֹ שֶׁל עוֹבַדְיָה,
שֶׁהִצִּילָה בָּנֶיהָ וְלֹא עָבְדוּ ע״ז עִם אַחְאָב.

"She monitors the ways of her household." This is the wife of Ovadiah, who saved her sons, and they did not serve idols with Achav.

"קָמוּ בָנֶיהָ וַיְאַשְּׁרוּהָ" — זוֹ שׁוּנַמִּית, שֶׁנִּקְרֵאת אִשָּׁה גְּדוֹלָה,
וּמִפְּנֵי מָה? מִפְּנֵי שֶׁהֶחֱזִיקָה בֶּאֱלִישָׁע לֶאֱכֹל.

"Her children rise up and praise her." This is the Shunamis, who is called a great woman, and why? Because she supported Elisha with food.

"רַבּוֹת בָּנוֹת עָשׂוּ חָיִל וְאַתְּ עָלִית עַל כֻּלָּנָה." — זוֹ רוּת הַמּוֹאֲבִיָּה, שֶׁנִּכְנְסָה תַּחַת כַּנְפֵי הַשְּׁכִינָה.

"**Many girls have done valiantly, but you excelled above them all.**" This is Rus the Moabite, who entered under the wings of the Divine presence.

"שֶׁקֶר הַחֵן וְהֶבֶל הַיֹּפִי" — שֶׁהִנִּיחָתָה אִמָּהּ וַאֲבוֹתֶיהָ וְעָשְׁרָהּ וּבָאָה עִם חֲמוֹתָהּ וְקִבְּלָה כָּל הַמִּצְווֹת. תְּחוּם שַׁבָּת, "אֶל־אֲשֶׁר תֵּלְכִי אֵלֵךְ" (רות א, טז), אִסּוּר יִחוּד עִם אִישׁ, "וּבַאֲשֶׁר תָּלִינִי אָלִין" (שם). תרי"ג מִצְווֹת, "עַמֵּךְ עַמִּי" (שם). עֲבוֹדָה זָרָה, "וֵאלֹהַיִךְ אֱלֹהָי" (שם), אַרְבַּע מִיתוֹת בֵּית דִּין, "בַּאֲשֶׁר תָּמוּתִי אָמוּת" (שם). לְפִיכָךְ זָכְתָה וְיָצָא מִמֶּנָּה דָּוִד שֶׁרִוָּה לְהקב"ה בְּשִׁירוֹת וְתִשְׁבָּחוֹת, לְפִיכָךְ נֶאֱמַר: "תְּנוּ לָהּ, מִפְּרִי יָדֶיהָ וִיהַלְלוּהָ בַשְּׁעָרִים מַעֲשֶׂיהָ."

"**Grace is deceitful, and beauty is vain.**" This is Rus, who left her mother, her ancestors, and her affluence, and came with her mother-in-law and accepted all of the mitzvos: the boundaries of Shabbos, "For where you go, I will go"; the prohibition of being alone with a man, "And where you lodge, I will lodge"; the 613 mitzvos, "Your people shall be my people"; idolatry, "and your G-d is my G-d"; the four deaths of *beis din*, "Wherever you shall die, I will die." Accordingly, she merited that Dovid came from her, [he] who pleased Hashem with songs and praises; therefore, it is written, "Give her of the fruit of her hands, and let her be praised in the gates by her deeds."

אֵשֶׁת חַיִל מִי יִמְצָא	A woman of valor who can find	אַבְרָהָם וְשָׂרָה	Avrohom and Sarah
בָּטַח בָּהּ לֵב בַּעְלָהּ	The heart of her husband trusts in her	שָׂרָה אִמֵּנוּ	Sarah, our matriarch
גְּמָלַתְהוּ טוֹב וְלֹא רָע	She does him good and not evil	רִבְקָה אִמֵּנוּ	Rivkah, our matriarch
דָּרְשָׁה צֶמֶר וּפִשְׁתִּים	She seeks wool and flax	לֵאָה אִמֵּנוּ	Leah, our matriarch
הָיְתָה כָּאֳנִיּוֹת סוֹחֵר	She is like the merchant ships	רָחֵל אִמֵּנוּ	Rochel, our matriarch
וַתָּקָם בְּעוֹד לַיְלָה	She rises while it is still night	בִּתְיָה בַּת פַּרְעֹה	Busya, daughter of Pharaoh
זָמְמָה שָׂדֶה וַתִּקָּחֵהוּ	She considers a field and takes it	יוֹכֶבֶד	Yocheved
חָגְרָה בְעוֹז מָתְנֶיהָ	She girds her loins with strength	מִרְיָם	Miriam
טָעֲמָה כִּי טוֹב סַחְרָהּ	She perceives that her merchandise is good	חַנָּה	Channah
יָדֶיהָ שִׁלְּחָה בַכִּישׁוֹר	She lays her hands to the distaff	יָעֵל	Yael
כַּפָּהּ פָּרְשָׂה לֶעָנִי	She stretches out her hand to the poor	אִשָּׁה אַלְמָנָה הַצָּרְפִית	Widow of Tzarfas
לֹא תִירָא לְבֵיתָהּ מִשָּׁלֶג	She is not afraid of the snow for her household	רָחָב הַזּוֹנָה	Rachav, the harlot
מַרְבַדִּים עָשְׂתָה לָּהּ	She makes for herself linens	בַּת שֶׁבַע	BasSheva
נוֹדָע בַּשְּׁעָרִים בַּעְלָהּ	Her husband is known in the gates	מִיכַל	Michal

סָדִין עָשְׂתָה וַתִּמְכֹּר	אִמוֹ שֶׁל שִׁמְשׁוֹן
She makes linen garments and sells them	Mother of Shimshon
עוֹז וְהָדָר לְבוּשָׁהּ	אֱלִישֶׁבַע בַּת עַמִּינָדָב
Strength and dignity are her clothing	Elisheva, daughter of Aminadav
פִּיהָ פָּתְחָה בְחָכְמָה	סֶרַח בַּת אָשֵׁר
She opens her mouth with wisdom	Serach, daughter of Asher
צוֹפִיָּה הֲלִיכוֹת בֵּיתָהּ	אִשְׁתּוֹ שֶׁל עוֹבַדְיָה
She monitors the ways of her household	Wife of Ovadiah
קָמוּ בָנֶיהָ וַיְאַשְּׁרוּהָ	שׁוּנַמִּית
Her children rise up and praise her	The Shunamis
רַבּוֹת בָּנוֹת עָשׂוּ חָיִל	רוּת הַמּוֹאֲבִיָּה
Many girls have done valiantly, but you excelled above them all.	Rus, the Moabite
שֶׁקֶר הַחֵן וְהֶבֶל הַיֹּפִי	רוּת הַמּוֹאֲבִיָּה
Grace is deceitful, and beauty is vain;	Rus, the Moabite
תְּנוּ לָהּ מִפְּרִי יָדֶיהָ	רוּת הַמּוֹאֲבִיָּה
Give her of the fruit of her hands, and let her be praised in the gates by her deeds.	Rus, the Moabite

Introduction

It all began a number of years ago. I had been married for a few years and had not yet had any children. I spent my days working as a computer programmer and my evenings wondering what to do with myself. I was bored. My husband spent his days (and nights) learning Torah and his evenings listening to me lament my lack of options.

I loved to learn Torah, but, as a woman, I knew that I had a much more important role in life. I knew I was supposed to have children, nurture my family with a warm home, and be gracious and hospitable. Unfortunately, neither my life nor my temperament really made that possible.

> Learning Midrash has added depth to my understanding of Torah and to my spiritual life.
>
>

One evening, my husband had enough. He walked over to our bookshelves, pulled off a large *Midrash Rabbah*, and handed it to me. "After you finish learning all of the Midrash with the commentaries on the book of *Bereishis*, we'll talk." Reluctantly, I began to learn. I never finished the *sefer* my husband handed me, but my love of Midrash was born. The Midrash added depth to all aspects of Torah and my spiritual life. More importantly, it made me focus on what it was I could achieve rather than what I might not be able to.

Fast-forward a few years. I now had a baby boy and was no longer working as a computer programmer. I had to juggle raising an active baby and teaching *Chumash* and Jewish philosophy in a girls' high school. I was far from bored. I spent every night learning and preparing my classes and trying to get my one-year-old to go to sleep.

Yet I was still filled with the same angst. What was wrong with me that I was not satisfied just taking care of my baby? How come I wasn't able to be more *aidel*, more passive and conciliatory to my husband or my peers? Why had I been stuck with such a large personality and so many opinions?

At that time, Hashem smiled down on me. I was teaching a group of high-school seniors the five *Megillos*: *Rus*, *Esther*, *Eichah* (Lamentations), *Koheles* (Ecclesiastes), and *Shir HaShirim* (the Song of Songs). Toward the end of the year, the girls asked to learn about other women in *Tanach*. I remembered a Midrash I had encountered before but had never studied in depth. It was a Midrash on *Eishes Chayil*.

This Midrash on *Eishes Chayil* takes each verse in the famous poem and compares it to a woman in Jewish history. I decided that it would be interesting to learn about the women in *Tanach* by learning what the Midrash teaches us about them.

As I prepared the familiar *pesukim*, I read the text and was amazed. The *eishes chayil*, the ideal woman, was not passive in the least. She was dynamic, intelligent, and active. She orchestrated, planned, and nurtured. She was a woman whom I could emulate. I knew that I would never achieve all she represented — but at least I was not out of the running before I even began.

> The *eishes chayil*, the ideal woman, is not passive in the least. She is dynamic, intelligent, and active. She orchestrates, plans, and nurtures.

Then I learned the Midrash. The text gave me encouragement and brought me to an understanding that changed the essence of my life. Each *pasuk* represented one — and only one — woman in *Tanach*. There was no ideal Jewish woman. Each woman had her own unique talents and place in history. Each was needed, and each was different. There were eighteen women described in the Midrash, and I could be like any or none of them. My job was to figure out who I was and be the best me I could be.

That year, I taught *Eishes Chayil* to my class and also to myself. I learned to accept myself and to think about how to become a better wife and mother using the talents and personality that G-d gave me.

Since then, life is ever-changing for me. Now, as a mother of more (and older) children, I am focusing more on my home. I am becoming the woman I could not relate to years ago. I happily bake cookies, sew costumes, and sing lullabies. Yet I can still look to *Eishes Chayil* to answer the challenges and questions that I now have.

It is my hope that *Eishes Chayil* will give you some of the inspiration that it gave me.

As we learn this material together, we will do several things:

- First, I would like to study the simple meaning of the text to understand how a married woman creates and nourishes herself, her family, and her society.
- Second, I would like to examine the lives of the great Jewish women to which the Midrash refers. Each woman can find her own role model and her own path to greatness.
- Finally, after each chapter, I include questions to help each woman on her journey of self-reflection.

What the words of *Eishes Chayil* say to me are not what they say to you, and that is the way it should be. Each of us is on our own journey and needs to find the tools and ideas that speak to us individually. There are questions to help any woman — regardless of her circumstances — to know herself better. There are questions for wives and mothers to clarify the dynamics in those important relationships, and questions to help us educate our daughters so that they may grow up to be vibrant, self-confident women as well. It may be helpful to keep a journal to write answers to these questions or to discuss them with a group of friends.

> Each woman is on her own journey and can find tools and ideas that speak to her individually.

I have postponed writing this book many times because I felt it arrogant to write anything about how to be the perfect wife and mother. My husband and children can attest to my not earning that title. From one imperfect woman to another, this is a book to help each of us on her journey of self-discovery and self-improvement using the words of Shlomo HaMelech, the commentaries, and the Midrash as our guide.

CHAPTER 1

First Impressions

For many of us, our perceptions of who we should be as women are very different from who we actually are. We wives and mothers have a litany of "shoulds" that we need to accomplish to feel worthy. Whether it is losing five pounds, decluttering the house, or devoting more time to davening and *chessed*, there is a gulf between our expectations of what we should do and the reality of what we actually do. This gap would be bad enough for any woman, but then, as G-d-fearing women, we add religious guilt to the mix — that we are somehow not living up to Hashem's plan for us. When we fail to live up to impossible, perfectionist standards, the guilt, shame, and pressure to change are overwhelming.

However, let's say our assumption about who we "should be" was grounded neither in reality nor in the Torah. Perhaps our visions were being driven by our own insecurities and popular culture. If we could recognize our own false ideas, we could replace them with healthier ideas that would lead to true happiness and fulfillment.

> It is important to study *Eishes Chayil* because many assumptions about who we "should be" are grounded neither in reality nor in the Torah.

This is why it so important to learn and study *Eishes Chayil*. We may think we know what it says, but it is only through proper study and analysis that we will discover if what we think is proper, truly is. We need to explode the myths we are using to guide our decisions and replace them with the eternal truths of the Torah that will give us clarity and hope — rather than disillusionment and pain.

Although I had never learned *Eishes Chayil*, I felt like I knew what it said. After all, I knew it by heart, having sung its verses at so many *kumzitzes* and every week on Friday night before *Kiddush*. It was a mainstay of the songs crooned at weddings and was the featured subject of many paintings. In truth, before I studied it, I did not really know what *Eishes Chayil* was about.

Despite my knowing all the words, I thought that the *eishes chayil* was demure and gentle, a woman with a perpetual smile, a starched apron, a warm cake in one hand and a *Tehillim* in the other. I thought that the *eishes chayil* would spend most of her time engaged in housework, child care, or meditative practice. I assumed that the family of the *eishes chayil* would look nothing like mine and would be remarkably sensitive, calm, and learned. In a few words, the *eishes chayil*, while praiseworthy and awe-inspiring, was someone I would never want to spend time with.

But I was wrong. The *eishes chayil* described in the verses and our sources looks nothing like the image I had painted in my head. As we will discover as we explore the verses of the poem line by line, the *eishes chayil* is no pushover. She is humble, strong, decisive, nurturing, and lives with faith. She is someone we would all enjoy spending time with — as well as someone whom we could strive to become.

Eishes Chayil Defined

Eishes Chayil, the last chapter of *Mishlei* (Proverbs), is a poem written about an ideal woman. The book of *Mishlei* is a book of insights, deep wisdom, and advice written by Shlomo HaMelech, the wisest person of all time.[1] The last chapter begins with the advice and reproof that Shlomo

---

1   *Melachim I* 5:11.

HaMelech's mother gave to him after he erred, and it helped him correct his ways.² After describing his mother's advice, Shlomo HaMelech transitions from discussing his mother, an *eishes chayil*, to describing the greatness of the *eishes chayil* in general.³ While much of the rest of *Mishlei* consists of suggestions and sharp advice, the text of *Eishes Chayil* is a description of a great woman, written only in positive terms.

The poem describes various traits of the *eishes chayil* in twenty-two verses, each of which begins with a different letter of the *Aleph-Beis*, in consecutive order.

Shlomo HaMelech wanted the poem of *Eishes Chayil* to catch the attention of those studying the book of *Mishlei*. It concludes the entire book of wisdom and is the only time where the letters of the *Aleph-Beis* are used in a poetic fashion to begin each line.

The *Aleph-Beis* was used to teach the importance of the *Eishes Chayil*. The *Aleph-Beis* is not a regular alphabet. In other languages and alphabets, ordinary letters are not imbued with meaning; they serve a function only when combined with other letters into words, sentences, and paragraphs.

In contrast, in the *Aleph-Beis*, even individual letters are imbued with inherent meaning. These letters are the building blocks with which G-d created the world. The Torah, Hashem's words to man, was written using the *Aleph-Beis*. The letters thus represent Creation and the Torah. By beginning each line of *Eishes Chayil* with a different letter of the *Aleph-Beis*, Shlomo HaMelech teaches us that the *eishes chayil* has a specific role in Creation and in the Torah. Her mission encompasses all of life, Creation, and the Torah.⁴ The more a woman lives according to the ideals of *Eishes Chayil*, the more she helps all of Creation fulfill its destiny.

> The mission of the *eishes chayil* encompasses all of life, Creation, and the Torah. The more we live according to its ideals, the more we help all Creation fulfill its destiny.

---

2   Rashi, *Mishlei* 31:1.
3   Malbim, *Mishlei* 31:10.
4   *Meam Loez, Mishlei* 31:31.

The Structure

For the most part, *Mishlei* is written in prose, as direct sentences of advice and wisdom. In contrast, *Eishes Chayil*, although it is part of *Mishlei*, is a poem. As a poem, it has a specific structure that adds an additional level of meaning to it.

Lines 1–3 (א–ג)	Definition of an *eishes chayil*
Lines 4–10 (ד–י)	Daily activities of an *eishes chayil*
Lines 11–18 (כ–צ)	Various roles of an *eishes chayil*
Lines 19–22 (ק–ת)	The result of a life of devotion

The first three verses of the poem introduce us to the *eishes chayil* and tell us who she is. Her three most important traits are described, and they lay the foundation for all the rest of her endeavors.

The next seven verses speak about the daily activities of the *eishes chayil* and how she spends her day from early in the morning until late at night.

In the next eight verses, the poem shifts focus from the minutiae of her day and looks at the many roles of an *eishes chayil*: vis-à-vis her family, husband, community, and herself.

The poem concludes with four verses in which her children and husband praise her and laud her for all that she has done.

Learning from the Structure

The structure of the poem itself tells us much about the Torah ideal for a woman. *Eishes Chayil* lists many professional and personal accomplishments. These accomplishments are rooted in the woman's deep faith in Hashem and her desire to do His will, as described in the first section.

By listing her daily routine in the second section, Shlomo HaMelech further highlights the greatness of the *eishes chayil*, as her day-to-day life truly reflects her top priorities. In other words, she does not get sidetracked from what she knows is truly important. With her priorities as her guide, the *eishes chayil* balances taking care of her family and husband with her own spiritual, emotional, intellectual, and physical needs every single day. No one area of concern is the subject of her full attention; all these areas are important.

This balancing act is expounded upon in the third section, in which the poem highlights how the *eishes chayil* is able to juggle multiple roles without neglecting any of them. The *eishes chayil* has the wisdom to balance her priorities at each stage of life with intelligence and sensitivity. She relates to different people accordingly, and she understands which proverbial hat she needs to wear in all of her interactions.

> The poem teaches us how to make our day reflect our priorities and how to juggle the roles of wife, mother, professional, and individual with wisdom and sensitivity.

At the end of the poem, we see the result of a life well lived. The *eishes chayil* leaves this world with the praise and admiration of those who truly matter and for whom she has built a legacy: her husband and her children. They acknowledge that her ultimate reward is in the World to Come because of the strong relationship she has built with Hashem. At the end of the day, that is the only praise that will ever matter.

Before you study the poem in depth, answer the following questions:

Self-Growth

1. When was I introduced to the verses from this poem?
2. How do I think an *eishes chayil* would occupy her time nowadays?
3. How do I think the *eishes chayil*'s family would relate to her?
4. What are four adjectives that come to mind to describe an *eishes chayil*?
5. Do I view myself as an *eishes chayil*? Why or why not?
6. What do I hope to gain from learning more about *Eishes Chayil*?

As Wives and Mothers

7. Are there any areas where my image of the ideal wife/mother does not match who I am?
8. What feelings arise because of any conflicts between my expectations and reality?

Teaching Our Daughters

9. What messages is my daughter getting from peers, school, and the community regarding what or who she should be like?
10. Are any of these message contrary to her best interests?

CHAPTER 2

The Midrash

The text of *Eishes Chayil* can teach women much about how to live full and meaningful lives. We were given even more rich material from which to learn in the form of the Midrash that was written to supplement the study of *Mishlei*.

Midrash is a compendium of rabbinic literature that highlights a different dimension of the Torah. It emphasizes the richness and textures of Torah texts and presents profound moral lessons and insights rooted in the words of the text.

While *Eishes Chayil* can be read as describing one woman, the Midrash looks at this poem through a different lens. The *Tanach* has many female heroines, each with her own strengths and gifts. The Midrash designates each line of *Eishes Chayil* as describing one of the female heroines in *Tanach*. Through learning about each heroine, we gain insight into her greatness as a role model and how to best bring the lessons of the *Eishes Chayil* poem to reality.

> When we learn about the heroines in *Tanach*, we gain role models and learn how to bring the lessons of *Eishes Chayil* into reality.

Before I learned the Midrash, I was familiar with a number of women described in *Tanach*. I knew about Sarah, Rochel, Miriam — all of whom (I felt) had minor roles in the development of the Jewish nation. Learning the Midrash about their histories gave me a new appreciation for their significant contributions to the development of our people.

The Midrash on *Eishes Chayil* also discusses women whom I never thought much about, like Shimshon's mother, and the woman from Shunam. Although mentioned briefly in *Tanach*, I was awed by their courage and character, and I learned important insights into my own life by studying their stories.

Learning from Exclusion

There was one woman who, to my surprise, was not mentioned at all in the Midrash. Devorah, the prophetess and Judge, is nowhere to be found in the Midrash on *Eishes Chayil*. How could this be?

If I had to vote for one woman who seemed to be a true role model, she would have been the one. Devorah lived during a tumultuous time in Jewish history. There was no monarchy, and the Jewish People were a confederacy of tribes ruled by a succession of judges. Every few years, as the Jews sinned, they would be attacked and oppressed by foreign rulers who taxed the Jewish population into poverty and waged battles to defeat them. After the Jews begged for Hashem's mercy, a judge would lead the tribes in battle and provide religious guidance for the loosely connected nation.

One of these judges was a woman named Devorah. She not only led the army in battle against a formidable opponent and won, she provided spiritual guidance as a prophetess to the women — and men — in the nation.

It struck me as strange that Devorah, a true female heroine — and a famous one — does not appear in the Midrash. Perhaps, one could suggest, the Midrash is trying to suppress the story of Devorah to keep women unempowered. However, this could not be the case since the Midrash highlights and praises many woman role models. What makes Devorah unique? Why is she excluded?

Devorah, while an exemplary leader, could never be a role model for the masses. In any group of people, only one person can become the leader. Someone — in fact most "someones" — need to be followers. As the *mishnah* in *Avos* says:

הֱוֵי זָנָב לָאֲרָיוֹת, וְאַל תְּהִי רֹאשׁ לַשּׁוּעָלִים.[5]
Be a tail to lions, and don't be the head to foxes.

It is unhealthy for all individuals in a society to want to be leaders because it is not a choice people can make about their own future. To be effective, leaders must be chosen based on their talents and potential to be of help. How can leadership be a person's goal? Rav Yaakov Weinberg, *zt"l*, explains another *mishnah* in *Pirkei Avos* in this vein:

בְּמָקוֹם שֶׁאֵין אִישׁ הִשְׁתַּדֵּל לִהְיוֹת אִישׁ.[6]
In a place where there are no leaders, strive to be a leader.

When there is a genuine need, a person should be willing to take on the responsibility to help others. However, implicit in this *mishnah* is that when there are adequate leaders, one should not aspire to this as a goal.[7]

Surely, Devorah was a Jewish heroine who stepped up to the plate when it was necessary, but her leadership was not a goal that the Midrash felt all women need to copy.

Most of our lives are quite different from hers. Devorah's battles were very public, while most of our battles take place in the privacy of our homes. There are no cheering crowds when we get up early to go to work, rock a shrieking baby, or bite our tongue to stop nasty comments from belittling others. We need role models to help guide us to victories in these "small" matters as well. The Midrash chose women who could serve as these kinds of role models. All the women listed in the Midrash fought and won personal battles in the way they conducted themselves in times of challenge. Their personal victories — though

---

5   *Avos* 4:15.
6   *Avos* 2:5.
7   *Rav Yaakov Weinberg Talks about Chinuch*, edited by Rabbi Doniel Frank, p. 159.

not well-known — changed the lives of their children and the course of history. The Midrash wants us to learn from these women that our personal, ordinary battles are meaningful. Our victories are as important to the future of our families as the battles fought by the women mentioned in *Tanach*. The women mentioned in the text are our role models because, at a certain level, we can all become them.

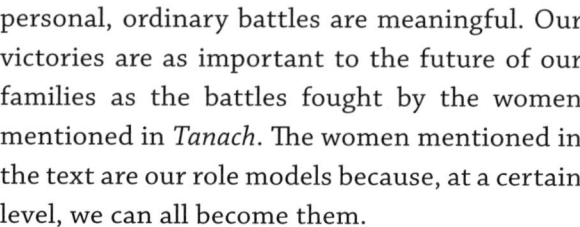

There are no cheering crowds when we get up early to go to work, rock a shrieking baby, or refrain from making a hurtful comment.

Living the Midrash

Although the battles of the women mentioned in the Midrash were private, the lessons we learn from them are not easy to implement. In particular, I found that understanding and incorporating the message of the first four women mentioned, our four *Imahos*, our spiritual matriarchs, was challenging — even as it was powerful and transformative.

The message of the *Imahos* required a paradigm shift from how I viewed my role and what I could expect from myself. More than anything else, the *Imahos* were never victims of circumstance. They took full responsibility for their actions and behaviors and kept the focus on themselves and what they could do with the life they had been given.

Living with this ideal made me uncomfortable with some of what I had learned, as I couldn't deflect my attention by thinking about how life would be better if only others would change. I had to confront the "real me" and what I needed to change about myself. I had to be honest about what I could or could not do and then communicate my needs when necessary.

For this reason, I chose to write this book solely from the perspective of a woman. It would be inconsistent with the message of the Midrash if I were to tell my husband or children how to change to suit what I was learning. The advice and character development that flows from the text of *Eishes Chayil* and from the Midrash could be beneficial for both men and women; both men and women are expected to grow as human beings and in their relationships. There is no reason that men or women should neglect their character development and rely on their partners to compensate for their lack. However, I have chosen to stay gender specific to stay true to this lesson of the Midrash.

There is a famous piece of wisdom attributed to Rabbi Yisroel Salanter, founder of the Mussar Movement, that encapsulates this message.

> *When I was a young man, I wanted to change the world.*
>
> *I found it was difficult to change the world, so I tried to change my nation.*
>
> *When I found I couldn't change the nation, I began to focus on my town.*
>
> *I couldn't change the town, and as an older man, I tried to change my family.*
>
> *Now, as an old man, I realize the only thing I can change is myself, and suddenly I realize that if long ago I had changed myself, I could have made an impact on my family.*
>
> *My family and I could have made an impact on our town.*
>
> *Their impact could have changed the nation, and I could indeed have changed the world.*

How to Learn the Midrash

When learning the Midrash, we will see that the ideals and values of the women discussed, particularly the *Imahos*, are very elevated. I find that this kind of truth is a danger zone for me. I have a tendency to be cynical, give up, or feel guilty when I can't reach the ideal. On some level, each of these approaches is safer, because when I am sarcastic, defeatist, or racked with guilt, I don't ever have to change. However, none of these tactics have ever worked. I have found that when trying new habits, being gentle and kind to myself actually has far better results.

When I look at the rest of *Mishlei* leading up to the chapter containing *Eishes Chayil*, it is filled with direct *mussar*. Shlomo HaMelech tells the reader what he should or should not do and the consequences of the decisions a person makes.

Eishes Chayil is very different. It doesn't say how we should act; it describes a person using only positive terms. The same is true with the stories of the women in the Midrash. Each line of the Midrash is positive and uplifting; it is written so that we can absorb the lessons without becoming defensive.

> There is no expiration date for the work described in *Eishes Chayil*. Have patience and use the lessons as a guide for positive growth, not as a tool to berate yourself.

When we learn the Midrash, we should keep this approach in mind. The impact of the work described in these pages is meant to last a lifetime. It is a process of growth; it cannot be perfected and there is no expiration date. This applies especially when we are learning about the lives of the *Imahos*; we should be patient with ourselves and use their lives as a guide for our own rather than as a tool with which to berate ourselves.

And now, I am excited to begin studying the text of *Eishes Chayil* and the Midrash together. I hope its study will be as positive an experience for you as it has been for me.

Questions

Self-Growth

1. With which of the women am I most familiar?
2. Are there any women listed whom I do not know?
3. Am I surprised by who was included?
4. With which woman do I best identify and why?
5. Which woman in the Midrash would be the best role model for Jewish women today?
6. Are there any women I would like to learn more about? Why?
7. Have I had any personal victories that have impacted my life or the lives of others in a positive way that were not publicized?

As Wives and Mothers

8. How do publicity and praise impact how I prioritize different responsibilities?

Teaching Our Daughters

9. What messages is my daughter getting from her peers, her school, and her community about leadership and competition? Do I agree or disagree with these messages?
10. How do I help my daughter develop a healthy sense of community responsibility and a Jewish perspective on leadership?

CHAPTER 3

A Woman of Valor – A Partnership

אֵשֶׁת חַיִל מִי יִמְצָא וְרָחֹק מִפְּנִינִים מִכְרָהּ.

*A woman of valor who can find?
For she is more valuable than pearls.*

Peshat

The words *"eishes chayil"* that begin the poem in *Mishlei* have become synonymous with the ideal Jewish woman. It is important, then, to understand what these two words mean before we can understand the whole first line of the poem. When I look in the authoritative translations, the words *"eishes chayil"* are translated as "a woman of valor." Have you ever met a woman of valor

> The words *"eishes chayil"* are often translated as "a woman of valor." "Valor" reminds me of knights and horses, not a nice Jewish woman. Why isn't she called righteous instead?

on the street? When I hear the word valor, I think of knights and horses, not of a nice Jewish woman. What does that translation mean? Why couldn't Shlomo HaMelech just call the woman righteous — an *ishah tzaddekes* — rather than calling her an *eishes chayil*?

Chayil Defined

Luckily, the word *chayil* is used elsewhere in the Torah. By looking at the context of the word in other *pesukim*, we can understand more about how it is being used in our poem.

In *Devarim* 8:17, the Torah warns us not to become arrogant when we are successful and not to say:

כֹּחִי וְעֹצֶם יָדִי, עָשָׂה לִי אֶת הַחַיִל הַזֶּה.

My power and the might of my hand
have gotten me this wealth.

Chayil in this context means wealth. Based on this usage, an *eishes chayil* could refer to a woman of wealth, but that does not seem to capture the essence of the ideal Jewish woman. We do not generally associate financial comfort with the measure of a person's spiritual attainments.

In contrast, when we look in *Shemos* 18:21, we find that *chayil* means men who possess outstanding character.[8] There, Hashem commands Moshe to find judges who are men of *chayil*.

וְאַתָּה תֶחֱזֶה מִכָּל הָעָם אַנְשֵׁי חַיִל יִרְאֵי אֱלֹהִים,
אַנְשֵׁי אֱמֶת — שֹׂנְאֵי בָצַע; וְשַׂמְתָּ עֲלֵהֶם,
שָׂרֵי אֲלָפִים שָׂרֵי מֵאוֹת, שָׂרֵי חֲמִשִּׁים, וְשָׂרֵי עֲשָׂרֹת.[9]

And you shall discern from all the people men of chayil,
who fear G-d, men of truth, who despise money;
and appoint them to be officers of thousands,
officers of hundreds, officers of fifties, and officers of tens.

---

8   *Akeidas Yitzchok, Shemos* 18:21.
9   *Shemos* 18:21.

The Ramban there explains that *chayil* implies that the person or thing is outstanding depending on its context.[10] With a judge, a *chayil* will have all the optimal traits for a judge listed in the *pasuk*. He will be G-d-fearing, honest, and industrious. The Ramban continues that the talented woman, the *eishes chayil*, will be an outstanding woman who has personal strength and is motivated — a *zerizah* who works hard and is productive.

Chayil can also have a third and equally important meaning. The *Daas Mikra* explains that the judges were called *chayil* because they feared G-d and were truthful.[11] Based on this context, the *eishes chayil* is a woman who fears Hashem and is honest and truthful.

> The three definitions of *chayil* paint a picture of a remarkable woman: wise, industrious, productive, and honest — who acts with purpose to meet the standards of G-d's will and Torah values.

What Is an Eishes Chayil?

These three definitions of *chayil* (wealthy, talented, and G-d fearing) combine to give us a picture of a remarkable woman: She is a woman with profound wisdom and understanding. She is a woman whose wealth stems from her industriousness and productivity. She acts with purpose, knowing that her life of honesty and integrity must meet the standards of Hashem's will and the Torah values He defines.

Becoming an Eishes Chayil

The first *pasuk* of *Eishes Chayil* tells us that it is difficult to find (or to buy!) an *eishes chayil*. Later, Shlomo HaMelech seems to contradict himself and says:

רַבּוֹת בָּנוֹת עָשׂוּ חָיִל.[12]

Many girls have become "chayil."

---

10   Ramban, *Shemos* 18:21.
11   *Daas Mikra*, *Mishlei* 31:10.
12   *Mishlei* 31:29.

Is the first *pasuk* correct or the later one? It is hard to imagine that Shlomo HaMelech, the wisest of all people, would contradict himself — especially within a span of twenty verses. What lesson is he trying to teach us?

The Malbim provides insight into solving this dilemma by contrasting two words in the first verse: the word *yimtza* — find, with the word *michrah* — price.[13] He explains that a *metziah*, a find, is something that one stumbles over without planning. Shlomo HaMelech tells us that the *eishes chayil* cannot be found by accident. In contrast, a *michrah* is something that can be purchased with money. The *eishes chayil* can also not be bought with money.

So how does one become an *eishes chayil* if it is a position that cannot be found or bought? The answer is found in the contradiction with the later *pasuk* that says:

רַבּוֹת בָּנוֹת עָשׂוּ חָיִל[14]

Many girls **have become** "chayil."

The girls had to work hard. The key to attaining this most precious of titles is to become a *chayil* — through hard work and fear of G-d.

Remaining an Eishes Chayil

When I was single, I was pretty sure that I was, and would continue to be, an *eishes chayil*. I made difficult decisions that were spiritually based, I learned Torah, sought guidance from spiritual mentors, did good deeds, and worked on my character. I was committed to living an ideal life based on the values with which I was raised and to which I had committed during my years in seminary and beyond. I had many friends who held the same confident outlook about themselves.

> The position of *eishes chayil* cannot be found or bought. The key to attaining the most precious of titles is to become a *chayil* — through hard work and fear of G-d.

---

13   Malbim, *Mishlei* 31:10.
14   *Mishlei* 31:29.

And then I got married. Suddenly, the idyllic perception of who I was took a hit. I found myself getting angry and annoyed in ways I had never experienced before. Suddenly, this other human being was triggering my worst behavior. And it could be over such stupidity. My husband and I disagreed about where his pajamas should be stored. As any rational human being will agree, they belong in a drawer! He felt that the logical place was in a pile near his bed, on the nightstand, on the floor, and on the table, so he could choose the right pair easily any time he wished. It wasn't just a difference of opinion. I was right and he was wrong. Worst of all, he wouldn't admit it, even if he agreed to keep his things contained in one spot or in the drawer. I got snippy and angry and insulting. My visions of my life as an *eishes chayil* dimmed quickly.

And then I had children who, thank G-d, were busy growing up while acting like children. My hopes of becoming an *eishes chayil* dimmed even more. In the mornings as I tried to get the kids out the door, or at bedtime when I was tired and my son started negotiating for a snack, a drink, and yet another book, I would lose it. I felt like my days of spiritual exploration and growth were a thing of the past as my hours were used up by my responsibilities to cook, shop, work, and play endless games of SORRY.

> The Midrash will teach us how to grow spiritually and be *chayil* (wealthy, talented, and G-d fearing) when life consumes us with responsibilities.

While it is challenging for a woman to act according to spiritual ideals when single, how is it possible for a woman to join the ranks of the *"rabos banos"* — the many girls — who have achieved this title when married and with kids? How can a woman continue to grow spiritually and be *chayil* (wealthy, talented, and G-d fearing) when confronted with the challenges of partnering with another human being who will push her buttons like no one else can? For help with this, we must turn to the Midrash.

Midrash – Avrohom and Sarah

"A women of valor who can find?"	אֵשֶׁת חַיִל מִי יִמְצָא
This is as it says:	זֶהוּ שֶׁאָמַר הַכָּתוּב
"They shall still bring forth fruit in old age"	עוֹד יְנוּבוּן בְּשֵׂיבָה וְגוֹ'
(Tehillim 92:15).	(תהילים צב:טו)
[This verse] parallels Avrohom and Sarah	כְּנֶגֶד אַבְרָהָם וְשָׂרָה
who were equivalent as one	שֶׁהָיוּ שְׁקוּלִים כְּאֶחָד
in charity and good deeds.	בִּצְדָקָה וּבִגְמִילַת חֲסָדִים.
And it was a good sign for the world.	וְהָיוּ סִימָן טוֹב לָעוֹלָם.
So too, G-d does not prevent righteous men	כָּךְ אֵין מוֹנֵעַ מִן הַצַּדִּיקִים
from marrying proper women	נָשִׁים כְּשֵׁרוֹת
that He matched to them	שֶׁהוּא מְזַוֵּג לָהֶם
as we found with the wife of Noach	שֶׁכֵּן מָצִינוּ בְּאִשְׁתּוֹ שֶׁל נֹחַ
that her deeds were equal to his deeds.	שֶׁהָיוּ שְׁקוּלִין מַעֲשֶׂיהָ בְּמַעֲשָׂיו
Therefore, she merited with him	לְפִיכָךְ זָכְתָה עִמּוֹ
to be saved from the waters of the Great Flood.	וְנִצְלָה מִמֵּי הַמַּבּוּל.

The First Pair

The Midrash starts off describing a couple, Avrohom and Sarah, as the people who best exemplify what is being described in the first *pasuk* of *Eishes Chayil*. It says that they were equal in their acts of righteousness and charity. The Midrash continues by stating that Hashem doesn't prevent righteous men from marrying women who are equally worthy and brings the example of Noach and his wife, Naama, both of whom were saved from the Great Flood.

The first line of the Midrash begs attention. For the rest of the verses of *Eishes Chayil*, the Midrash brings one woman to represent the character trait that the *pasuk* is addressing. The first *pasuk* is the only one that does not fit the pattern. Instead of citing one person, the Midrash mentions two, one of whom is a man! Why is the first *pasuk* different? Why not just mention Sarah as the *eishes chayil,* as is done in all the rest of the *pesukim*? Why does Avrohom need to be mentioned at all?

The Midrash compounds the mystery by mentioning a second couple, Noach and Naama, in addition to the first. The Midrash states that Naama, Noach's wife, was also his equal in good deeds, and she merited to be saved from the Great Flood because of her actions. No other *pasuk* has two personalities used to describe it, yet here we have four. If the Midrash thought that Noach and Naama were a good example, why did it begin with Avrohom and Sarah? After all, as we will see, the Midrash mentions Sarah in connection with the next *pasuk*.

The First Test

To understand why Sarah and Avrohom exemplify the character trait of *Eishes Chayil*, we must look at their lives.

Sarah and Avrohom were born in an era of wealth and prosperity when everyone worshipped idols. The head honchos, the people who controlled the money and power, believed that society would crumble without paganism. Avrohom challenged this notion by declaring his belief in one G-d. The emperor, Nimrod, tried to stop this new idea from spreading and promptly threw Avrohom into a flaming furnace, hoping to eradicate this idea forever. Avrohom was saved through a miracle and escaped the furnace without even a sunburn.

Avrohom's brother, Haran, was asked whom he supported. Did he stand with Nimrod, the powerful king, or his brother Avrohom, the monotheistic rebel? Haran vacillated as to what he believed: "Paganism? Monotheism? Paganism? Monotheism?"[15]

When Haran saw Avrohom exit the furnace alive, he declared his faith in one G-d and was promptly thrown into the furnace. Since Haran's faith was weak, he did not merit the miracle of being saved. Haran left three surviving children: Milkah (who married Haran's brother Nachor), Sarah (who married Avrohom), and Lot (who fled the region with his uncle). Sarah became Avrohom's partner in the mission

---

15 *Bereishis Rabbah* 38:16.

to teach others about the existence of one G-d. Avrohom and his family moved to Charan — far away from the dangers of Nimrod — where they remained for some time.[16]

As a Partner

Despite the dangers and opposition of the most powerful men in that era, Avrohom continued to proclaim his belief in one G-d. He set out to introduce others to this understanding. According to the Midrash, Avrohom opened the original "bed-and-breakfast" with a tent that always welcomed passing travelers to come, rest, eat, and learn. He hoped that through his generosity and kindness, he could introduce others to the truth of Hakadosh Baruch Hu.[17]

> In their outreach work, Sarah and Avrohom worked independently, each in his own sphere of influence, to accomplish the common goal of bringing glory to G-d's name.

Sarah, his wife, who had lived through her father being killed for his support of one G-d, was always right beside him. As Avrohom introduced the pagan men to Hashem, Sarah worked to teach the pagan women about one G-d. Rashi, the medieval commentator, explains:

אַבְרָהָם מְגַיֵּר אֶת הָאֲנָשִׁים, וְשָׂרָה מְגַיֶּרֶת הַנָּשִׁים.
וּמַעֲלֶה עֲלֵיהֶם הַכָּתוּב כְּאִלּוּ עֲשָׂאוּם.[18]

Avrohom converted the men and Sarah converted the women. And the Torah attributes it as if they made them.

In their outreach work, Sarah and Avrohom worked independently, each in his own sphere of influence, to accomplish the common goal of bringing glory to G-d's name.

---

16   Ramban, *Bereishis* 11:28.
17   *Talmud Bavli, Sotah* 10b.
18   Rashi, *Bereishis* 12:5.

As a Supporter

Sarah also supported Avrohom's needs, even when it involved sacrifice. Sarah was barren for many years, and she decided that although she couldn't have children, Avrohom should have an heir. She encouraged Avrohom to marry Hagar, her maid. She did not want Hagar to be a surrogate mother providing a child for Sarah to raise; this was not becoming of Avrohom. Rather, she wanted Hagar to become a full-fledged, legitimate second wife who could bear a child for Avrohom. For Avrohom's sake, Sarah elevated her servant to be her equal and rival so that Avrohom could perpetuate his legacy in this world by having a legitimate child.[19] Hagar then bore a child named Yishmael and mocked Sarah for her infertility.[20]

> Sarah spent the hottest day of the year, without air-conditioning or refrigeration, preparing a banquet for Avrohom's visitors whom she would not even meet.

The years passed, and Sarah continued to support Avrohom. When Avrohom was ninty-nine years old, he was circumcised. G-d made a miracle and made the day unnaturally hot so that no human being would travel in the desert and bother Avrohom during his recovery. Indeed, the sun beat down, and no man ventured forth in the heat of the desert. Yet Avrohom sat waiting for guests, longing to fulfill the kindness of hospitality.[21]

To help relieve Avrohom's anguish, Hashem sent three angels to visit him to help him feel better. The angels asked Avrohom, "Where is Sarah?" Avrohom answered, "She is in the tent."[22] On the hottest day of the year, without the benefit of air-conditioning or refrigeration, Sarah was preparing a banquet for the visitors. Sarah was not only willing to be the proactive outreach professional working with women as Avrohom's equal, and she was not only willing to elevate another

---

19   Ramban, *Bereishis* 16:2.
20   Ramban, *Bereishis* 16:4.
21   Rashi, *Bereishis* 18:1.
22   *Bereishis* 18:9.

as a partner in their home to bring the joyful sounds of children into her home, she was also happy to assist Avrohom in his work, hosting his guests as a cook without making an appearance to see who was visiting.

A year after the angels visited, Sarah was blessed with a son named Yitzchok.[23]

As a Challenger

Perhaps the greatest gift that Sarah gave to Avrohom as his partner was to challenge him, even though it caused conflict. Yishmael, Hagar's son, was uncontrolled and aggressive. He behaved in a manner that was antithetical to all that Avrohom stood for. Sarah recognized that Yishmael's presence in her home threatened the spiritual growth of her own child, Yitzchok, and therefore the future of the Jewish People; she knew that Yitzchok was destined to be Avrohom's spiritual heir and would be one of the Patriarchs.[24]

גָּרֵשׁ הָאָמָה הַזֹּאת וְאֶת בְּנָהּ.[25]
"Expel this woman and her son."

Sarah demanded that Avrohom force Hagar and his son Yishmael to leave.

Avrohom was torn by this demand. With the expulsion of Hagar, he would also be rejecting his son. As a man of kindness, he felt this went against all he believed.[26]

Hashem told Avrohom clearly:

כֹּל אֲשֶׁר תֹּאמַר אֵלֶיךָ שָׂרָה שְׁמַע בְּקֹלָהּ.[27]
Anything that Sarah says to you, heed her voice.

---

23 *Bereishis* 21:2.
24 Rashi, *Bereishis* 21:9.
25 *Bereishis* 21:10.
26 http://www.yutorah.org/lectures/lecture.cfm/738430/HaRav_Avigdor_Nebenzahl/The_Trials_of_Avrohom#.
27 *Bereishis* 21:12.

Rashi explains that Hashem instructed Avrohom to listen to Sarah's words because she was a prophetess.[28] Although Sarah was asking Avrohom to do something that was difficult, she did so with his best interests at heart. Avrohom could pay attention to Sarah's concerns since they came from her spiritual depths, not from a petty place.

> Perhaps the greatest gift Sarah gave Avrohom was to challenge him to ensure his actions were in line with his desire to fulfill Hashem's will.

The Foundation of a Jewish Home

Sarah is called the *akeres ha-bayis* — the foundation of all the Jewish People.[29] The *Yefas Toar* explains that she is given this title because she was *Ikar Bais Yisroel*, the primary source for the Jewish People.[30] She gave Avrohom an indispensable gift that allowed him to create the Jewish nation. She made herself a partner, whether it meant working independently, in his service, or even by challenging him directly. His goals were her goals, driven by Hashem's goals — and that understanding guided her actions.

Achieving Greatness

With this understanding of the relationship of Sarah and Avrohom, and Sarah's choices in that relationship, we can better understand the *pasuk* and why both Avrohom and Sarah are mentioned in the Midrash. For a woman to achieve her greatest spiritual heights, she must be challenged to grow as part of a team and still maintain her internal spiritual compass. A woman who can achieve this is as rare as pearls and is hard to find. The Midrash began with a couple because greatness cannot be achieved in solitude. Becoming an *eishes chayil* is not an abstract quality of holiness; rather, it is a very practical realization of a relationship with shared spiritual goals.

---

28   Rashi, *Bereishis* 21:12.
29   *Midrash Rabbah, Parashas Vayera* 53:6.
30   *Yefas Toar*, ibid.

What allowed Sarah to juggle the different roles in her life were the values she shared with Avrohom, which guided her life decisions as a member of a team. Her actions were never driven by petty motivations; they came from a place that was larger than both her and Avrohom Avinu. At times, Sarah acted independently, speaking to women about belief in one G-d. Other times, she was cooking in the tent to serve guests. At yet other times, she disagreed with the *gadol hador*, the most righteous man of the generation (who had discovered Hashem on his own!), to expel his own son against his initial will. She filled all of these roles with grace because it was all done as Avrohom's partner and was guided by her devotion to fulfill Hashem's will.

> For a woman to achieve her greatest spiritual heights, she must be challenged to grow as part of a team yet still maintain her internal spiritual compass.

The Midrash does not let us mistakenly assume that this partnership was based on love. Of course there was deep love; however, this incredible partnership was most importantly based on good deeds and fear of Heaven. For this reason, the Midrash mentions another couple to teach us that a relationship based on common goals is a requirement to become righteous, rather than being a unique characteristic of just one couple (Avrohom and Sarah).

By starting this way, the Midrash tells us that all *tzaddikim* and their wives, like Noach and Naama, are partners. *Tzaddikim* and their wives each work to live a life of meaning. They are not living to make themselves happy or even to make each other happy. They are living to make Hashem happy. This is the glue that keeps their marriage strong. And this is the essence of an *eishes chayil*.

Getting Practical: Making Marriage a Partnership

An *eishes chayil*, as we defined before, is a woman who uses all of her talents to do the will of G-d. We have now seen that it is not enough to become an *eishes chayil* without responsibility to and for others. A woman must use her talents as part of a team to create an even bigger source of holiness in this world.

How do we make ourselves into women who dedicate our lives to G-d, and how do we turn our marriages into partnerships? How do we embrace the multiple roles that are required of us, such as the acts of service (the laundry and cooking) and the spiritual activities (prayer), while maintaining focus on our relationship through resolving conflicts about important issues? How do we make all of these things holy parts of our relationship rather than reflections of our ego?

> How do we embrace the multiple roles that are required of us and make them holy, and not merely reflections of our egos?

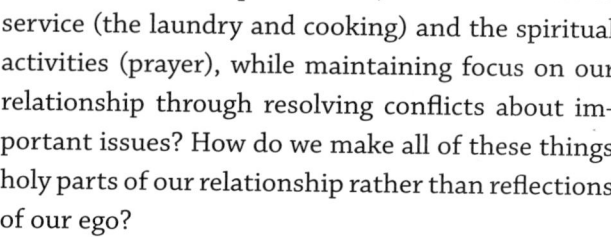

Defining Our Own Values

Sarah Imeinu was a prophetess who had a clear picture of the values that informed her role in her marriage. The first step we can take is to stay connected to our values and who we truly are. This work begins long before marriage, with us clarifying and identifying our core values so that we know ourselves and have a strong internal compass to guide us.

I have a friend who told me how detrimental it was for her when she ignored her internal voice and sought approval for her decisions. It was Yom Tov, and my friend had no energy left to clean up after the meal. She knew that if she didn't lie down, she would say something she regretted, but she also felt guilty leaving the mess knowing her husband might clean it all himself. Instinctively, she asked her husband if it was okay for her to rest, hoping he would affirm that she should take the break she needed. Much to her chagrin, her husband asked for more help because he was also tired. She ended up feeling hurt, saying the regrettable things she had hoped to avoid, and he felt confused and tricked. After all, she had asked for his input!

Later, after much reflection, my friend realized that she hadn't checked her own internal voice and had wanted her husband to make a decision that was her responsibility. Had she felt more confident, they both would have acted in a way that reflected their mutual priority — to be kind and supportive of each other.

I witnessed another scenario that highlighted for me how dangerous losing this sense of self can be. I was at a class on Jewish law when we learned a halachah that was straightforward and impacted each woman directly. A woman commented that her husband, who was learning in yeshiva, was never careful about this law. Therefore, she could not or would not be careful about it herself because she followed her husband's lead and did not want to question him.

> Sarah Imeinu teaches that a woman can and must continue to think and be present for all decisions.

This decision gave me pause. I had always learned, as we will discuss in a later chapter, that my husband should be the spiritual leader in our home. I realized then that there is a caveat to this rule. I cannot abandon my knowledge of right and wrong whenever it disagrees with my husband. Sarah Imeinu teaches that a woman can — and must — continue to think and be present for all decisions. By doing so, she provides a balance in the relationship so that no person's will becomes greater than the will of G-d Himself.

The Values Danger Zone

There is a flip side to using my internal compass in my marriage. With all my spiritual awareness, I can assume that it is my job is to check the spiritual practice and health of my spouse, whether by monitoring his minyan attendance or tracking his time spent learning Torah.

> Being a partner does not mean that we get to judge and monitor our spouses.

When I first got married, I was anxious about whether my husband was doing the right thing. This hit especially hard after the newlywed glow wore off. I went from thinking my husband was the epitome of perfection to realizing he had flaws like anyone else. At times, I would nag him. Other times, I would try positive reinforcement and encouragement. Both approaches annoyed him. I thought that I was being feminine and smart when really I was just manipulative, parental, and disrespectful of my

husband's individuality. Rather than bringing us closer and helping us achieve greater spiritual heights in our home, it was a wedge that did not allow either of us to grow. Being a partner does not mean that we get to judge and monitor our spouse.

Transitioning from that newlywed navigating married life to a true partner required me to grow up and accept my husband for who he was, rather than try to change him into who I wanted him to be. I had to learn when it was my business to speak up because it impacted me and our home, and when an issue was his alone to confront.

Partnership Tools

Avrohom Avinu and Sarah Imeinu were lucky. When they had a spiritual conflict about whether to expel Yishmael from their home, Hashem Himself made the decision for them. Few other couples in the history of the world have had it so easy. There are some other alternatives that can help us make our married lives one of spiritual growth and partnership rather than of conflict.

An important step is to find spiritual mentors — rabbis, *rebbetzins*, or people whom we respect — who can act as sounding boards when we have concerns. This does not replace the internal compass that we need to maintain, but it can help us move from an emotionally driven decision to one that is well thought-out and grounded in our values.

> Tools for partnership incude (1) finding spiritual mentors, (2) setting common spiritual goals, and (3) regularly checking in about the goals.

Another important tactic is to share common goals with our spouses so that our life is guided by a purpose greater than either of us. Hopefully, for most couples, the goals they share and establish are ones based on meaningful values rather than on superficialities. When there is the inevitable disagreement, they have their values to guide them, rather than basing a decision only on personality and will.

Like most couples, when my husband and I dated, we spent many hours discussing our dreams and goals. When I first got married, I had all the intentions of earning a substantial income for many years. I had dreamed that my husband would learn Torah, and I felt computer programming was the ticket to a secure future. I majored in Computer Science and spent my summers interning in the field to make my career possible. After sitting behind a desk alone for many hours and meeting tight deadlines that required overtime, I discovered that working as a full-time computer programmer made me miserable. Instead, I found a passion for teaching, albeit with a paycheck that was much smaller than the one I earned in the tech world. Thankfully, my career was never a core value in my marriage. My husband and I could make the changes necessary yet still stay true to what was really important to us.

The heady conversations while dating set the course for the beginning of the marriage. The years go by and things change, most often in ways that were never expected. A couple may have planned to live near their parents but can't find work and have to move to find employment. They may dream of a large family, but are now raising a few precious children. The bills mount, a relative gets sick, and suddenly their carefully made goals no longer fit their life.

Hopefully, most couples have spiritual goals that help them navigate many of the unforeseen changes. A couple is committed to raising a family that serves Hashem. They aspire to build a home full of kindness. Changes in life circumstances most often do not impact these kinds of values. However, even spiritual goals may change. A wife and husband can decide that they want a Shabbos table with many guests — and then they have children who are introverted and get overwhelmed by noise. A husband's dream may be to teach Torah, and his wife may dream of helping make that a reality — until they discover that he has no talent in the classroom.

How does a couple weather disappointments and changes when life does not match the goals they had initially set?

Reestablishing Common Goals

While couples set up goals when they marry, regularly revisiting their goals throughout married life will help make sure the goals reflect their current reality and what Hashem wants from them on an ongoing basis. There is no formula for conversations. How my husband and I evaluate our goals will be different from what is useful for another couple. I have a friend who, together with her husband, crafts a family mission statement that they revisit regularly. I know another woman who sits down, formally, twice a year for a goal check-in. Some couples make time for this conversation in less formal ways. However it is done, the priority is to track shared goals and how they are working for each spouse and, please G-d, the expanding family. By discussing abstract goals regularly, we can celebrate our accomplishments, make course corrections when necessary, and abandon the goals that no longer fit.

With these relevant and honest shared goals, as life changes we can measure what we do using a steady barometer. Our roles and responsibilities will be flexible as the family and the time require. As long as we always view our marriage as a team working toward something bigger than ourselves, we will be successful.

The Limits of Common Goals

While these conversations are theoretically nice, they involve two real and very different people. I will never have the exact same goals as my husband. We are both individuals, with two different missions in life, trying to reach our potential. If I try to force my husband to make my life goals his, and he tries to make me embrace his goals as my own, we are going to end up as two unhappy people. Instead, we have learned to be comfortable having his goals, her goals, and our goals. One of our shared goals is to help the other reach his individual goals. Through maintaining our individuality during this process, we become greater as individuals and as a team than either of us can become on our own.

The life of Avrohom Avinu and Sarah Imeinu was one of shared goals and partnership. Their ability to work together and transcend petty concerns is remarkable. They represent a level

Avrohom Avinu and Sarah Imenu are the ultimate role models. We need a road map to teach us how to become like them. This is provided by the subsequent pesukim.

of greatness that is, as the *pasuk* notes, rare and "more precious than pearls." We can look to Avrohom and Sarah as the ultimate role models, but we still require a road map to teach us how to become like them.

The subsequent *pesukim*, with this *pasuk* as our vision, provide that guide to help us achieve this goal. By working slowly and patiently to attain this idea, we will each become an *eishes chayil*, no matter the circumstance. And like the *eishes chayil*, each of us will be a rare and valuable gift to the world.

Summary

"A woman of valor who can find?"   אֵשֶׁת חַיִל מִי יִמְצָא
Avrohom and Sarah   אַבְרָהָם וְשָׂרָה

From the Pasuk We Learn

An *eishes chayil* is a remarkable woman: She is wise, industrious, productive, and honest; she acts with purpose to meet the standards of Hashem's will and Torah values. This title can only be attained through hard work.

From the Midrash We Learn

Avrohom and Sarah were the ultimate partners. From them we learn that an *eishes chayil* does not exist in a vacuum. True greatness comes through partnering with our spouse to create a home based on shared spiritual goals. Partnership requires us to be comfortable working together, working separately, being secondary, or having conflict to stay true to our shared vision for a home based on Hashem's will.

Practical Steps

1. Find spiritual mentors.
2. Stay true to our own personal value system.
3. Establish shared spiritual goals.
4. Regularly reevaluate shared goals as life and circumstances change.

Questions

Self-Growth

1. What are some of my life goals?
2. How do I prioritize my goals? Which goals are nonnegotiable and which are flexible?
3. What goals do I need my spouse to share? What goals can be mine alone?

As Wives and Mothers

4. Do my husband and I share common goals?
5. Have we articulated these goals to each other?
6. Have we discussed and updated our goals recently?
7. Do we have a predetermined time to discuss these ideas?
8. How do we resolve an issue when our goals conflict?
9. How do I distinguish between an issue that impacts me and when I am being judgmental and parental toward my husband?

Teaching Our Daughters

10. How do I teach my daughter worthy life goals?
11. How do I teach my daughter to have her own life goals rather than parroting what others say?

CHAPTER 4

Trust

בָּטַח בָּהּ לֵב בַּעְלָהּ וְשָׁלָל לֹא יֶחְסָר.

*The heart of her husband trusts in her,
and he lacks no wealth.*

Peshat

The second *pasuk* continues with another foundational principle: trust. The *pasuk* tells us that the heart of the *eishes chayil*'s husband trusts in her and, as a result, lacks no riches. The *pasuk* connects emotional trust to financial reward. Why would this be so? Furthermore, why is trust so important that it is the second principle upon which a marriage depends?

What Is Trust?

In *Chovos HaLevavos*, Duties of the Heart, Rabbeinu Bachaya Ibn Pekudah describes the trust a person has in Hashem.[31] In his preface to

---

31   *Chovos HaLevavos*, The Fourth Gate: The Gate of Trust, chapter 1.

his treatise on *bitachon* (trust), he defines what it means to trust in another. He writes that *bitachon* is the confidence that someone else will work on our behalf without having to make promises or guarantees — just because he is looking out for our best interest — and he will do so to the best of his ability with kindness and generosity.

While only Hashem can truly care for each of our needs, a person can try to be trustworthy for a partner. Living with someone we can rely on to look out for us and our needs creates a beautiful marriage.

> Trust (*bitachon*) is the confidence that someone else will work on our behalf without having to make promises or guarantees, just because he is looking out for our best interest.

The Trust of a Husband

The *pasuk* states that the heart of a husband trusts in his wife. There are obvious areas of trust that need to be established for a marriage to work. For there to be trust, a spouse must be faithful, and there can be no physical or verbal abuse in a relationship.

There are some behaviors that may seem subtle but are also essential to building trust, which in turn leads to a strong marriage. The *Meam Loez* describes a wife who evokes this level of trust.[32] He says that the *eishes chayil* can be trusted socially, financially, and spiritually. Both spouses in a marriage must earn this level of trust. The examples I give below involve women because they draw a clear distinction to how the *eishes chayil* acts.

> The *eishes chayil* can be trusted socially, financially, and spiritually.

Reuven married Channah, who became sarcastic when people annoyed her. Every few weeks, someone in shul would start to avoid Reuven. Reuven was often wondering what he could have done wrong that would have put a distance between him and his neighbor. He would soon find out the cause of the sudden chill in his relationship:

---

32 *Meam Loez, Mishlei* 31:11.

Channah had once again been catty to a friend. Even though he could trust his wife for larger issues, in his heart, Reuven knew he could not trust Channah to keep the peace in the neighborhood.

Dovid had a different problem. He had a stable job, as did his wife. Every month, though, a credit card bill would arrive that exceeded their take-home pay. There were charges for clothing they could not afford, charges for takeout because his wife would forget to cook dinner on the night she had committed to do so, and late fees for bills that she had agreed to pay. When he talked to his wife, she blamed society, her neighbors' expectations, and her busy schedule. Dovid loved his wife and appreciated her hard work, but in his heart he could not trust her financially.

Levi had yet a different issue. He was a man who had spent his life following halachah. The food he ate was kosher, he kept Shabbos, and he tried to instill a love of Torah in his children. Whenever he walked into his own kitchen, however, there were problems. It was never anything overt, but there were questionable practices he would avoid if he could: For example, an open dairy pot would be boiling next to a sizzling hot meat frying pan, or a bag of shredded cheese was spilled onto the counter that was supposed to be used for meat dishes only. Nothing was ever non-kosher, but too many questions arose that could have been solved with a little more care. When asked, Levi would say he trusted his wife to keep kosher, but in his heart, he had an uncomfortable feeling about trusting her completely with spiritual matters.

The *eishes chayil*, in contrast, according to the *Meam Loez*, is trustworthy for big issues as well as small ones. She gives her word, makes responsible financial decisions, creates a warm rapport with neighbors and friends, and admits when she makes a mistake. Her husband knows intellectually and emotionally that the *eishes chayil* can be trusted — no matter what.

The Heart: The Seat of Trust

The *Daas Mikra* explains that this is why the *pasuk* says that the husband's trust lays in his heart. In the Torah, the heart sometimes means the seat of emotion, and sometimes it refers to the source of rational thought.[33] The husband of the *eishes chayil* trusts his wife because he both depends on her emotionally and because he knows intellectually that she can be trusted based on her consistent behavior.

Everyone gets married believing that her spouse will try to do what is best for her. Without trust, no one would risk getting involved in such an important relationship. This trust is emotional and helps the relationship begin on the right foot.

As life continues, that initial trust is often tested. Whenever a spouse acts with thought and care for the other, the emotional trust is reinforced by a rational proof. The more a spouse acts trustworthy, the more a spouse trusts, both intellectually and emotionally. In contrast, when a spouse is dishonest or hurtful, the trust is tested. If the poor behavior continues, trust may be broken, and the relationship will flounder as each spouse tries to protect his own interest. In the place of trust comes hurt, anxiety, and guardedness.

> When a person acts with thought and care, the spouse will trust both intellectually and emotionally. When, however, a spouse is dishonest or hurtful, trust is broken. In the place of trust comes hurt, anxiety, and guardedness.

Roadmap to Wealth

Trust, then, is one of the foundations of a marriage. Without trust, a person cannot be vulnerable in the relationship. The relationship can limp along but without the depth and connection that is possible with trust. Trust is obviously an important component of a marriage, so why does the *pasuk* tell us that this trust leads to wealth?

Imagine this example: You hire your children's favorite babysitter so that you can attend a friend's wedding. At the wedding, you get a chance to catch up with old friends and are refreshed by the energetic dancing. You come home invigorated from an evening free of responsibility and tension.

---

33   *Daas Mikra, Mishlei* 31:11.

Now imagine the opposite scenario. You hire a new babysitter who has never watched your children before. During the wedding, you get one call, then another, as you referee an argument long-distance. In the background, you hear the baby screaming and realize the babysitter is not able to feed the baby with the bottle you left for her. You come home exhausted, not having enjoyed yourself and not having had a chance to catch up with your friends.

The *Metzudas Dovid* explains that trust in a wife leads to a similar situation for her husband because he can focus on his work without anxiety.[34] A man, without a trustworthy partner, will be nervous that his children are not eating well, need help with homework, may be eating non-kosher food, or that the bills are growing faster than he can earn money. A man may be learning Torah or busy at work, but his mind is at home. He calls at every chance he gets to see if everything is okay. The constant anxiety makes him unable to focus on whatever it is he should be doing.

> With trust and confidence in one's spouse, everything in life is more beautiful and happy.

Rashi says that *shalal*, material goods, is not just referring to money.[35] Rashi says the husband of an *eishes chayil* will not lack any good. Nothing can be enjoyed when there is a state of constant anxiety. With trust and confidence in one's spouse, everything in life is more beautiful and happy.

Midrash – Sarah

To what extent can a husband trust in his wife and, conversely, to what extent can a woman trust her husband? No one plans to betray or deceive her spouse. We are all reasonable people who wouldn't purposely be negligent and untrustworthy. To what extent is trust supposed to permeate a Jewish marriage? How do we intentionally make this fundamental trait a

---

34 *Metzudas Dovid, Mishlei* 31:11.
35 Rashi, ibid.

part of our marriage? The person who can best guide us how to trust and be trusted is Sarah Imeinu, as she is described in the Midrash.

The Midrash says:

"The heart of her husband trusts in her."	בָּטַח בָּהּ לֵב בַּעְלָהּ
This is Sarah our matriarch,	זוֹ שָׂרָה אִמֵּנוּ
on whose behalf Avrohom got rich,	שֶׁהֶעֱשִׁיר אַבְרָהָם בִּשְׁבִילָהּ
as it is written,	שֶׁנֶּאֱמַר
"And to Avrohom he was good	וּלְאַבְרָהָם הֵיטִיב
on her behalf"	בַּעֲבוּרָהּ
(Bereishis 12:16).	(בראשית יב:טז)

The Midrash describes that just like our *pasuk*, Sarah was so trustworthy that Avrohom became rich because of her. The Midrash is rather cryptic and does not really explain how Sarah demonstrated this trust, why Avrohom became wealthy as a result, or what we can learn from her behavior.

Sarah's Trustworthiness

To understand the Midrash, we must go back to the *pesukim* that the Midrash cites. The Midrash quotes a *pasuk* from an episode in *Bereishis*. By studying that verse and its surrounding story, we can construct a picture of what trustworthiness really means.

This story takes place during a time of upheaval in Avrohom and Sarah's life. Avrohom and Sarah had been living in Charan and were converting pagans to monotheism. When Avrohom was seventy-five years old, Hashem appeared to him and told him to travel to a foreign, unnamed land.[36] Avrohom and Sarah abandoned their lives and families in Charan to travel, assuming the destination of choice was Canaan. Upon their arrival in Canaan, they wandered, never settling in one location, and waited for the revelation that would tell them they had arrived at the destination of their long, challenging journey.[37]

---

36 *Bereishis* 12:1.
37 Ramban, ibid.

Soon after their arrival, Canaan was ravaged by a famine. Life became unbearable, and Avrohom and Sarah were forced to travel to Egypt for food.[38]

As they neared Egypt, Avrohom realized that Sarah's external beauty was a threat to his life. The Egyptians were known for their immorality and would find a way to murder Avrohom so they could gain access to his wife. Avrohom asked Sarah to tell the Egyptians that they were siblings so that the Egyptians would not kill him.[39] Rashi explains that Avrohom was so concerned for their safety that he hid Sarah in the cargo to prevent anyone from seeing her.[40]

When Avrohom and Sarah arrived in Egypt, the customs officers opened all of their crates and discovered...Sarah! She was whisked off to Pharaoh's harem whereupon Avrohom informed the officers that he was Sarah's brother. The Egyptian began to shower Avrohom with gifts, hoping to buy his approval of his "sister's" treatment. Meanwhile, Sarah was a prisoner. Faithful to Avrohom, she did not reveal his deception despite the great danger in which she had been placed.

The *Midrash Tanchuma* relates that Sarah began to pray for salvation from Hashem; miraculously, an angel appeared. As soon as Pharaoh neared her, she gave the command, and the angel injured Pharaoh and everyone in the palace, preventing him from carrying out his plan.[41] This continued until Pharaoh discovered that Avrohom had lied about being Sarah's brother and not her husband. Pharaoh was furious and ordered Avrohom, Sarah, and their whole retinue deported from the country.

What about this story makes Sarah the paragon of trust?

Imagine if we were in the same situation. Your husband asks you to lie to the police to protect both of you. Somehow, you are the one who ends up in jail while he collects a large cash reward for your capture. What would be your reaction? Would you keep quiet about your

---

38   *Bereishis* 12:10.
39   *Bereishis* 12:11–13.
40   Rashi, *Bereishis* 12:15.
41   *Midrash Tanchuma, Lech Lecha*, chapter 5.

husband's role in landing you in jail when it was his idea in the first place? Would it even be correct to let your husband use you to save himself? Why is Sarah a model for being trustworthy? She keeps Avrohom's secret — but at what cost?

I believe that Sarah was a model of trustworthiness because Sarah trusted Avrohom to the extent that she was willing to risk her life for him, and she knew he was worthy of that trust. She would never betray his trust, nor did her trust in him ever waver. Even when Avrohom was profiting from her suffering, she did not betray him. She knew — with all of her being — who Avrohom was and that she would act with him in accordance with the trust she had in him. She summoned her spiritual strengths and trust in G-d to help her through this crisis rather than panicking and attacking Avrohom out of fear. She was then worthy of salvation through an open miracle that would not have occurred had she betrayed her husband.

> Sarah never betrayed Avrohom. She knew who Avrohom was. She would act with him in accordance with the trust she had in him.

Getting Practical: Building Trust

The lesson of this *pasuk* is that the *eishes chayil* is a trustworthy spouse. The Midrash adds that it is not enough to be trusted; the *eishes chayil* must also trust.

Building Emotional Trust

The primary trust that underlies a strong marriage is an emotional trust. Marriage is the most intimate of all relationships because both the husband and wife are completely vulnerable to what the other partner says and does.

To be trustworthy in a marriage, a person has to know that the ego of the spouse is exposed, and it requires gentle handling. When a spouse demeans, insults, or is sarcastic, something precious in the relationship is destroyed. We want our spouse to trust us enough to share his inner world. Being that vulnerable is scary and difficult; if we want that level of emotional intimacy, we have to earn it.

Earning emotional trust means that we need to be trustworthy even when we are angry or frustrated. If my husband forgets to call me when he knows he is going to be late, I can choose to discuss it with him sensitively and calmly, or I can react harshly. I've tried it both ways. While judgmental anger and frustration may feel righteous in the moment, it never has the long-term results I want.

> Earning emotional trust means that we need to be trustworthy even when we are angry or frustrated.

Creating emotional trust in a relationship is a two-way street and requires that we also allow ourselves to be vulnerable and share parts of ourselves that are tender and sensitive. The more we hide important details of our thoughts and feelings, the more walls we build between us and our spouse. These walls lead to a lack of trust, as without sharing, we do not truly know each other. After all, how can I trust someone whom I only know superficially? We can sense when something is hidden, and it soon feels safer to retreat and hide more. The cycle only gets worse and worse.

Our trustworthiness can be tested in so many ways. Like Sarah, the trust between a husband and wife must extend even to the moments when we are put in an uncomfortable spot: Our spouse has to know in his heart and mind that we are only looking out for what is best for him and that we will be his first defenders.

- There is a neighborhood party and I am late. Do I blame my husband, or do I apologize as a team without finger-pointing?
- I am annoyed at my husband. Do I share the juicy details with friends or respect the dignity of our relationship and keep it private?
- A relative is criticizing my husband's abilities. Do I commiserate? Do I listen without responding, or do I leave the situation?

It is challenging, but when we make trust a priority, we can be our spouse's best advocate and most ardent supporter regardless of what other people think about us.

Trust as Partners

One level of trust is built when we are emotionally trustworthy; another level comes when we are reliable partners in building a home. Our spouse relies on our commitments to plan his life and schedule. He wants and needs to trust us. In our marriage, we are co-parents, we share financial responsibilities for family expenses, and we are legally responsible for what happens in our home. It makes things difficult if we make a commitment and then fail to keep it. It is better to promise less and be honest about our limitations than to promise a lot and fail to see something through.

> Our spouse plans his life and schedule as part of a team. When we honor our commitments, we are reliable partners in building a home.

Everyone overcommits at some time. Sometimes I overcommit because I misjudge the timing; other times it's because I didn't want to look bad or say no. We need to pay attention to how often we don't follow through to make sure that being trustworthy is a higher priority for us than avoiding conflict and looking good. Trust is too important a value to risk for short-term gains.

Learning How to Trust

The Midrash describing Sarah added to our understanding of trust in a marriage that it is not enough to be trustworthy; we must also learn to trust our husband.

How does a woman develop a relationship with her husband that is so strong that she would risk her life for him as Sarah did?

Furthermore, is it even proper for a modern woman to act like Sarah? After all, our husband is not as holy as Avrohom. When is it appropriate to trust an imperfect human, and when should we be wary and recognize that our priority is to protect ourselves?

Bringing Hashem into the Picture

Building trust is a lifelong work and requires a strong foundation of spiritual devotion. Sarah's first action when taken to the palace was not to panic and blame Avrohom. She recognized that she needed to bring G-d into the situation and ask Him for help. This, then, is the first step we must all take. The car breaks down, dinner is burnt, or the fridge light is on over Shabbos. It may be his fault, it may be our fault, but whose fault it is is not important. There is a Hand greater than either of us at play here. Like Sarah, we can turn the outcome over to Hashem before we get into blame and distrust. With His help, we will be able to solve a problem in the best possible way. When we are confronted by something that annoys or scares us, a prayer for direction can never hurt.

> Like Sarah, when a problem arises, we can turn the outcome over to Hashem before we get into blame and distrust.

Paying Attention to Build Trust

The next step is to proactively work to learn how to trust in our husband. When we get married, we are essentially marrying a stranger. No matter how long we have dated or how much we have talked, nothing is the same as living with a spouse in a committed relationship. We do not spend our time when dating discussing capping the toothpaste or picking up laundry off the floor, but these small things can become the battleground that tests the trust in a relationship. Every day of a marriage has many opportunities to build trust — or betray it.

Trust comes slowly through repeated acts of devotion that we notice and appreciate. We need to value and acknowledge to ourself — and to our spouse — each time they have our best interests at heart so that we develop a deeper emotional connection and more trust in them. If we dismiss all positive acts of devotion as "expected" (for example, "a husband is supposed to bring his wife flowers for Shabbos — he doesn't get any points for that!") and focus on the mistakes, we will never come to the beautiful level of trust that is the foundation of healthy marriages.

To reach trust, we also need to treat our husband as the mature partner that he is. If our husband buys a different brand of tuna than the one we prefer, we can learn to live with it. If his bedtime routine for the kids is more fun and less timely than ours, we can choose to allow him to discover his own voice. If we try to micromanage or control through belittling, suggesting, or judging, we are not only destroying his trust in us, but we are sabotaging the chance to develop trust in our spouse as a partner.

Setting Boundaries

Trust develops in other ways as well. Healthy boundaries allow there to be a vulnerable place for trust to develop. How to speak is one area where boundaries can be set: Early on, couples establish acceptable ways of communicating and sharing responsibilities. We cannot speak sarcastically or demean our husband, nor can we allow ourselves to be spoken to in that way. When our boundaries are violated (for example, if a husband pressures his wife to do something she feels uncomfortable with or if he often speaks to her in a belittling way when he has a bad day) we need to find a way to communicate this so that the relationship can grow. If we respond hysterically or violently, or if we do not address the issue at all, we are undermining the trust our marriage requires in order to work.

Setting boundaries creates a sacred space where love and holiness can flourish.

Setting boundaries is not about being right or taking what the other says or does personally. It is also not a missed opportunity to become holy and righteous by ignoring our needs. Setting boundaries creates a sacred space where love and holiness can flourish.

Aside from how we communicate, healthy boundaries should be set with how we relate to (other) members of the opposite gender. Because we care so much about our spouse and our relationship, we need to consider what constitutes a violation of that sacred trust and set safeguards against it. At work or in the community, in our day and age, even the most well-intentioned spouse can find himself or herself in problematic scenarios with members of the opposite gender. Mistakes and misunderstandings — even "minor" ones — can rip the fabric of a home because they touch on our trust of our most intimate partner. When we acknowledge our need to build safeguards for trust, we can discuss our needs without fear of sounding harsh and judgmental. Some of these may include: filters on the Internet, limiting emotionally close relationships with members of the opposite gender, and how we interact on social media and in person. When these boundaries come from a desire to be close and to trust rather than from a lack of trust, they are relationship-builders.

Communicating about Boundaries

There will be times when we feel hurt or annoyed by behavior patterns, and a lack of trust develops. Ignoring these negative feelings does not help us, our husband, or our marriage. It takes thought as to how and when we start these discussions that are likely to be awkward and uncomfortable.

Timing is everything. The house will not burn down if we do not respond in the heat of the moment. Waiting to feel calm and process our emotions helps the conversation have a productive outcome. Checking that we are not overreacting is an important step. Saying a short prayer first helps keep the focus on what is important, and paying attention to what our husband is doing at the time ensures that both halves of the conversation will be heard and said. The goal is not to make the other person feel bad or to vent; it is to build a strong marriage and let our husband know our needs.

These conversations can make us feel exposed, which can be scary and threatening. What if my husband gets angry? What if he denies my feelings? What if he points out where I have been wrong? What if he needs something from me that I can't or don't want to give him? What if he says no? What if he doesn't change? What then?

Any and all of these things may or may not happen. We don't

communicate our needs to control and manipulate the other person. We do so because it is the right thing to do in a relationship in order to build trust. If the outcome of a conversation is not what we had hoped, we now have information that can help us make decisions and that teaches us something. If it works out, our relationship can grow in a different direction. The outcome of the difficult conversation is up to Hashem, not us. We can only try our best.

The work of setting boundaries is not a one-day or a one-week endeavor. It is a process like that of becoming a partner that, as discussed in the first *pasuk* of *Eishes Chayil*, takes a lifetime. There will be times when it is easier and times when it seems like there is no hope. No one is perfect — not us and not our husband — and there will be successes and disappointments. All we can be expected to do is to continue to try and to do so with a prayer on our lips.

Being trusted and developing trust is not easy. Sarah Imeinu could risk her life, and Avrohom Avinu could risk his, because of the trust that existed between them and the trust they had in Hashem. We are not on that level, but we can take steps to be trustworthy and learn to trust by making it a priority in our lives. When we do, we will see huge dividends. Trusting and being trustworthy allows us to become the *eishes chayil* described in the rest of the *pesukim* and brings joy and richness to our lives — both materially and emotionally.

 Summary

"The heart of her husband trusts in her."   בָּטַח בָּהּ לֵב בַּעְלָהּ
Sarah, our matriarch   שָׂרָה אִמֵּנוּ

From the Pasuk We Learn

An *eishes chayil* is a woman who is trustworthy. She acts with her husband's and family's best interests in mind: spiritually, financially, socially, and emotionally.

From the Midrash We Learn

Sarah Imeinu trusted Avrohom Avinu at a great risk to her life. From Sarah we learn that it is not enough to be trusted. An *eishes chayil* builds a home where trust flourishes, and both husband and wife trust each other.

Practical Steps

Becoming trustworthy
1. Speak kindly and with respect even when upset.
2. Be loyal to our husband and respect his privacy.
3. Share our true self and be willing to be vulnerable.
4. Be responsible financially and with our time commitments.

Trusting our husband
5. Notice acts of kindness.
6. Don't micromanage; allow our husband to make mistakes and make adult choices that we don't agree with.
7. Set boundaries.
8. Communicate when trust has been violated so that it can be rebuilt.

Questions

Self-Growth

1. How do I make an effort to be a loyal friend?
2. Am I trustworthy? How do I decide which commitments to pursue and honor?
3. What helps me be kind in my speech and tone and allow for mistakes in others?
4. How do I make honesty a priority for me? Do I notice when I change facts or lie?
5. How can I respect others' loyalty to their spouse and encourage that? How do I make sure my friends don't need to choose between their loyalty to their spouse and to me?
6. How do I communicate my needs respectfully and set boundaries to rebuild trust?

As Wives and Mothers

7. How can I live up to my commitments so that I am trustworthy?
8. How can I make sure that I am looking out for the best interests of my husband and family in the way I spend money and with my other behaviors?
9. How do my husband and I learn about each other and our authentic selves even though it feels vulnerable?
10. What are safeguards that my husband and I have for relationships with members of the opposite gender, on the Internet, and in other areas of temptation?
11. What are my guidelines when I will talk about my husband to other people?

Teaching Our Daughters

12. How do I help my daughter learn to communicate her needs to set boundaries?

13. How do I help my daughter learn to value the sanctity of a marriage before other friendships and relationships?
14. How do I help my daughter learn to be a trustworthy friend?

CHAPTER 5

Consistent Kindness

גְּמָלַתְהוּ טוֹב וְלֹא רָע כֹּל יְמֵי חַיֶּיהָ.

*She does him good and not evil
all the days of her life.*

Peshat

Eishes Chayil began by laying the foundation for the ideal marriage with partnership and trust. The third ingredient of successful marriages can only be understood by analyzing this *pasuk* and the Midrash carefully.

Why So Many Words?

The *pasuk* begins by stating that the *eishes chayil* does good and not bad for her husband all the days of her life. Shlomo HaMelech could have simply said, "She does him good." Why does he mention that she does not do bad? Also, what is the point of informing us that the *eishes chayil* does this good each and every day of her life?

A Typical Day

To answer these questions, just think back to some of the ordinary bad days that happen in any home. It's the early morning and one of the kids is running a fever, another lost his only clean sock, and you need to get to work in fifteen minutes. Your husband walks through the door at that moment and asks what he can take for lunch.

> How can we "do good" and respond with kindness even when we are harried and stressed?

Doing good and not evil applies at this moment, too. It means that even when things are stressed, the *eishes chayil* does good and responds with kindness.

Let's play the situation differently. The husband (not yours, I'm sure) walks through the door and starts criticizing his wife for the chaos. He is stressed and is taking out his frustration on the easiest and nearest target. Does a wife doing good and not bad to her husband apply on this day as well? Wouldn't it suffice to just not do bad? Who could expect a wife to "do good" at this moment?

The Ideal

The *pasuk* tells us that we have to strive for a different ideal. The *eishes chayil* pays back good — and not bad — each and every day of her life. Her kindness for her husband is consistent and independent of her emotions — even his behavior!⁴² It happens all the days of her life: Her kindness is independent of her mood, her health, or her other stresses. It happens because it is how she has trained herself, who she has become, and who she is — irrespective of externals.

A friend of mine came close to articulating this ideal to me when she described her attitude in her marriage. Her husband often comes home late from work on *erev Shabbos*, after the kids have all been bathed and the table has been set. She told me that no matter what time her husband walks through the door, or even if he decided to sleep in the office

---

42   *Metzudas Dovid, Mishlei* 31:12.

over Shabbos, how she reacts is still her problem, not his. She, not he, is in control of how she responds and how she greets him. She is able to do good — and not bad — every day because she does not put her destiny in the hands of another person's behavior.

This concept seems superhuman. How can a wife not respond when slighted in this most intimate and emotional of all relationships? Furthermore, how can she even "do good" in these situations? For guidance, we can once again turn to the Midrash:

Midrash – Rivkah

"She does him good and not evil."	גְּמָלַתְהוּ טוֹב וְלֹא רָע
This is Rivkah, our matriarch,	זוֹ רִבְקָה אִמֵּנוּ
who did kindness to Yitzchok	שֶׁגָּמְלָה לְיִצְחָק
at the time when Sarah, his mother, died.	בְּשָׁעָה שֶׁמֵּתָה שָׂרָה אִמּוֹ

How Is Rivkah a Model?

This Midrash is rather cryptic; after all, Sarah died three years before Rivkah arrived. What kindness did she do when Sarah died?

Sarah's Tent

We must turn to another Midrash for the answer.[43]

The Midrash explains that there were four unique qualities to Sarah's tent:

1. A cloud hovered over the entrance to the tent.
2. All doors were open wide.
3. Challah stayed fresh from week to week.
4. A candle was lit from one Shabbos to the next.

Each of these things disappeared when Sarah died and returned with Rivkah's arrival and marriage to Yitzchok.

---

43 *Bereishis Rabbah* 60:16.

The Significance of Sarah's Tent

According to the *Yefas Toar* commentary on the Midrash, each of these aspects of Sarah's tent represented another component of her holiness:[44]

The Cloud

First, there was a cloud at the entrance of her tent. This cloud was not produced by humid conditions that followed Sarah. Rather it was the cloud of the *Shechinah* (Hashem's presence that found an earthly abode near Sarah.) Sarah, and all the matriarchs, were *nevi'os*, prophetesses.[45] They merited receiving prophecy and being surrounded by the Divine presence because of their extraordinary devotion to the Divine will and their perfection of thought and character.

> The hovering cloud, open doors, fresh challah, and lit candles in Sarah's tent each represented another component of her holiness.

The Tent Doors

Second, Sarah's tent was open wide. This does not mean that her tent was drafty. It states in *Pirkei Avos*:

יְהִי בֵיתְךָ פָּתוּחַ לִרְוָחָה.[46]
Let your house be opened up wide.

There are two very important reasons to have guests. The first is to be influenced by the good people who will visit and the second is so that we can do the mitzvah of *chessed*, loving-kindness. Both Sarah and Rivkah were not only concerned with the intellectual pursuit of spirituality through prophecy; they were also generous by sharing their home and taking care of strangers.

---

44   *Yefas Toar, Bereishis Rabbah* 72:6.
45   *Bereishis Rabbah* 72:6.
46   *Avos* 1:5.

The Blessing in the Challah

Third, a special blessing was found in the challah. Challah bread represents one's livelihood. Sarah, and later Rivkah, brought blessing into the livelihood of their homes by being careful with how they managed the finances. This special care was the blessing that they put into their challah.

The Lit Candles

Finally, the fourth component of Sarah's (and, later, Rivkah's) tent was constantly lit candles. The Gemara relates that if a home can only afford one set of candles, either for Shabbos or for Chanukah, the candles should be used for Shabbos. The rationale is that Shabbos candles are lit for *shalom bayis*, domestic harmony.[47] In Sarah's home, the Shabbos candles remained lit all week. In other words, in her home, serenity and calm reigned supreme. Stress and divisiveness never entered her doors. The warmth of her *shalom bayis* illuminated her home all week.

> Yitzchok was raised by a mother who was spiritual, generous, industrious, and warm. When she died, all the characteristics that transformed her tent into a home died with her.

This was the home in which Yitzchok was raised. His mother was spiritual, generous, industrious, and warm. When she died, all the characteristics that transformed her tent into a home died with her.

Rivkah's Kindness

It was into this void that Rivkah found herself beginning her marriage with Yitzchok. She could not help but be compared to her perfect mother-in-law. Many daughters-in-law would have insisted on forging their own identity. Rivkah did what was the greatest kindness to Yitzchok. She perpetuated Sarah's legacy and reinstituted the practices that made the tent holy. She became the spiritual heir of Sarah by being

---

47   *Talmud Bavli, Shabbos* 23:2.

spiritual, generous, industrious, and warm, like her predecessor. She made her home an extension of Sarah's legacy. These kindnesses, which permeated her home day in and day out, brought her husband comfort and made her the second of our matriarchs.

While this may, in and of itself, have been remarkable, what made it even more exceptional was how the life story of Rivkah and Yitzchok played out and how Rivkah responded and acted throughout.

Core Disagreements

Yitzchok and Rivkah were married for twenty years and still had not had children. They prayed with all of their being to merit a child; miraculously, Rivkah became pregnant. But this was not an ordinary pregnancy. She felt as if a war was taking place inside of her.[48] She asked other women if they ever had such physical pains, and they told her that her suffering was unique.[49] Rivkah resolved to ask a *navi*, a prophet, for his prayers and insight.[50] The Ohr HaChaim explains that she wanted to know why she would miraculously conceive if she or the baby was going to die.[51]

The *navi* who responded to her pleas gave her insight into what her children would become.

וַיֹּאמֶר ה' לָהּ, שְׁנֵי גוֹיִם בְּבִטְנֵךְ, וּשְׁנֵי לְאֻמִּים, מִמֵּעַיִךְ יִפָּרֵדוּ;
וּלְאֹם מִלְאֹם יֶאֱמָץ, וְרַב יַעֲבֹד צָעִיר.[52]

And Hashem said to her: Two nations are in your womb,
and two peoples shall be separated from your insides;
and the one people shall be stronger than the other people,
and the elder shall serve the younger.

On that day, Rivkah learned that she was not carrying ordinary children. Her pregnancy was the beginning of an epic battle for supremacy. In the end, the righteous younger son would prevail over the elder son.

---

48   *Bereishis* 25:20–22.
49   Ibn Ezra, *Bereishis* 25:22.
50   Rashbam, ibid.
51   Ohr HaChaim, ibid.
52   *Bereishis* 25:23.

A prophecy was shared with her, and now she was to go home. Could she share this prophecy with her husband? Rivkah concluded that he was a greater prophet than she was, and if it was intended for him to know this information, G-d Himself would have told him. And so, Rivkah kept the news to herself.[53]

When the children were born, and later as they grew, this necessary secret changed how Yitzchok and Rivkah dealt with their children. Yitzchok loved Esav. Hashem allowed Yitzchok to be fooled into believing Esav was righteous and good. Rivkah saw past the ruse of her eldest son and loved Yaakov fiercely because of his goodness and purity.[54]

> Despite disagreeing about a fundamental issue, the Shabbos candles in Rivkah's home stayed lit from one week to the next.

The Torah does not relate whether the couple discussed the difference in their opinions regarding their children. But the Midrash tells us that Rivkah's home had Shabbos candles lit from one week to another. Despite disagreeing about such a fundamental issue, Rivkah was able to perform only kindness and never harm her husband throughout their marriage.

Halachah above All

Fast-forward fifty years. Rivkah had orchestrated that Yaakov receive his father's blessing rather than the blessings be given to the wicked Esav. Yitzchok had the divine veil lifted and finally saw Esav for who he was. He recognized and acknowledged what Rivkah had seen all these years.

Rivkah then had another prophecy; this time, that Esav planned to kill Yaakov as soon as his father died.[55] Realizing that Yitzchok's life could end at any moment, she told Yaakov to flee from the

---

53   Ramban, *Bereishis* 27:4; *Chizkuni*, *Bereishis* 25:27.
54   *Baalei HaTosfos*, *Bereishis* 25:28.
55   Rashi, *Bereishis* 27:42.

murderous temper of his brother.⁵⁶ Yaakov wanted to go, but there was still a problem. He couldn't leave without bidding his father farewell. Disappearing without informing Yitzchok was a cruel punishment to inflict on his father. Telling Yitzchok about Esav's intentions would also pain his father. According to the Ohr HaChaim, had Rivkah (or Yaakov) told Yitzchok about Esav's evil plot, it would have been *rechilus*, a violation of the Torah laws forbidding gossip in which a person causes conflict between two parties.⁵⁷

Rivkah thought of a plan to accomplish her goals while saving her husband from undue suffering and anger. She complained that Yaakov might marry a local Canaanite woman who served idols. Yitzchok agreed with her assessment and sent Yaakov to Rivkah's childhood home to find a wife.

Note what happened. For sixty-three years, Yitzchok has disagreed with Rivkah's opinion of her children. He finally understood her love of Yaakov, and yet Rivkah does not use Esav's plan to prove that she had always been right. Rivkah could have been self-righteous; instead, she was guided by *yiras Shamayim* (fear of Heaven) and acted with self-control based on Hashem's will rather than her emotions. It was crucial to her that she not hurt her husband — or break halachah.

> Rivkah could have been self-righteous, but instead was guided by *yiras Shamayim* (fear of Heaven) and acted with self-control based on Hashem's will rather than her emotions.

This vision and commitment to Hashem's will allowed there to be *shalom bayis*, domestic harmony, for all the years of her marriage. Rivkah was less concerned about her feelings and more concerned about doing what was right. She was guided by the cloud inherited from Sarah, which hovered over her tent. She had a connection to Hashem that guided her in all she did. This allowed her to act with kindness no matter the circumstances.

---

56   *Bereishis* 27:42–46.
57   Ohr HaChaim 27:46.

Getting Practical: Consistency in Marriage

The hallmark of the actions of Rivkah and the *eishes chayil* in our *pasuk* was their consistency throughout changing life events. We all have good moments. The question is, how do we make our home a safe haven — for our husband, our children, and ourself — no matter the circumstances? How do we choose kindness despite provocation to do otherwise?

Like we learned from Sarah, and now from Rivkah, the first step is to work on our own spiritual connection with Hashem. The more profound a connection that we have with Him, the less trivial details about others will bother us. When we connect to Hashem, our relationships with others flow from that source. When we lose that connection, we are threatened by every insult, perceived or real, that we experience.

We are all capable of becoming like Rivkah: to be able to do good even when we feel provoked, even if we are not (yet!) prophetesses. We can train ourselves to deal — successfully — with challenging situations.

For a number of years, I was an elementary school teacher whose duty it was to monitor kids on the playground during recess. One of the biggest problems that kids have at recess is that the minute they get insulted, they respond with a fist or a nasty comment, and things escalate quickly as each person acts in line with his initial reaction. I had to break up many fights that started small and quickly got out of control.

This doesn't only happen with children; adults can act very much like children in this regard. When a person feels threatened or insulted, he can respond quickly with a put-down or aggressive response.

My job during recess duty was to help students recognize that between every action and reaction there is an invisible space of time where choices can be made. That space is where our free will resides. Even if a child thought he was being insulted, he could choose to talk to a teacher or walk away rather than fight back. I had to teach the kids that there would always be things happening that would set them off emotionally. When someone excludes you from a game, the initial reaction is to feel hurt. No matter how much planning and talking we do beforehand, we will not change that reality. That initial feeling isn't good or bad; it just is.

However, the moment *after* that initial feeling is a special time. The moment between when we feel and before we act is a time to decide how to act. When we react out of fear and emotion, we demean ourselves and cause us to lose respect for ourselves. When we respond from a thoughtful, spiritual place, we end up respecting ourselves more.

Having an empowering response to a difficult emotion does not come naturally. It requires pre-planning. As a teacher, I was taught to role play different scenarios to enable the students to become comfortable with different reactions they could have to emotional situations. I've seen that it works.

> We don't lose our calm over the large, shocking things, but over the small things. We can plan responses so that we can make good choices when we are triggered.

As adults, there are some things in life that are unpredictable. Sometimes, our reaction may be out of our hands as our emotions are so powerful they overtake us. There are many other things, however, that we can predict. The first time our husband says something we find insulting (like asking us to call his mother for her meatball recipe), it is a shock. The second time, we know it is in the realm of possibility. The annoyances over which we abandon our calm are often not the large, shocking things. It's the small things like showing up late, not helping out, or ignoring us. For those things, we can plan responses so that when we have a moment to think, we can make good choices.

I was discussing this idea with a friend when she gave me a great example that I worked on in my own life. Every night, she felt triggered during homework time. She would end up shouting at the kids because they wouldn't get their work done or because they were talking over each other while she was trying to get dinner on the table. Finally, she had enough of feeling lousy about her reactions and made a plan. She drew up a schedule, got dinner done the night before, and had snacks ready when the kids got home from school. She made sure that she had also eaten so that she could have patience. Homework is still not stress-free because, after all, it is still homework, but she has addressed the key problems that made the time so challenging and left her feeling inept. Things changed when she didn't take the negativity as a given, and she worked on contributing factors so that she could be in a more positive frame of mind.

All the Days of Her Life

Thus far, we have been discussing the first half of the *pasuk* — that the *eishes chayil* does good and not bad. The second half of the *pasuk* also has much to teach us. It says that the *eishes chayil* acts kindly all the days of her life. This does not only mean that the *eishes chayil* responds with kindness on days when she is in a bad mood. It teaches us that she makes kindness a regular habit on ordinary days as well. The candles of *shalom bayis* in the tents of Sarah and Rivkah were lit from one Shabbos to another — including the ordinary days of the week.

> Days that seem ordinary are the foundation of our lives and can be made special with attention and forethought.

In Judaism, the ordinary is extraordinary. We say a blessing before we drink water, smell herbs, and hear thunder. There are blessings to thank G-d for clothing, for shoes, and the ability to stand. Each experience in life, even the most mundane and ordinary, has the capacity to be elevated to the spiritual with mindfulness and attention.

Days that seem ordinary are the foundation of our lives and can be made special with attention and forethought. Every day can be filled with joy so that our home is a warm and happy place. On ordinary days, we can decide to make our marriage a priority and make our relationship stronger by doing special — yet ordinary — things.

Saying thank you, making a favorite supper, or expressing our love — for no reason — during a telephone call are kindnesses. Leaving a note, helping out with a smile, and letting our spouse get the last word are also kindnesses that can be done any day. When we listen, attend, care, and partner, we are acting like the *eishes chayil*.

Kindness – Any Day and Every Day

Acting kindly can stem from our emotions. When we are in a good mood, we act generously; but when we are not, we may not think of others. Alternatively, we can make a disciplined decision so that kindness is a fixture in our homes. In this scenario, being kind becomes part of our spiritual practice rather than a response to those around us. When we focus on being kind and make it a goal, the tone in our home changes.

Rivkah was able to be a kind, loving, and supportive wife in the most trying of circumstances. Her commitment to halachah and to her character development allowed her to transcend issues that rocked the spiritual world. It is for this reason that she became the second of our matriarchs and the second woman listed in the Midrash.

We can look to Rivkah as a source of inspiration as we try to make our homes become like that of Sarah and Rivkah, with the *Shechinah* dwelling within and with a warm feeling within our walls — all week long.

Summary

"She does him good and not evil." גְּמָלַתְהוּ טוֹב וְלֹא רָע
Rivkah, our matriarch רִבְקָה אִמֵּנוּ

From the Pasuk We Learn

The *eishes chayil* is kind — independent of her mood, her health, or her other stresses. It is who she trained herself to be, who she has become, and who she is — irrespective of externals.

From the Midrash We Learn

Rivkah had a home marked by its tranquility, despite her fundamental disagreements with her husband, Yitzchok, about how to raise their children. From Rivkah we learn that being kind is not based on personality. An *eishes chayil* can act consistently kind if she focuses on doing Hashem's will by commiting to observe halachah and prioritizes her own character development.

Practical Steps

1. Prioritize working on oneself rather than focusing on the shortcomings of others.
2. Plan responses to the challenging behaviors of others.
3. Set yourself up for success by making sure that unneeded stresses are minimized.
4. Sprinkle life with warmth and kind actions every (ordinary) day to create a loving home.

Questions

Self-Growth

1. How can I become more disciplined about doing kindness for those I know (at home and at work), as well as for strangers whom I meet?
2. How do I nurture my spiritual and emotional life so that people's behaviors do not disturb me?
3. What are some things that annoy me and cause me to react in a hostile and unkind manner? What is an alternate way of reacting?

As Wives and Mothers

4. How can I increase the small favors I do for my husband, based on what he would appreciate?
5. Is my home marked by a feeling of warmth and kindness? How have I achieved this, or how can I achieve this?
6. How can I work on accepting my husband's needs fully and without being critical? How do I communicate this with him?
7. What are some things that have been repeated areas of conflict in my marriage? Can I maintain my kindness even when these issues arise?

Teaching Our Daughters

8. How do I help my daughter learn to be kind, giving, and generous even when it is uncomfortable? What limits should I help her set regarding when she can give and when she needs to take care of herself and her family's needs?
9. How do I help my daughter learn to pause and react thoughtfully while respecting her own needs and feelings?

CHAPTER 6

Initiative

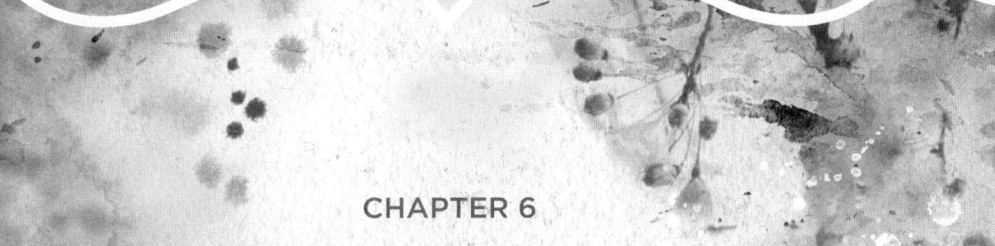

דָּרְשָׁה צֶמֶר וּפִשְׁתִּים וַתַּעַשׂ בְּחֵפֶץ כַּפֶּיהָ.

She seeks wool and flax and works willingly with her palms (hands).

Peshat

The first three *pesukim* of *Eishes Chayil* dealt with the characteristics that serve as the foundation of a successful marriage. These characteristics, embodied by our first two matriarchs, Sarah and Rivkah, are partnership [אֵשֶׁת חַיִל], trust [בָּטַח בָּהּ], and consistent kindness [גְּמָלַתְהוּ טוֹב].

The next series of *pesukim,* seven in total, describes character traits that refine a woman, improve her life, and create a strong home. Each of the seven *pesukim* involves a woman's participation in the finances and practical management of her home. Her involvement in the financial stability of the home is an indication of her commitment to ensuring the strength of her family in all areas.

Seeking

This section begins by informing us that the *eishes chayil* seeks wool and flax and then processes them with a joyous attitude. There are many hobbies a person may have. Some collect baseball cards, others collect stamps. Why is the *eishes chayil* collecting wool and flax? The first word in the *pasuk*, "*darshah*" (she seeks), is also strange. Why must the *eishes chayil* "seek" out the threads? Why doesn't she go down the street to the local wool and flax store to pick up a few spools?

Woman's Responsibility in the Home

The answer lies in a woman's responsibilities to her household, as defined by the Talmud. Before the nineteenth century, every home had a spinning wheel and loom. At any spare moment, the woman of the household could be found sitting at the spinning wheel or loom, adding another few inches to a piece of fabric that could be used for clothing. Without this work, the family would not be clothed. The Talmud relates that one of a wife's duties in the home was to spin yarn. However, the wife's responsibility was only to spin.[58] If her husband did not provide the raw materials, then she would have no obligation to produce any thread.

> The *eishes chayil* is not only concerned about whether or not she has the obligation to spin.

In our case, the *Metzudas Dovid* explains,[59] the *eishes chayil* is not concerned about whether or not she has the obligation to spin. The *eishes chayil*'s husband is not providing the wool or flax, yet she steps in and does her husband's job so that she can do hers, that of spinning. She goes above the call of duty by being *darshah* — seeking — to fill the needs of her household.

---

58   *Talmud Bavli, Kesuvos* 59b.
59   *Metzudas Dovid, Mishlei* 31:13.

A Mind of Their Own

The *pasuk* then says that her palms work willingly. It sounds like her hands have a mind of their own and want to do the work of spinning for her!

Spinning is tedious work that requires long periods of sitting and doing mindless, routine activity. There are far more interesting ways for the *eishes chayil* to occupy her time. Yet, as the Ibn Ezra explains, it is as if her hands are possessed with a passion to do the work.[60] Her husband is supposed to bring home wool; her friends' husbands do and her brothers-in-law do, but her husband does not. Any woman could feel resentful or play the part of the martyr. "Ah well, you know that you do not bring the wool," sigh… "I guess I'll have to find some myself and…" sigh… "then my work can begin." But that is not her reaction. Instead, she chooses to do her work with a positive attitude.

Initiative

What is reflected in this *pasuk* is joy at being a partner in building the home. This *eishes chayil* does not worry about whose turn it is to do any given job. She looks at what she is capable of doing and does it wholeheartedly. She does not check whose night it is to do the dishes or complain about having to work to pay for the kids' tuition. She is excited by the prospect of building her home using her independent talents.

> This *eishes chayil* does not worry about whose turn it is to do a job. She looks at what she is capable of doing and does it wholeheartedly.

This level of industriousness requires independence. It requires the *eishes chayil* to have a vision of what she wants her home to be like and be happy to do that which she is capable of to bring that vision to fruition.

---

60 Ibn Ezra, *Mishlei* 31:13.

Midrash – Leah

The Midrash highlights one Jewish woman who took the initiative to bring about her vision despite others' perception of her and a lack of support. That woman is Leah, the third of our *Imahos*. The Midrash says:

"She seeks wool and flax."	דָּרְשָׁה צֶמֶר וּפִשְׁתִּים
This is Leah, our matriarch,	זוֹ לֵאָה אִמֵּנוּ
who accepted Yaakov	שֶׁקִּבְּלָה לְיַעֲקֹב
with a pleasant countenance.	בְּסֵבֶר פָּנִים יָפוֹת
As it is written, "And Yaakov came home	דִּכְתִיב וַיָּבֹא יַעֲקֹב
from the field in the evening,	מִן הַשָּׂדֶה בָּעֶרֶב
and Leah went out to greet him,	וַתֵּצֵא לֵאָה לִקְרָאתוֹ
and she said to him, you should come to me	וַתֹּאמֶר אֵלַי תָּבוֹא
because I paid for you…"	כִּי שָׂכֹר שְׂכַרְתִּיךָ וְגו'.
(Ibid. 29:16).	(שם כט:טז)
Therefore, she merited	לְפִיכָךְ זָכְתָה
to have come from her kings and prophets.	וְיָצְאוּ מִמֶּנָּה מְלָכִים וּנְבִיאִים

An Uncertain Future

This Midrash chooses one specific episode in Leah's life that shows that she took initiative to implement her vision. It tells us how Leah greeted Yaakov one evening and told him to come to her tent. As a result, she had children from whom came the kings and prophets. To understand this event and what the Midrash means, one must understand what led up to her actions and subsequent reward.

Marriage to Yaakov

Lavan, Rivkah's brother, had two daughters. The elder daughter was Leah and the younger daughter was Rochel, whom the Torah tells us was beautiful.⁶¹ Rochel was destined to marry Yaakov, a holy man who devoted his life to the service of Hashem.

The Torah also tells us that Leah's eyes were weak. Rashi explains what caused her weak eyes: The people of her neighborhood predicted that she would marry her first cousin, Esav (Yaakov's older brother), a wicked and violent man. Leah's deepest desire in life was to be a partner in building a home devoted to Hashem and to spread the message of monotheism to the world. She was distraught at the prospect of being married to a man who was the antithesis of her life's goals. She cried and prayed to be saved from this horrific fate.⁶²

Yaakov arrived at Lavan's house while fleeing Esav. He became engaged to Rochel and worked for Lavan for seven years to earn the right to marry her. Leah's opportunity to escape marriage to the evil Esav came when Lavan decided that Leah (and not Rochel) should marry Yaakov, since Leah was older and should be married first. Lavan tricked Yaakov into marrying Leah. Seven days later, Yaakov married Rochel as well. ⁶³

Children

While Leah married Yaakov for noble reasons, he was not happy with her. The Midrash relates that Yaakov called Leah a cheat and was even ready to divorce her.⁶⁴ The Midrash goes on to describe how the neighbors began to hate Leah and resent her for what she did to Rochel.⁶⁵ They had always thought she was holy; now they ostracized her.

Hashem saw Leah's isolation and the pure motivation for her actions and allowed her, although she was born a barren woman, to conceive.

---

61   *Bereishis* 29:17.
62   Rashi, ibid.
63   *Bereishis* 29:20–30.
64   *Bereishis Rabbah* 70.
65   *Bereishis Rabbah* 71.

conceive.⁶⁶ Leah named her eldest son Reuven to acknowledge that Hashem *ra'ah*, He saw, the pain she suffered because her husband did not love her. Reuven's birth was quickly followed by two brothers, Shimon and Levi.⁶⁷

Then Leah had a fourth son, Yehudah. Her joy knew no bounds. All four *Imahos* (matriarchs) were prophetesses.⁶⁸ Leah knew that Yaakov would have four wives and that he would have twelve sons. She knew that, by right, she should only have had three sons, yet Hashem had granted her a fourth. After this fourth son, Leah stopped having children.⁶⁹

Sacrifice

During the time when Leah had four sons, Rochel did not have any children. Rochel decided to give Yaakov her maid, Bilhah, as a wife in the hopes that Bilhah would be a "surrogate" mother and that Rochel would merit having her own children one day as a result. Rochel was replicating the actions of Sarah, who had Avrohom marry her maid and then merited to bear Yitzchok. Through this sacrifice for Yaakov, Rochel hoped that she too would merit bearing her own children.⁷⁰ Indeed, Bilhah had two sons whom Rochel helped raise.

Leah saw that Rochel had helped Yaakov have children and thought that she too should try to help Yaakov fulfill his destiny of having twelve sons.⁷¹ Introducing a rival wife was unnecessary. Leah did not need merits to have more children, as Rochel did, for Leah already had more than her share of children. Yet Leah encouraged Yaakov to marry her maid, Zilpah. In doing so, Leah showed **why she** is one of the *Imahos*. Leah introduced another wife who **could** compete for her husband's time and affection for a greater spiritual good.

---

66   Ramban, *Bereishis* 29:31.
67   *Bereishis* 29:30–34.
68   Rashi, *Bereishis* 29:35.
69   *Bereishis* 29:34.
70   Rashi, *Bereishis* 30:4.
71   *Bereishis* 30:3–12.

Leah named each of Zilpah's two children names that reflected how happy she was to play a part in bringing Yaakov's children, the *shevatim*, into the world. She called the oldest Gad, from the root *bagad*, which means "luck comes"; and the second she called Asher, which means happiness, because she felt so happy that she was able to contribute to the birth of more *shevatim*.

> When Leah encouraged Yaakov to marry her maid Zilpah, she introduced another wife into the family for a greater spiritual good.

After the birth of two children to Bilhah and two to Zilpah, Leah's eldest son, Reuven, went out to collect *dudaim*, special flowers. Rochel requested these *dudaim* from Leah. Leah did not initially want to give up her son's gift but did so for the opportunity to spend the night with Yaakov.[72] It is at this point that our Midrash begins.

"She seeks wool and flax."	דָּרְשָׁה צֶמֶר וּפִשְׁתִּים
This is Leah, our matriarch,	זוֹ לֵאָה אִמֵּנוּ
who accepted Yaakov	שֶׁקִּבְּלָה לְיַעֲקֹב
with a pleasant countenance.	בְּסֵבֶר פָּנִים יָפוֹת
As it is written, "And Yaakov came home	דִּכְתִיב וַיָּבֹא יַעֲקֹב
from the field in the evening,	מִן הַשָּׂדֶה בָּעֶרֶב
and Leah went out to greet him,	וַתֵּצֵא לֵאָה לִקְרָאתוֹ
and she said to him, 'You should come to me	וַתֹּאמֶר אֵלַי תָּבוֹא,
because I paid for you...'"	כִּי שָׂכֹר שְׂכַרְתִּיךָ וְגוֹ'

Leah went out to the road to inform Yaakov of the change in plans for the evening and that she had exchanged her son's gift to spend the time with him.

After Yaakov returns home with Leah, it is written:

וַיִּשְׁמַע אֱלֹהִים אֶל לֵאָה וַתַּהַר וַתֵּלֶד לְיַעֲקֹב בֵּן חֲמִישִׁי.
And Hashem hearkened to Leah, and she became pregnant and gave birth to a fifth son.[73]

---

72   *Bereishis* 30:14–15.
73   *Bereishis* 30:17.

The commentaries ask: What exactly did Hashem hear at this point, since there was no conversation to be overheard? Rashi explains that Hashem heard how much Leah wanted there to be more *shevatim* born to Yaakov. As a reward for her pure motivations, Yissachar, a fifth son, was conceived on that night.[74]

Reward

The Midrash continues:

לְפִיכָךְ זָכְתָה וְיָצְאוּ מִמֶּנָּה מְלָכִים וּנְבִיאִים.
Therefore, she merited to have come from her kings and prophets.

The Gemara tells us that the sons of Yissachar were not ordinary members of the Jewish People. Leah's actions resulted in the descendants of Yissachar becoming the intellectual aristocracy of all the tribes.[75] The descendants of another of Leah's sons, Yehudah, became the kings. These two brothers (along with Zevulun, another of Leah's sons) camped together on the east of the Mishkan, the holy Tabernacle. They resided in the place that symbolized Torah.[76] Another of Leah's sons, Levi, lived in the camp that surrounded the Mishkan. The *Leviim* taught Torah and performed auxiliary duties in the Mishkan. The most famous *Levi*, Moshe, was the ultimate prophet; he spoke face-to-face with Hashem and transmitted His Torah to the Jewish People.[77] The *Kohanim*, who descended from Levi, served in the Mishkan as priests and created a strong relationship between Hashem and the Jewish People.

---

74 Rashi, *Bereishis* 30:17.
75 *Talmud Bavli*, *Eruvin* 100b.
76 *Kli Yakar*, *Bamidbar* 2:4.
77 *Bamidbar* 12:6–8.

Leah's sons merited living in the most illustrious locations in the camp and occupied many of the most prominent political, religious, spiritual, and educational roles — because of the dedication of their mother. Leah did not want children to fulfill her maternal instinct nor did she want children so that they could wield power. She wanted children who would elevate the world to a higher level of spirituality. Her children then became the conduits of spirituality through their service as *Kohanim*, *Leviim*, kings, and scholars.

> Leah's sons occupied many of the most prominent political, religious, spiritual, and educational roles — because of the dedication of their mother.

Getting Practical: Initiative in Marriage

In this *pasuk*, the *eishes chayil* invests her energies in a goal — even though it is not her responsibility to do so. She voluntarily chooses to seek wool and linen to spin, even though it is her husband's responsibility. Similarly, Leah also invested in her goal of bringing *shevatim* into the world even though it caused her inconvenience and discomfort: her husband wasn't initially supportive of her, and her friends and family mocked her for her efforts.

It is easy to do the right thing when our husband is behind us and we are going with a popular decision. It is far more difficult to do something when we feel we shouldn't have to do it or if others do not have to do similar things.

This *pasuk* reminds us that our focus should always be on doing the next right thing. We must continually focus on what we can contribute to better a situation rather than focusing on our spouse or friends to give us what we want. We cannot change our spouse nor can we change our children or our parents. The only ones we can change are ourselves. When we take responsibility for our own choices and behavior, we can make better decisions. We can start taking initiative.

In the *eishes chayil*'s case, the initiative involved taking on financial responsibility. In Leah's case, it involved helping Yaakov have more children. Doing the next right thing applies to other areas as well. At times, we may feel hurt or insulted by others — we want our spouse to notice us, help us, or provide for us. If we focus on what our spouses are not doing for us, we will lead miserable lives, lives that will be at the mercy of someone else, with us as victims of that person's choices. We instead can think about how we can change our own circumstances. When we do for ourselves or for others what we want others to do for us, we initiate positive actions that will bear fruit. When we decide to be proactive to get results that are important to us and our home, our attitude to our responsibilities changes.

The clerk in a store will work the exact amount of hours for which he is paid — no more and no less. If he is honest, he will work productively for all of those hours. He will not work overtime and he will not try to be creative and try to improve the store. The owner of the store, however, thinks very differently than an employee. He is there when the first customer arrives and stays until late at night, working as hard as he can to increase his profit.

In our homes, we can decide to be workers or owners. As employees, we will constantly be looking for someone else to take over our work, and we will feel like we are being cheated if it is not a fifty-fifty split. As owners, we will invest ourselves and our energies into making our home the best place it can be. We will take responsibility for what happens in our home — and in our destiny. As owners, we do whatever it takes to be successful.

On a personal level, I put the lesson of this *pasuk* and Midrash into action and found it to be empowering. I built up my courage to act with initiative in other more meaningful decisions.

For a few years, I wanted my living room to be repainted. Our home repair budget was already spent on other projects, and my husband's schedule was booked solid. For years, I looked at the walls with a mixture of disgust and martyrdom knowing that I could not get what I wanted.

Then I learned this *pasuk*, and I reevaluated whether I really needed my husband to save me and paint the walls or if I was able take the initiative myself and accomplish something that was important to me. I talked to a few friends who had painted, went to the hardware store to get supplies and advice, and did the prep work to get the walls ready to begin.

When my husband found an hour or two to help out, I was very grateful — but I remained in charge of the project. When the walls were all done, I didn't feel weak and helpless, I felt like I could do anything and that I was a lot more capable than I had thought! Now if I see the garbage is overflowing, rather than getting annoyed and asking to be saved, I take it out myself. If I want my children to hear a specific *dvar Torah* at the Shabbos table, and it wasn't in my husband's plans but he doesn't mind, I take initiative, and I don't nag him about it. I have learned that when necessary, I can be "Leah" for those things that I feel are important.

A Progression of Growth

Taking initiative is the important "next step" in the progression of the *eishes chayil*:

1. First, like Sarah and Avrohom, the *eishes chayil* establishes what she values [אֵשֶׁת חַיִל — *eishes chayil*].
2. Next, she builds a relationship of trust and kindness [בָּטַח בָּהּ לֵב בַּעְלָהּ — Her husband's heart trusts her, and גְּמָלַתְהוּ טוֹב וְלֹא רָע — she does good and not evil].
3. Now, she has to put those principles into action. She can choose to make the fulfillment of her dreams dependent on someone else, or she can choose to lead the efforts.

> When we throw ourselves into a cause, we are not being taken advantage of. We are leading by example.

Taking this kind of initiative can be overwhelming. It means that we are fully responsible for what happens to us and cannot blame others. We are open to being taken advantage of if others rely on us too much.

Still, the benefits of taking the first step far outweigh any risks. The Midrash says that Leah merited children who were leaders; her children were a direct result of her actions. It tells us this information because it applies to our lives as well. When we throw ourselves into a cause, we are not being taken advantage of; we are leading by example. The result is that others who respect us will learn and also lead by example. Our children will witness our efforts, and they will try to improve their family's lives and the lives of those in their community. They will initiate changes that will create a lasting legacy for their family, certainly something for which we should be willing to risk getting messy and doing hard work.

Summary

"She seeks wool and flax."
Leah, our matriarch
דָּרְשָׁה צֶמֶר וּפִשְׁתִּים
לֵאָה אִמֵּנוּ

From the Pasuk We Learn

The *eishes chayil* takes on responsibilities to fulfill her vision of life regardless of the fact that they may be outside societal expectations and/or her comfort zone. She looks at what she is capable of doing and does it wholeheartedly.

From the Midrash We Learn

More than anything else, Leah wanted more *shevatim* to be born to Yaakov. She was willing to sacrifice her own comfort to see that happen. If we have a vision of what we want our home to be like, we can take initiative to make it happen. We can sacrifice temporary discomfort for long-term gain, and our children will learn from our example.

Practical Steps

1. Focus on the next right thing to do.
2. If we want something, think about what we can do to make it happen in a way that does not involve nagging or hustling.
3. Stretch ourselves to take initiative in areas in which we have previously relied on others, whether because of fear or laziness. Ask for help and support when we need it.

Questions

Self-Growth

1. What steps can I take to fulfill my life goals?
2. Are there things that I would like to see done that I expect others to do?
3. How do I take initiative when others around me are not?
4. Am I feeling resentful that I'm doing things that I feel others should be doing instead? How can I change this dynamic?
5. Are there things that I can do for myself that I am waiting for others to do for me?

As Wives and Mothers

6. What steps need to be taken in our family to fulfill the goals we have set? Which of these jobs can I do?
7. Have I assumed that there is a division of labor in my home (i.e., taking out the trash, making dinner), and have I discussed whether my spouse holds the same views?
8. How do I develop a positive, proactive attitude toward my home and family responsibilities?
9. Are there areas in which I compare my husband and what he does for our family with other men and what they do for theirs?
10. What are some responsibilities that I cannot do without losing my patience and calm? Have I discussed my needs with my husband?

Teaching Our Daughters

11. How do I help my daughter learn to be proactive and take responsibility for what she wants in life without nagging or having expectations of her parents and others to do things for her?

CHAPTER 7

Effort

הָיְתָה כָּאֳנִיּוֹת סוֹחֵר מִמֶּרְחָק תָּבִיא לַחְמָהּ.

*She is like the merchant ships;
she brings her bread from afar.*

Peshat

In the previous *pasuk*, Shlomo HaMelech praised the *eishes chayil* for doing things that were beyond her responsibility. In this *pasuk*, Shlomo HaMelech praises the *eishes chayil* by comparing her to a merchant ship who travels to faraway ports to get bread.

This *pasuk* is hard to understand. The *eishes chayil* is being compared to a ship, an inanimate object. What is this *pasuk* trying to teach us?

Commitment

The *pasuk* compares the *eishes chayil* to a ship to demonstrate how much effort she is willing to invest on behalf of her family. The previous *pasuk* described her independence; this *pasuk* describes the lengths to which she goes **to do the work**.

In the last *pasuk*, the *eishes chayil* collected the raw material so she could spin fabric. She took on a job that she was not required to do as she remained in the comforts of her neighborhood to help with the finances and assist her husband and his enterprises. Here, the Malbim notes, the *eishes chayil* travels far away from her home, like a merchant ship at sea, in order to do business in areas where the demand for her product is bigger and she can earn greater profits.⁷⁸

> The *pasuk* compares the *eishes chayil* to a ship to demonstrate how much effort she is willing to invest on behalf of her family.

In his *sefer Chanoch L'Naar*, Rav Shmuel Shaul Siriro explains that while merchants own many ships to increase their profits, the *eishes chayil* herself is the אֳנִיּוֹת סוֹחֵר — the merchant ship. She does not hire merchants to run her ship, rather she does the work herself; she is in control of her business and her vessel.⁷⁹ By being so involved with the sale of her goods, she is able to alter her tactics on a moment's notice to adjust them according to her needs. The *eishes chayil* is also compared to multiple ships, to אֳנִיּוֹת. Successful merchants will simultaneously invest in multiple ventures to maximize profit and minimize risk. Here, too, the *eishes chayil* is involved with many different ventures in the hope that some will bear fruit.

Modesty vs. Effort

A question still remains.

It appears from the text that the *eishes chayil* is being praised for traveling far from home which seems to contradict the Jewish value of *tznius*, modesty. It says in *Tehillim*:

כָּל כְּבוּדָּה בַת מֶלֶךְ פְּנִימָה.⁸⁰

The honor of a princess is inward.

---

78 Malbim, *Mishlei* 31:14.
79 Rav Siriro, *Chanoch L'Naar*, quoted in *Sefer Eishes Chayil*, p. 119.
80 *Tehillim* 45:14.

Being like a ship or a merchant is neither princess-like nor private. How can we reconcile this contradiction?

The *pasuk* in *Tehillim* is letting us know what gives a woman exalted status. It is not her professional status or her communal commitments; a woman's honor comes from what she contributes to her home. The biggest priority for any woman and the source of her dignity is what she achieves within the four walls of her home.

The *Meam Loez* explains that this *pasuk* is not the ideal for a woman who has sufficient income and many children.[81] This *pasuk* is talking about what happens when the family's income does not match its expenses.

What should a woman do when there is a crisis that upends the prudent planning and responsible choices her family has made? In this case, although it means leaving the place where she is most honored, the *eishes chayil* is willing to make the sacrifice because she can contribute to her family's survival. We see later in the poem that the *eishes chayil* does not choose to stay in this kind of profession, where she must regularly leave her family; rather, she modifies her professional opportunities based on her family's needs and the opportunities she has. At this time, with the circumstances she is presented, she makes choices that take effort and sacrifice.

> What should a woman do when there is a crisis that upends the prudent planning and responsible choices her family has made?

Throughout Jewish history, there have been women who have made this kind of sacrifice. It is not a choice to be taken lightly. The wives of the Chazon Ish and the Chofetz Chaim owned stores that required them to purchase merchandise and sell goods to support their families so their husbands could learn Torah and achieve the greatness that they did. Many women today act like merchant ships so that their children can go to school and so that their families can have food on the table. Life circumstances can make extraordinary efforts become necessary.

---

81   *Meam Loez, Mishlei* 31:14.

My husband's grandmother and grandfather came to the United States after Kristallnacht. Grandma Alice was used to a life of luxury. Her husband had been the largest employer in the town from which she moved. When she recalled memories of Pesach from her childhood, she would recount how exhausting it was, as a child, to oversee the maids' efforts. Yet all that changed when she moved to the United States. She had to wash floors and clean houses, and her husband had to muck out horse stalls to pay the rent. Grandma Alice never discussed those experiences with bitterness. She was able to do what was necessary to help her family survive. She lived this *pasuk* — as an *eishes chayil*.

Financial Responsibility

The Meiri, unlike other commentaries, does not interpret the *pasuk* to mean that the *eishes chayil* actually engages in commerce far from home.[82] He interprets the line allegorically, uncovering its deeper meaning. The Meiri explains that the *eishes chayil* acts carefully to support her family. She looks for sales, is frugal about where she shops for clothing and food, and researches the quality of products before investing in them. This care with her family's finances may mean that she has to act like a merchant ship and go from store to store rather than buying everything in the most convenient place. She puts forth the effort because it helps her family stay solvent, have food to eat, and have clothing to wear.

This message is as applicable today as it has been in the past. If we are buying food or products for our home, we need to keep in mind the value of the dollar we are spending. It can be as simple as checking the price per ounce on ketchup and not buying detergent in an expensive convenience store. It can also mean that we need to buy based on our income rather than on what our neighbors are getting. We may want a fancy Bugaboo stroller, but if it means going into debt, we need to sacrifice and buy a stroller we can afford. We cannot spend money on decorating our home if it

---

82   Meiri, *Mishlei* 31:14.

means that other bills will not be paid. Living within our means requires increasing our revenue streams — the money coming in, and carefully evaluating our expenses — the money going out.

A Common Message

All commentaries seem to understand one important message from this *pasuk*. The *eishes chayil* is aware of her reality and acts to the best of her ability within that framework. She puts forth maximum and diverse efforts to make sure that her top priority is achieved: ensuring that her family is safe and fed. She works tirelessly, and she employs all reasonable means to achieve her goals even when it is challenging. How is a woman supposed to know when she needs to go outside her comfort zone and when she should continue to act as she has in the past? The Midrash chooses Rochel as the role model to teach us how to implement this idea in all areas of our lives.

> The *eishes chayil* is aware of her reality and acts to the best of her ability within that framework. She puts forth maximum and diverse efforts to make sure that her top priority is achieved: ensuring that her family is safe and fed.

Midrash – Rochel

"She is like the merchant ships."	הָיְתָה כָּאֳנִיּוֹת סוֹחֵר
This is Rochel, our matriarch,	זוֹ רָחֵל אִמֵּנוּ
who was embarrassed	שֶׁהָיְתָה מִתְבַּיֶּשֶׁת
regarding the children every day.	עַל הַבָּנִים בְּכָל יוֹם
Accordingly, she merited	לְפִיכָךְ זָכְתָה
to have a son come from her	וְיָצָא מִמֶּנָּה בֵּן
who resembled a ship	שֶׁהוּא דּוֹמֶה לַסְּפִינָה
that is filled with all the best of the world;	שֶׁהִיא מְלֵאָה כָּל טוֹב שֶׁבָּעוֹלָם
so Yosef upheld	כָּךְ יוֹסֵף
all of the world in his merit	מִתְקַיֵּם כָּל הָעוֹלָם בִּזְכוּתוֹ
and sustained the world	וְכִלְכֵּל אֶת הָעוֹלָם
in the years of famine.	בִּשְׁנֵי רְעָבוֹן

The Midrash states that Rochel is compared to a merchant ship because she was embarrassed about the children, and somehow this embarrassment led her to have a son who was like a ship that supported the world.

Like the *pasuk* upon which it is based, this Midrash is hard to understand and does not seem to relate to the very *pasuk* to which it refers! To understand the Midrash, which will allow us to understand our *pasuk*, we must examine each line of the Midrash.

Rochel's Embarrassment

שֶׁהָיְתָה מִתְבַּיֶּשֶׁת עַל הַבָּנִים בְּכָל יוֹם.
Who was embarrassed regarding the children every day.

The first question that must be addressed is how and when was Rochel embarrassed. The Torah relates the episodes in Rochel's life that gave her a horrific sense of shame — shame that we would not have predicted, knowing her life story.

Rochel was engaged to Yaakov, who worked seven years for the privilege of marrying her. Yaakov and Rochel anticipated that Lavan, Rochel's father and a known swindler, would try to prevent them from marrying. They exchanged secret codes to be shared under the wedding canopy so that any nefarious plans Lavan may have had would be thwarted.⁸³

> Rochel felt a horrific sense of shame — shame that we would not have predicted, knowing her life story.

The day of the wedding arrived. Lavan decided to trick Yaakov into marrying Leah, Rochel's older sister. Rochel saw that her older sister was being led into the wedding hall, and her heart broke for her. She knew that Leah would stand under the wedding canopy and be embarrassed publicly because she did not know the codes that Yaakov would request to confirm her identity. Rochel

---

83   *Talmud Bavli, Bava Basra* 123a.

quickly taught Leah the secret codes and watched as her older sister married the man she had waited seven long years to marry.

At the time, Rochel could assume that she was forfeiting the life she had anticipated for herself. She did not know if she would be forced to marry Esav, whom Leah was originally supposed to marry; or if Yaakov, so disgusted with both sisters' deception, would leave them both and travel elsewhere to marry.

In the end, Rochel did marry Yaakov one week later, joining her sister Leah as a wife — a sister who would now compete with her for her husband's time. Within seven months of the marriage, Leah had her first son. Three more sons followed in quick succession, while Rochel remained barren.[84] At this point, the Torah tells us that Rochel became jealous of her sister.[85] Rashi explains that Rochel was jealous of Leah's good deeds. Rochel assumed that Leah was more righteous and merited having children because of her spiritual greatness, while Rochel was less righteous and did not deserve having children.[86] She began to feel ashamed over her obvious rejection by Hashem and embarrassed that everyone would assume that she was flawed spiritually and therefore did not merit to have children.

> When Rochel gave Leah the codes, it was most likely that she was forfeiting the life she had anticipated for herself.

Seeking Help

At this time of hopelessness, Rochel came to Yaakov and demanded that he pray for her: "If you do not, I am dead."[87] Yaakov became angry with Rochel and told her that children were a gift from Hashem and that he, as her husband, had no power to grant her request. (The Ramban adds another dimension to Rochel's request: Rochel came to Yaakov to

---

84   *Bereishis* 29:31–35.
85   *Bereishis* 30:1.
86   Rashi, ibid.
87   *Bereishis* 30:1–3.

coerce him to pray. He turned to her and said that she needed to pray for herself if she truly wanted a child.)⁸⁸

Efforts and Reward

לְפִיכָךְ זָכְתָה וְיָצָא מִמֶּנָּה בֵּן.

Accordingly, she merited to have a son come from her.

In the next *pesukim*, Rochel becomes active in her pursuit of children.⁸⁹ She gives Yaakov her maidservant, Bilhah, as a wife, just as Sarah had given Avrohom Hagar as a wife so many years before. She did so hoping that the merit of helping Yaakov have children through Bilhah would help her have her own children.⁹⁰ A few years later, Rochel acts again. She requests the *dudaim*, a known herbal remedy for infertility, that Reuven had collected for his mother Leah.⁹¹ The *Seforno* says that Rochel was doing something necessary to achieve her goals: She was putting in effort, *hishtadlus*, rather than waiting for miracles.⁹²

The results of these efforts were not immediate. Leah had two more children, and Rochel remained barren.

Finally, after six long years:

וַיִּזְכֹּר אֱלֹקִים אֶת רָחֵל.⁹³

Hashem remembered Rochel.

The commentaries note that Hashem remembered three things:

1. First, the *Seforno* says Hashem remembered her *hishtadlus* (her efforts), both that she encouraged Yaakov to marry Bilhah and that she acquired the *dudaim* from Leah.⁹⁴

---

88 Ramban, *Bereishis* 30:1.
89 *Bereishis* 30:3–6, 14–15.
90 Rashi, *Bereishis* 30:3.
91 *Seforno*, *Bereishis* 30:14.
92 *Seforno*, *Bereishis* 30:22.
93 *Bereishis* 30:22.
94 *Seforno*, *Bereishis* 30:22.

2. Second, Hashem remembered the heartfelt prayers she offered that her efforts be successful.⁹⁵
3. Third, Rashi adds that Hashem remembered her selflessness and fear of G-d when she gave Leah the passwords on her wedding night.⁹⁶

> The three merits of Rochel: She was proactive (with Bilhah and the *dudaim* flowers), she prayed, and she was selfless on her wedding night.

In the merit of these three things, Rochel had a son. She called her son Yosef:

אָסַף אֱלֹקִים אֶת חֶרְפָּתִי.⁹⁷
Hashem gathered my embarrassment.

Rochel was embarrassed because she felt that her prayers and motives were less pure than her sister Leah. The birth of Yosef proved that to be false.

Rochel was like a merchant who knew that she was the captain of her own destiny. She tried all means possible to bring Yosef's soul down to this world. The *eishes chayil* goes to distant ports to obtain that which is rare and valuable, just as Rochel's actions were unique and precious to Hashem. Because of these actions, she merited a unique son who is known as *Yosef HaTzaddik*, Yosef the righteous one.

A Ship Filled with Goodness

שֶׁהוּא דּוֹמֶה לַסְּפִינָה, שֶׁהִיא מְלֵאָה כָּל טוֹב שֶׁבָּעוֹלָם.
*Who resembled a ship that is filled with
all the best of the world.*

The Midrash continues explaining the *pasuk* in *eishes chayil* by stating that in the merit of Rochel's deeds, Yosef became like a ship filled with good merchandise.

---

95 *Seforno, Bereishis* 30:22.
96 Rashi, ibid.
97 *Bereishis* 30:23.

The Gra on *Sefer Yonah* tells us that a ship is a metaphor for life. The goal of a ship is not to remain at sea; the captain tries to steer it from one port to another. During its journey, the ship will meet with storms that will threaten its existence. The captain must keep a steady hand to bring the ship to its destination.[98]

> A person's life is like a long sea voyage. Our body is the ship; it carries us through the rocky waters of life.

A person's life is like a long sea voyage. Our body is the ship; it carries us through the rocky waters of life. We are met with challenges that could drown us. Our soul is the captain; it is entrusted with the mission of guiding our ship to our true destination: *Olam Haba*.

The Midrash tells us that Yosef was a ship. He was sold into slavery in Egypt by his brothers, and he faced challenges and temptations.[99] He used his soul to guide him through those tumultuous times so that he would not lose his place as one of the *shevatim* and his place in the World to Come.[100]

Yosef was brought down to Egypt in chains. Despite his superficial appearance as a slave, all who saw him recognized him as one who possessed greatness. One of the first who recognized his stature was a noble named Potifar, who appointed him as manager of his estate.[101] The wife of Potifar desired Yosef and tried to seduce him. Yosef almost succumbed, but he overcame his temptation and conquered his desires.[102] For this reason, Yosef is called a *tzaddik*, a righteous man.[103] Like his mother, Rochel, who transcended her own desires by helping her sister, Yosef transcended his desires by remembering his commitment to Hashem.

---

98 *Peirush HaGra al Sefer Yonah* 1:3.
99 *Bereishis* 37:27–28.
100 *Talmud Bavli, Sotah* 36b.
101 *Bereishis* 39:1–4.
102 *Talmud Bavli, Sotah* 36b.
103 *Zohar, Vayeitzei* 134.

Supporting the Whole World

> כָּךְ יוֹסֵף מִתְקַיֵּם כָּל הָעוֹלָם בִּזְכוּתוֹ,
> וְכִלְכֵּל אֶת הָעוֹלָם בִּשְׁנֵי רְעָבוֹן.
>
> *So Yosef upheld all of the world in his merit and sustained the world in the years of famine.*

As a result of his choice to refuse the advances of Potifar's wife, Yosef was framed for a crime and thrown into jail.[104] While there, he was asked to interpret two of Pharaoh's recurring dreams. He did so and revealed to Pharaoh that there would be seven years of agricultural surplus followed by seven years of famine. Pharaoh appointed Yosef as his viceroy to help steer his nation through this challenge.[105]

Chazal tell us that because Yosef dominated his will and resisted the advances of Potifar's wife, he was allowed to dominate the nation of Egypt.[106] Now in his role as viceroy, he needed to provide food for the whole world. He used two tactics to achieve this goal. First, like his mother had done, Yosef prayed. He prayed that he should be able to provide food for the country.[107] Next, in addition to prayer, Yosef used his skill to organize a comprehensive system so that all in the region could survive.[108]

> Like a merchant who searches out the best ports, Yosef and Rochel both sought whatever means possible to fulfill their purpose in this world.

Like Rochel, Yosef used all the tools he had to accomplish what he needed. He had the merit of his self-restraint, prayer, and efforts on his side. Like a merchant who searches out the best ports, Yosef and Rochel both sought whatever means possible to fulfill their purpose in this world.

---

104 *Bereishis* 39:20.
105 *Bereishis*, chapter 41.
106 *Tanchuma Yashan Naso* 32; *Zohar, Vayera* 239.
107 *Torah Shleimah, Bereishis* 20, Letter 79.
108 *Bereishis* 41:45–49.

Getting Practical: Effort in a Marriage

This *pasuk* teaches us that we must be fully committed to achieve the goals we have set for ourselves and our homes. We must expend all efforts to reach our goals, sometimes sacrificing things that are of lower priority at the moment. Rochel teaches us what these efforts include.

We must (1) verify that our course of action is correct, (2) pray for Hashem's help, and (3) put forth our maximum efforts to reach our goal.

Doing What Is Right

Our first course of action must be to verify that our goals are what Hashem wants from us. Rochel and Yosef made choices based on what they knew Hashem wanted from them, rather than on what they wanted. Initially, it looked like Rochel was abandoning any hopes of getting married by allowing her sister to marry Yaakov instead of her. Next, it looked like she was rejected by Hashem when she did not have children. Because he ran away from Mrs. Potifar, Yosef was thrown in jail, and it looked like he had doomed himself to life in a dungeon. People may have seen their actions as foolish and dangerous, but Hashem viewed things differently. In both cases, Hashem gave Rochel and Yosef their hearts' desire — children and life — because of the risks they took.

Hashem gave Rochel and Yosef their hearts' desire — children and life — because of the risks they took.

Sometimes, it may appear that the consequences of our (correct!) choices are terrible. We may feel like we are losing all hope if we stay committed to halachah and *derech eretz*, refined behavior. When we choose a career, we may be asked to compromise on halachah to fit in, we may be tempted to gossip to ingratiate ourselves to our coworkers and boss, or we may get criticized because we cannot work as many hours because of our family commitments and because of Shabbos and Yom Tov.

On the surface, it looks like we are ruining our lives by sticking to our values. However, surface appearances are not reality. The reality is that Hashem controls the world. Our hard choices — which cause us pain in the short term — will be the source of our ultimate salvation.

The Role of Prayer

After establishing that we have worthwhile goals, we must pray.

Chazal teach us that all the matriarchs were initially barren so that they would pray. They explain:

הקב״ה מִתְאַוֶה לִתְפִלָּתָן שֶׁל צַדִּיקִים.[109]

Hashem desires the prayers of the righteous.

Hashem created this lack to force the *Imahos* to daven to Him. There are two ways to create something new in this world — with prayer and without prayer:

- With prayer, the new innovation will be powerful and strong.
- Without prayer, the new innovation will be weak and mediocre.

The most important innovation ever to be created in the world was the creation of the Jewish People through the birth of the *shevatim*. Hashem wanted the Jewish nation to be as strong as possible. Each matriarch was barren so she would pray. These prayers created the most perfect nation possible. If we have goals that align with Hashem's will, the best results will only come about through prayer.

> If we have goals that align with Hashem's will, we want the results to be as perfect as possible. This can only be achieved through prayer.

People have many customs they perform in the hope of miracles and salvations. Every Shabbos after Pesach, pictures abound of all the

---

109 *Talmud Bavli, Yevamos* 64a.

different forms in which challah can be baked, in accordance with the custom to help us merit financial security. When someone is diagnosed with an illness, women organize groups to bake challah. *Tzedakah* organizations claim great salvation will result if you contribute to their cause. These customs have merit, but they are not magic incantations that give us what we want while absolving us of the need to ask for it directly from Hashem.

At times, we may seek the blessing of a *tzaddik*, a righteous man, to help in a challenging situation. In this case as well, we can't rely on the *tzaddik's* prayers without contributing our own. It is our responsibility to do everything we can — which includes offering our own prayers. The Ramban explains that the mitzvah of prayer from the Torah is that when we have a problem, an *eis tzarah*, we turn to Hashem and ask for help.[110] If we only ask others for prayers, we have neglected a powerful tool in our arsenal. The Ramban explains that this is why Yaakov rebuked Rochel when she asked him to pray for her to have children. Rochel was relying on the prayers of Yaakov to give her children without contributing her own.[111] In the end, it was Rochel's personal prayer that brought about her salvation.[112]

> The mitzvah of prayer from the Torah is that when we have a problem, an *eis tzarah*, we ask Hashem for help. If we only ask for others' prayers, we have neglected a powerful tool in our arsenal.

If we have a need, whether it is with our marriage, our children, or our finances, we have to first ask Hashem for help and recognize that He is the One who put us in this circumstance and wants us to strengthen our relationship with Him. Our prayers are what give the outcome its ultimate strength.

---

110 Ramban, *Hasagos l'Sefer HaMitzvos, Mitzvas Asei* 5.
111 Ramban, *Bereishis* 30:1.
112 *Ha'amek Davar, Bereishis* 30:22.

Taking Action

After we have determined that what we want is right and we have prayed for help, we must take action to reach our goals. What we actually do is not as important as the fact that we are doing something, as this shows we are not relying on open miracles.

When Rochel requested the flowers from Leah, she did not think that those flowers would be more powerful than the prayers of her husband, Yaakov. Having enough grain to feed the whole known world was a miraculous feat, whether or not Yosef collected wheat for seven years in storehouses. Rochel and Yosef knew that physical *hishtadlus* — efforts — would be wholly ineffective without Hashem's involvement, yet they also recognized that it was necessary to do the *hishtadlus*. Why? In order to show they were open to miracles and their salvation would have a natural explanation.

> Our *hishtadlus* actions should be reasonable. Like Rochel and Yosef, each of us needs to figure out a reasonable course of action to accomplish what we hope to achieve.

Of course, our *hishtadlus* actions should be reasonable. Like Rochel and Yosef, each of us needs to figure out a reasonable course of action to accomplish what we hope to achieve. Our efforts truly do not get us what we want. Hashem, Himself, determines the outcome.

As Dovid HaMelech says in *Tehillim*:

אִם ה' לֹא יִבְנֶה בַיִת שָׁוְא עָמְלוּ בוֹנָיו בּוֹ. [113]

*If Hashem does not build a house,
then in vain its builders toil with it.*

This means that anything that happens in this world is based on what Hashem wants, no matter how much work and effort a person expends. The fact that Hashem is responsible for the outcome does not absolve us from the work. By doing our part, we allow miraculous bounty to flow into our homes.

---

113 *Tehillim* 127:1.

At times, like the *eishes chayil*, we may have to pursue opportunities that were not in our plan, or our image, of who we thought we should be. It was probably not easy for the *eishes chayil* to act like a merchant ship. When Yosef was living in his father's home, he would never have dreamed of being a manager of an Egyptian estate. Hashem changed his life so that he could develop the skills he needed to best fulfill his potential in this world.

When we are confronted with challenges that require us to leave our comfort zone, we need to (1) make sure it is halachically permissible by consulting with a *rav*, *rebbetzin*, or mentor; (2) pray for guidance; and (3) work hard and then embrace the new opportunities with which we are involved.

This will help us become who Hashem wants us to be rather than being stuck with who we thought we should be.

This *pasuk* and the Midrash helped me navigate a tough decision recently. As my kids get older, *baruch Hashem*, the cost of tuition, food, clothing, and camp continues to increase. With the growing monthly expenses, my husband and I had to decide how to deal with this new reality. I had seen others who, when faced with a similar reality, stayed frozen in their current plight. They made no changes as things got worse. I had always loved teaching children Torah, but I knew it was irresponsible to ignore the many signs that it was time to make a change.

After consulting with mentors who encouraged the move, this *pasuk* gave me the peace of mind to transition from something that seemed ideal to me to a new, albeit temporary, situation. I davened for guidance and a clear sign, and I emailed a former professor asking for help. Within five days, he had arranged an interview with an acquaintance, and I accepted a job working full time in a local public school. I also took the opportunity, as the Meiri explained this *pasuk*, to evaluate my budget and how I, with a little effort and less focus on what others were doing, could cut down on my expenses.

With the knowledge that Rochel and Yosef confronted far more difficult situations with courage, I took the job and implemented my new budget guilt free, knowing that Hashem was opening up a new path for me to traverse. I can't know why I needed the change, but I had the strength to put forth the effort on behalf of my family because that was the call of the moment. I needed to rise to the occasion, and *Eishes Chayil* helped me do it.

There are many things we may want and feel like we need. Nothing valuable happens without effort. Only through following Hashem's will, praying, and putting in hard work will we have a home that reflects our dreams and goals.

Summary

"She is like the merchant ships."   הָיְתָה כָּאֳנִיּוֹת סוֹחֵר
Rochel, our matriarch   רָחֵל אִמֵּנוּ

From the Pasuk We Learn

The *eishes chayil* makes extraordinary choices and sacrifices when her family's stability and needs require her to do so. Rather than being a victim of her circumstance, the *eishes chayil* makes very difficult choices to help the family's income meet its expenses.

From the Midrash We Learn

Rochel wanted children and taught her son Yosef — and by extension all of us — how to achieve what may seem impossible.

When there is a pressing need, there are steps we can take to determine how and when to act:

1. Evaluate whether the decision is Hashem's will by clarifying that it conforms with halachah.
2. Daven to Hashem for guidance and assistance.
3. Be proactive, even if we are not expected to be.

Practical Steps

Take Financial Responsibility
1. Evaluate present circumstances honestly and see if changes are needed.
2. Create a realistic budget and shop based on income rather than peer pressure.

Be Proactive
3. Don't get stuck in a problem. Talk to mentors to help figure out the next best step.

4. Regularly daven and ask for help.
5. Take a reasonable course of action that is neither defeatist nor panicked.

Questions

Self-Growth

1. How have I, or how will I, recognize when it is time to make a change based on my current reality?
2. How do I choose safe and helpful people with whom to share my concerns?
3. When do I reach out to others to share my concerns and seek guidance?
4. How do I make prayer for help and guidance a regular part of my life?
5. What reasonable actions do I need to take to help with my areas of concern? Are these in my comfort zone? How do I determine if an action is too extreme or if it shows faith in Hashem?
6. Have I ever been asked to compromise on halachah for a "greater" good? How do I decide what is the right thing to do?
7. What resources do I have for learning more about being financially responsible?
8. Do I have a budget and a clear idea of my income and expenses? How is that impacting my life?
9. How do I decide what to buy and when to buy it?

As Wives and Mothers

10. Has there ever been a time that my family's needs were not met? How did I deal with this? How would I like to deal with this in the future?
11. How do I make decisions about what is a luxury and what is a necessity? Where is the best place to shop for food, clothing, etc., that fits my budget?

Teaching Our Daughters

12. How do I help my daughter learn the value of hard work and investing her time and efforts?

13. How can I be a safe place for my daughter to come with her concerns? How can I help her learn how to identify healthy people to approach if she has a problem?

14. How can I help my daughter learn how to bring prayer for help into her life as a first step in solving problems?

15. How do I help my daughter recognize situations in which she is being asked to compromise halachah — for a job, friends, or a *shidduch* — and she should say no?

16. How do I help my daughter learn to live within her means? What tools and information does she need to learn to properly manage the finances of her home?

CHAPTER 8

Preparation

וַתָּקָם ׀ בְּעוֹד לַיְלָה וַתִּתֵּן טֶרֶף לְבֵיתָהּ וְחֹק לְנַעֲרֹתֶיהָ׃

*She rises while it is still night
and gives food to her household
and a portion to her maidens.*

Peshat

The previous two *pesukim* have focused on the *eishes chayil*'s work ethic while she is at work and at home. In this *pasuk*, Shlomo HaMelech discusses one of the recipes for her success: preparation.

Women have multiple commitments every day. We are often the ones called when our child gets sick in school, we are the caretakers of elderly parents, we have many household responsibilities, and we are often expected to pull equal weight at our job. Trying to balance it all is very stressful. With all the stress, our core values can sometimes fly out the window. While we want to be a trustworthy and kind partner, often, in the heat of the moment, a worse side of ourselves reacts. This *pasuk* teaches us how to plan our day so we can maintain our equilibrium. It teaches us how to minimize the chaos so we can do that which is important in a manner that reflects who we are.

This *pasuk* teaches us that for the *eishes chayil* to be successful, she needs to have a plan for each day so that it flows predictably and smoothly. There are three parts to the plan:

> This *pasuk* teaches how to minimize the chaos so we can do that which is important in a manner that reflects who we are.

1. Time management
2. Tools
3. Help

The Three-Part Plan for a Successful Day

TIME MANAGEMENT: UP WITH THE SUN

The *pasuk* tells us:

וַתָּקָם בְּעוֹד לַיְלָה.

She rises while it is still night.

Rav Siriro relates that the *eishes chayil* wakes up when it is not day and not night; she arises at dawn so that she won't be disturbed from getting done what is necessary.[114] There are two times a mother can wake up: before her children and after her children. On the days I get up before my children, my day goes more smoothly. I can help my children greet the morning in a positive way, keep track of when the bus is coming, and remember who still needs breakfast. When the kids wake up before me, I end up rushing — and the stress impacts all of us.

Getting up early is not just a question of setting an alarm clock. It also means planning my day — and my evening — so I can get adequate sleep and wake up on time the next day. After a long day, when things are finally quiet, I find it tempting to while away the hours at night. I can

---

114 Rav Siriro, *Chanoch L'Naar* quoted in *Sefer Eishes Chayil*, p. 122.

easily spend the time thoughtlessly doing chores or reading and playing on the computer.

Despite the temptation to use my evenings mindlessly, this quiet time is a perfect opportunity to make every subsequent day better than the one that just ended. It is a chance to stop and reflect on how my day went and think about how to make the next one even more meaningful. It is a time to process my feelings and experiences — and a chance to think about the positive things I have done.

> Getting up early requires going to sleep on time. It forces us to recognize that we are worthy no matter what we accomplish in a day.

Winding down purposefully at night has another important function. It helps me recognize that I am worthy no matter what I accomplish during the day. No matter what time at night I go to sleep, there will always be more to do. When it is time to go to sleep, based on my plan, I can go to sleep because if something did not get done, it was not meant to be done. I can return the task back to Hashem and scratch it off my own to-do list for that day.

Getting up when it is dark has another implication. It can also mean that we make sure that we leave adequate time to take care of our responsibilities before we become rushed. If I need to get to an appointment, I can plan my day so I won't be late. This leaves me able to deal with others in a calm, respectful manner without unnecessary stress.

TOOLS TO START THE DAY

The second component of the *eishes chayil*'s preparation discussed in the *pasuk* is that she makes sure she has the things she needs at the beginning of the day. The *pasuk* says that she arranges the meals for her family before they are needed:

וַתִּתֵּן טֶרֶף לְבֵיתָהּ.
She gives food to her household.

This idea extends beyond having food ready. The *eishes chayil* makes sure that the lunches are packed, homework is signed, and clothing is taken out of the dryer and laid out for the next day. This groundwork prevents panic and chaos, as things are set aside well in advance of when they are needed. There are no children yelling, "I NEED UNIFORM PANTS!!" and no rushed attempts to locate bread for sandwiches right before car pool is due to arrive.

Making lunches is definitely one of those tasks that I dread, and I know many of my friends feel the same way. I leave it to the last minute because I hope that somehow lunches will make themselves. As mothers, we understand instinctively how much we need to invest in our children's spirituality. We want our children to love Judaism and have a meaningful life. But lunches? It is a mindless chore. In the rush, we often do not even get to hear a proper thank-you (like the one we sometimes get at dinner time for the food we cooked).

Children's physical needs are a spiritual goal.

The Ralbag states that as much as the *eishes chayil* is concerned with the spiritual well-being of her children, she is equally concerned for their physical well-being.[115] When a person is healthy, he can be productive and successful. Otherwise, nothing can get done. Lunches, then, are on the *eishes chayil*'s radar to be prepared in advance — as a spiritual goal.

Rav Siriro notes that the *eishes chayil* is not shy to hire help.[116] She may let her maid clean the bathroom or have her assistant answer emails, but she alone makes sure her children have food. This is such a priority that she does not entrust it to others.

HELP: MANAGING THE HOUSEHOLD

The *eishes chayil* realizes that there is a limit to what she can realistically accomplish in one day. She hires as much help as she can afford — enough to ensure that everything necessary gets done and her home runs smoothly. Doing the work perfectly, by herself, is less important than being available emotionally and spiritually for herself and her family.

---

115 Ralbag, *Mishlei* 31:15.
116 Rav Siriro, *Chanoch L'Naar* quoted in *Sefer Eishes Chayil*. p. 122.

The *eishes chayil* views herself as a manager — a job that needs to be done right. Managing others is, in itself, an art. The Meiri comments that to maximize her time and the help available, she sets forth clear expectations.[117] She communicates what she needs and how she wants it done. Valuable time is not wasted on having to redo the work that her employees were supposed to do. She also makes sure that her employees have the tools they need to do their job. The cleaning supplies are available and snacks are ready, if needed.

The *eishes chayil* knows that she needs to motivate her support staff differently than she motivates her children.

Her children each receive what they need:

וַתִּתֵּן טֶרֶף לְבֵיתָהּ.
She gives food to her household.

She gives to her children based on their tastes. One child may like Pringles, while to the other she gives Bisli. These small touches and individualization communicate her love for each of her children's unique qualities.

In contrast, the *eishes chayil* only gives:

וְחֹק לְנַעֲרֹתֶיהָ.
An allotted portion for her maids.

> For a woman to achieve all her goals, she needs to stay calm. She needs to prepare how to stay calm by managing her time, resources, and help.

According to Rabbi Haim Messas in *Nishmat Haim*, the *eishes chayil* understands that it is detrimental to play favorites with employees.[118] Each worker receives an allotted portion, which motivates the **team to work well together without competition and backstabbing**.

This *pasuk* teaches us that for a woman to achieve all her goals, she needs to remain calm. This can be achieved by planning and preparing in advance and by

---

117 Meiri, *Mishlei* 31:15.
118 Rabbi Haim Messas, *Nishmat Haim*, quoted in *Sefer Eishes Chayil*, p. 128.

managing her time, resources, and help. This kind of preparation is not merely limited to her daily responsibilities. The Midrash explains how Basya, the daughter of Pharaoh, epitomized this level of forethought and preparation in spiritual matters as well.

 Midrash – Basya

"She rises while it is still night."	וַתָּקָם בְּעוֹד לַיְלָה
This is Basya,[119] daughter of Pharaoh.	זוֹ בִּתְיָה בַּת פַּרְעֹה
She was a non-Jew who became a Jew,	גּוֹיָה הָיְתָה וְנַעֲשֵׂתָה יְהוּדִיָּה
and her name is mentioned	וְהִזְכִּירוּ שְׁמָהּ
among the righteous ones,	בֵּין הַכְּשֵׁרוֹת
since she dealt with Moshe.	בִּשְׁבִיל שֶׁעָסְקָה בְּמֹשֶׁה
Accordingly, she merited	לְפִיכָךְ זָכְתָה
to enter into paradise in her life.	וְנִכְנְסָה בְּחַיֶּיהָ לְגַן עֵדֶן

This Midrash is not only hard to understand, but it also does not even seem to be related to our *pasuk*. Basya, who converted to Judaism, merited entering the World to Come "alive" because of her dealings with Moshe. Most people die before they enter Gan Eden; only a handful of people in the history of the world entered Gan Eden alive. What is the connection between these two facts? How do Basya's dealings with Moshe demonstrate foresight, and why did they lead to an eternal life different from the rest of the women mentioned in *Eishes Chayil*?

> How do Basya's dealings with Moshe demonstrate foresight, and why did they lead to an eternal life different from the rest of the women mentioned in *Eishes Chayil*?

---

119 The woman discussed in this Midrash is often referred to as Basya based on a phrase from Chazal that calls her the daughter of Hashem. There is a *pasuk* in *Divrei HaYamim* that lists her name as Bisya. To avoid confusion, for this essay, Bas Pharaoh will be referred to as Basya.

Basya's Choice

The Torah never refers to Basya by her name. In the Torah, she is called Bas Pharaoh — the daughter of Pharaoh. In *Divrei HaYamim* (Chronicles), the *pasuk* tells us that Basya bas Pharaoh married Mered and was the matriarch of a family of prophets and scholars.[120] Chazal inform us that Basya bas Pharaoh is the same Bas Pharaoh mentioned in the Torah story.[121]

When we first meet Bas Pharaoh in the Torah, her story can be interpreted as a somewhat unremarkable tale of a pampered woman looking to fulfill a maternal instinct. A rich princess is strolling, accompanied by servants, to bathe in the Nile River. At this time, there was a royal decree that all Jewish baby boys should be drowned in the river. While Bas Pharaoh was bathing, she heard a baby boy crying. The baby's mother had placed him in a basket in the river rather than allowing the Egyptians to drown him. Basya realizes that the baby is Jewish, but she has pity on him and chooses to raise the child as her own.[122]

This simplistic interpretation of the story does not address some crucial details. Basya was a princess, her father's eldest.[123] Her father had been told by his astronomers that a Jewish baby boy would be born who would destroy his kingdom.[124] As a result, he commanded the Egyptians to throw every baby boy into the river to protect his empire.

It was in Basya's best interest to ensure that all boys would be killed. Yet when she chanced upon an abandoned baby, she did not kill it — or even report it to the authorities. She saved the baby from certain death.

The *pasuk* further confuses the issue by informing us that when Basya went down to the river, she immediately recognized that the

---

120 *Divrei HaYamim* 1:14.
121 *Talmud Bavli, Megillah* 13a.
122 *Shemos* 2:5–10.
123 *Shemos Rabbah, Parashah* 18:3.
124 *Talmud Bavli, Sotah* 12b.

child was a Jew. The Midrash tells us that she wanted an Egyptian woman to nurse the baby, but the baby refused.[125] Rather than kill or abandon the child, she dispatched a Jewish girl to find a Jewish woman to nurse the child. She then had this child raised in his Jewish home for two full years.[126] Basya could have demanded that the baby remain in the palace with the nursemaid, but she instead ensured that the child's foundation be one of Jewish values by having him cared for in a Jewish home.

With these additional details provided by Chazal, Basya was obviously acting with very different motivations than her father. She was sending a clear and public message to her nation and to the Jews that Pharaoh's command was not to be taken seriously. Basya was seemingly a leading participant in the overthrow of her own father's regime.

Chazal tell us that the day Moshe was placed in the river was not an ordinary day in Basya's life. Basya had come to realize that her father was a cruel, evil man. She realized there was only one Hashem and that her father's religion and claim to power were farcical. On that day, Basya went to the river to wash away all the sins of her past and to convert to the Jewish faith.[127] She knowingly abandoned the paganism of her father's home for the belief in one G-d. As she accepted this new

> When Basya converted to a belief in one G-d, she simultaneously accepted upon herself to overthrow her father's reign of tyranny.

faith, she simultaneously accepted upon herself to overthrow her father's reign of tyranny.

As the Midrash on *Eishes Chayil* says:

שֶׁעָסְקָה בְּמֹשֶׁה.
That she was busy with Moshe.

---

125 *Shemos Rabbah, Parashah* 1:25.
126 Ibid., *Parashah* 1:26.
127 Ibid., *Parashah* 1:23.

She was not busy with the feeding and care of a baby to fulfill a maternal instinct. She was busy preparing this child to be the leader of the Jewish People: the leader who would lead the Jews from Egypt to Har Sinai, where they would renounce her father's paganism once and for all.

Basya's Rewards

Eighty years later, Moshe enters Pharaoh's court and tells him to release the Jews from slavery. If he does not, all firstborns, both male and female, will die. Indeed, on that night, Hashem Himself killed all the firstborns throughout Egypt. Only one firstborn, Basya, was saved from this fate.[128] Basya had awoken to the truth of Hashem's Oneness eighty years before, during the darkest, most bitter part of the Jews' exile. It had seemed then that there was no hope or future in being a Jew. Yet this awakening in the darkness is what allowed her to be saved so many years later.

Basya's awakening in the darkness of exile is what saved her so many years later.

The light in Basya's life continued after the redemption from Egypt. In *Divrei HaYamim*, we are informed that Basya married Mered.[129] Chazal inform us that Mered was another name for Kalev, the prince and leader of the tribe of Yehudah.[130] Together, they merited having children who became prophets and Torah scholars.

What Is Gan Eden?

The Midrash tells us that her true reward was that she entered Gan Eden while alive. What is Gan Eden and what does it mean that Basya entered it "alive" because of her involvement with Moshe?

Before Adam's sin, he lived in Gan Eden, where his physical and

---

128   *Shemos Rabbah, Parashah* 18:3.
129   *Divrei HaYamim* 1:14.
130   *Talmud Bavli, Megillah* 13a.

spiritual desires were equally balanced.[131] Through positive choices, his spiritual will was meant to purify his physical being until he achieved perfection and brought about the ultimate reward: *Olam Haba*, the World to Come. Adam's sin changed this delicate balance and made the physical more prominent. The soul could never purify the body and bring it to perfection. In this new world, *Olam Haba* could never be reached. To achieve spiritual perfection, Adam first needed to die so that through death and the decomposition of his body, the soul and body could separate. Only once the body was purified and the goals of mankind were achieved would the body and soul reunite for their ultimate reward in the World to Come, in *Olam Haba*.

> Through her hard choices, Basya's soul had already perfected her physical being in this world. Thus, she was able to enter Gan Eden alive with no need to experience death.

All of Adam's descendants also need to die to rid themselves of their physicality. Their souls then enter Gan Eden where they await *techias hameisim*, the resurrection of the dead, and *Olam Haba*.

Basya was different from almost all of mankind in that she overcame her physicality while alive when she was willing to forgo all the pleasures of this world for what was true and spiritual.[132] She was a princess with every luxury available to her. Yet she regarded her life of privilege as meaningless and worked to undermine her own status and comfort by caring for Moshe. Unlike the rest of humanity, Basya did not have to die for her body to be perfected to be ready for *Olam Haba*. Through her hard choices, her soul had already perfected her physical being in this world. Thus, she was able to enter Gan Eden alive with no need to experience death.

Getting Practical: Preparation in Marriage

In this *pasuk*, *Eishes Chayil* teaches that we must prepare in advance if we hope to be successful.

---

131 *Derech Hashem*, part 1, chapter 3.
132 Email correspondence with Rav Asher Balanson.

Chazal teach:

אֵיזֶהוּ חָכָם הָרוֹאֶה אֶת הַנּוֹלָד.[133]
Who is wise? The one who foresees the future.

Chazal define wisdom as the ability to understand the future consequences of what is happening now and to be careful as a result.[134] The *eishes chayil* has this kind of wisdom. She understands that in both the physical and spiritual realm, everything she does or does not do has consequences. Her greatness comes from not only understanding that there will be ramifications for her behavior but from making positive changes to ensure the best outcomes.

> In both the physical and spiritual realms, there are consequences for choices. The *eishes chayil* makes positive changes to ensure the best outcomes.

On a practical level, the *eishes chayil* is teaching us that we must prepare for the next day by laying the groundwork so things can stay calm. Laundry needs to be folded, lunches have to be made, and help should be hired before the crisis hits and the carpool appears in our driveway.

On a spiritual level, we must also be like Basya and prepare ourselves for our spiritual goals as well. We must plan how we will react when our toddler tracks *chametz* through the house, our charming eight-year-old has witty comebacks filled with chutzpah, or our husband is late and forgets to call. With planning, we can *act* with dignity rather than *react* to challenges that arise.

Building a Nation

Basya anticipated great things from the Jewish People. She prepared herself to be involved in the creation of a nation. Initially, she made choices that were difficult but were ultimately to her benefit. She made these choices because she recognized the value of what she was helping to create.

---

133   *Talmud Bavli, Tamid* 32.
134   Rashi, ibid.

We, too, have the opportunity to help form a nation. Our children will one day, with the help of G-d, have their own families and bring about their own potential. By investing our time and effort in them as children, we are preparing them for the greatness that awaits them. Our seemingly mundane involvement with the day-to-day running of our home has significant long-term implications. Our spiritual involvement with them will also bear fruit.

Indeed, we must remember that all of our mundane preparations are, in fact, spiritual. They give our children a sense of their destiny and their importance to us. I attended a funeral for a brilliant woman who was an accomplished musician. The eulogies spoke of her being a valedictorian, her accomplishments as a flutist, and her sharp memory. Her daughter, a woman in her thirties, broke down as she spoke of the homemade lunches she brought to school. Her mother always made sure to cut her sandwiches in triangles the way she liked and made sure her fruit wouldn't turn brown. The daughter said to the crowd how she knew that it did not matter if her mother needed to cross a desert or the sea — if she forgot her lunch, her mother would be there.

> When we invest our time and effort in our children, we are preparing them for the greatness that awaits them.

In the end, our acts of devotion for our children are remembered. They are important: they tell our children how essential they are to the world and help them fulfill their potential. We need to have faith in these results and plan our day accordingly.

Accepting Help

Creating the life and future of our dreams requires planning. It also requires help from others. The *eishes chayil* hires maidens to help with her chores; Basya asked Yocheved to help nurse and care for Moshe for the first two years of his life.

For some women, it can be incredibly shameful to admit they need help. They do not **want** anyone to know that they are not perfect and need others to **make** it through the day.

The *eishes chayil* (and Basya) had a broader vision. They did not judge their need for help. They sought out messengers from Hashem who would help them fulfill their mission in life. In our life, no one is perfect, and we should be open to help when we need it. We wouldn't begrudge someone else for needing help, and we can't judge ourselves harshly when we have the same need. Sometimes, these messengers come in the form of spiritual guides, sometimes in the form of friends, sometimes in the form of therapists, and sometimes even as cleaning ladies. Being open to receiving help is a sign of wisdom and of seeking a connection to Hashem and is not a weakness.

> Seeking help is a brave choice: a recognition of Hashem's guidance, not one of which to be ashamed.

Basya, and the *eishes chayil*, understood what great things awaited her and her family when she prepared for the future. Let us have equal amounts of confidence and joy anticipating the wonderful destiny that awaits us as well.

Summary

"She rises while it is still night." וַתָּקָם בְּעוֹד לַיְלָה
Basya, daughter of Pharaoh בִּתְיָה בַת פַּרְעֹה

From the Pasuk We Learn

The *eishes chayil* ensures a successful day by laying the groundwork for technical success. Her plan includes:

1. Time management: Waking up early to ensure she has the time to do the necessary tasks before they become urgent needs
2. Tools: Preparing necessary supplies for the coming day
3. Help: Effectively recruiting and managing others to help with her responsibilities

From the Midrash We Learn

Basya made the difficult choice of breaking from her family to ensure her spiritual future. From her we learn that an *eishes chayil* makes decisions while focusing on their future consequences. When we plan for — and invest in — our own or our children's spirituality or physical needs, we reap the benefits for many generations.

Practical Steps

1. Providing for physical needs is a spiritual job.
2. Time management

   A. Wake up early, before the children.
   B. Plan our evenings so we are not overtired.
   C. Wind down at night purposefully to allow for self-reflection and planning.
   D. Affirm that what we have done during the day is sufficient.
   E. Plan the day with enough time to complete necessary tasks.

3. Tools

   A. Have necessary supplies (laundry, food, etc.) before they are needed.

4. Help

   A. Seek and accept help as needed with grace, faith, and consideration.
   B. Communicate needs to employees in a polite and clear manner.
   C. Provide essential supplies for employees to do their job.
   D. Motivate employees with fair and equitable treatment.

PREPARATION   145

Self-Growth

1. What time do I need to get up in the morning to ensure that my day is calm and flows peacefully?
2. What time do I need to go to sleep to ensure that I can be awake and start my day on the right foot?
3. What are the three most important things I want to do each morning and evening to ensure that I have a meaningful and productive day?
4. Do I need help in any area to maximize my future? How will I find the best person to help me?
5. How do I manage my time so that I am punctual and can complete my responsibilities calmly?
6. How do I manage any employees or household help? How do I help them be as productive as possible?
7. Are there things I am sacrificing now because I anticipate long-term benefits?
8. What can I do today to create a more positive and meaningful tomorrow?

As Wives and Mothers

9. What does my family need in order to have a successful day?
10. What do I need to do beforehand to make that happen?
11. What strengths do my children possess that I can nurture so they will be prepared for their roles as adults?

Teaching Our Daughters

12. How do I teach my daughter to prepare so that her days are calm?
13. How do I teach my daughter to think about consequences and the long-term results of her behavior now?

CHAPTER 9

Vision

זָמְמָה שָׂדֶה וַתִּקָּחֵהוּ מִפְּרִי כַפֶּיהָ נָטְעָה כָּרֶם.

She considers a field and takes it; with the fruit of her palms she plants a vineyard.

Peshat

In the previous *pasuk*, we learned about how the *eishes chayil* prepares for her day. This preparation is one small part of how she creates the life of which she dreams.

This *pasuk* discusses how the *eishes chayil* first considers buying a field, buys it, and then purchases a vineyard with the profits of her new undertaking.

Changing Plans

At first glance, in this *pasuk* the *eishes chayil* seems to enter a more common business venture: agriculture. The *eishes chayil*, who traveled near and far, is leaving her merchant ships to invest in property. Why does the *pasuk* emphasize that this move is done with forethought, and why does she make the transition from merchant to farmer? What is the timeless lesson contained in this seemingly financially focused *pasuk*?

The Malbim explains the greatness the *eishes chayil* demonstrates here and the lesson we may all learn from it.[135] The *eishes chayil*, according to the Malbim, has a vision of what she wants her life to be like. She is able to pursue this vision when the need arises because she has a clear understanding of her life's goals.

Life Goals

The *eishes chayil*'s main goal had never been to earn a large salary or become a famous professional. She had been buying and selling merchandise because that was what her life demanded of her, and it suited her needs and the needs of her family. One day, she happened upon a field and thought, "Will investing in this field be better than what I am currently doing?"

The *eishes chayil* knows that her primary goal is to serve Hashem to the best of her ability. She is constantly looking for better ways to care for her family, perform mitzvos, and be meticulous in her own behavior. As a result, she is always looking at each new opportunity in her life through the prism of how it will impact her service of Hashem.

She now has the option to buy a field and is able to examine the pros and cons of the decision analytically and non-emotionally.

> The *eishes chayil* is always looking at each new opportunity in her life through the prism of how it will impact her service of Hashem.

She asks herself, "Will I be able to care for my family better?"

Yes, she would not be so far from home.

"Will I be able to do more mitzvos?"

Yes, having a field would allow her to provide food for her family as well as for the poor. There are also many mitzvos, such as leaving a corner of the field for the poor, that can only be done when owning a field.

Finally, "Can I be more modest?"

---

135   Malbim, *Mishlei* 31:16.

Again, yes — not interacting with so many strangers is more refined than the constant haggling and socializing that is a must in the business world.

The *eishes chayil* realizes that leaving the exciting world of trade will allow her to serve Hashem better. She recognizes that pursuing this new venture seems to be Hashem's will. If it's Hashem's will, then it will happen. And because the *eishes chayil* has pure motivations, indeed Hashem helps her buy the field and profit from this change.

Dedication

The *Metzudas Dovid* and Rabbi Haim Messas add another dimension to the greatness of the *eishes chayil*'s behavior. The *Metzudas Dovid* says that once she recognized that owning a field would be better for her and her family, she worked toward this goal unceasingly. She invested her time and effort into making it happen.[136]

> The *eishes chayil* did not need to max out her credit cards or drastically alter her lifestyle. She lived within her means so that she could invest when the opportunity arose.

Rabbi Messas points out that the *eishes chayil* had money available for this transaction.[137] She did not need to max out her credit cards or drastically alter her lifestyle. She had always lived within her means; therefore, she had the extra money needed to make the investment when the opportunity arose.

The lesson of this *pasuk* is not that the *eishes chayil* had good business sense, nor is it that a woman should switch careers regularly. The message is that the *eishes chayil* bases her decisions on whether her actions in life are in accordance with *ratzon Hashem*, the will of Hashem.

This lesson is equally relevant to all women, no matter their career or life circumstance. Every woman has crossroads where she needs to decide what to choose next. Do I volunteer out of the home or stay

---

136 *Metzudas Dovid, Mishlei* 30:16.
137 Rabbi Haim Messas, *Nishmat Haim,* quoted in *Sefer Eishes Chayil,* p. 138.

home at nights with my children? Do I switch to a job that is better paying or stick with the job that gives me flexibility? Do I shop for an upcoming Yom Tov or go to a Torah class? Sometimes the choice is obvious, but other times the choices are hard to make because there are many forces driving us in our decision-making. The *eishes chayil* is telling us to keep Hashem's will as our primary motivator.

At times, Hashem's will is not clear to us. Which yeshiva do I choose for my son? When do I say no to a *chessed* and when do I push myself? Often, we are choosing between two right things; this is the most difficult.

At times like these, we can look back at the previous *pesukim* and the role models we have learned about. The four *Imahos* each made prayer the first step when they were confronted with a challenge. If we don't know what to do, we can ask Hashem to help us do His will and to give us clarity. As we have also learned thus far, we can seek guidance from spiritual mentors who may have insights into our situation.

> When a decision is choosing between two right choices, we can learn from our four *Imahos*. We can pray, seek guidance from spiritual mentors, and then do our best.

Next, we can try to do our best. When I was younger, I thought these difficult life decisions were like a trick multiple-choice quiz administered by an all-powerful G-d. Making the right choice was a test of my devotion to Hashem since I should be able to figure out what was the right thing. As I got older, I realized this black-and-white thinking stemmed from a lack of *bitachon* (faith in Hashem). If He wanted me to have more information to make my decision, I would have it. Instead of fretting about the complexity of an issue, I learned to wait for more information to come. Often, the hardest decisions resolved themselves easily with just a little bit of time. When I started trying my best, asking for guidance, and praying, I realized that Hashem was caring for me in spiritual matters as well.

The Midrash discusses one woman who set up her life so she could make difficult life decisions based on Hashem's will alone. She was rewarded far more than anyone could anticipate. If we follow her example, we will also be able to benefit from choices made with Hashem in mind.

Midrash Yocheved

"She considers a field and takes it."	זָמְמָה שָׂדֶה וַתִּקָּחֵהוּ
This is Yocheved,	זוֹ הִיא יוֹכֶבֶד
from whom came Moshe	שֶׁיָּצְאָה מִמֶּנָּה מֹשֶׁה
who was equivalent to all of Yisroel,	שֶׁהוּא שָׁקוּל כְּנֶגֶד כָּל יִשְׂרָאֵל
who are called a vineyard,	שֶׁנִּקְרְאוּ כֶרֶם
as it says, "Because a vineyard of Hashem	שֶׁנֶּאֱמַר: "כִּי כֶרֶם ה' צְבָאוֹת
is the House of Yisroel"	בֵּית יִשְׂרָאֵל"
(Yeshayah 5:7).	(ישעיה ה:ז)

The Midrash lists Yocheved as the woman who best represents this *pasuk*. As a result of her decisions, she merited to have Moshe, who was equivalent in greatness to all of the Jewish People. The choices that led to this reward were entirely in the spirit of the *eishes chayil* and were driven by her desire to serve Hashem, regardless of all other factors.

Yocheved's Challenge

After the death of Yosef and his brothers, the Jewish nation multiplied and spread throughout Egypt.[138] Pharaoh wanted to stem their growth but did not want to publicly kill all the baby boys, as this would seem cruel and unnecessary.[139] Instead, he devised a plan so he would not be linked to a decision which his nation would condemn. He called Shifrah and Puah, the Jewish midwives, and commanded them to kill all Jewish baby boys born under their watch.

---

138 *Shemos* 1:6–14.
139 Ramban, *Shemos* 1:10.

VISION   **151**

Chazal tell us that these midwives, who were known as Shifrah and Puah, were called by other names: Yocheved and Miriam. They were a mother and daughter team from the tribe of Levi.[140] According to Rashi, Yocheved beautified the infants while Miriam comforted the newborns. When Yocheved/Shifrah and Miriam/Puah received Pharaoh's order, they devised their own plan.[141] Rather than killing the babies, Yocheved and Miriam gave them and their mothers food and drink to ensure the newborns' survival and the growth of the Jewish People.

> Pharaoh asked Yocheved and Miriam to kill all baby boys. Instead, they provided the baby boy and his mother food and drink to ensure the newborns' survival and the growth of the Jewish People.

Rewards of Shifrah and Puah

The *pasuk* tells us explicitly that Hashem rewarded the midwives for their actions.[142] The *pasuk* that describes the reward seems out of order.[143] First, the *pasuk* says that Hashem did "good" to Yocheved and Miriam, then it says that Hashem increased the nation, and finally, it says that Hashem made houses for the midwives. The *pesukim* seem to be written stating the result, then the cause, then the result. The *pesukim* should have first stated the cause — the nation increasing, and then mentioned the results — Hashem doing "good" for the midwives and making them houses. Why is the chain of events interrupted with the seemingly unrelated fact that the Jewish nation grew?

The Ohr HaChaim teaches that the increase in the nation was not the cause of Yocheved and Miriam's reward, but was — in and of itself — their reward.[144] The nation's growth was the good that Hashem did for the midwives. The biggest reward the midwives

---

140   Rashi, *Shemos* 1:15.
141   *Shemos* 1:17.
142   *Shemos* 1:20.
143   *Shemos* 1:20–22.
144   Ohr HaChaim, *Shemos* 1:20.

could receive was that the Jewish nation increased! A distant second to that was the personal reward of houses that were built for Yocheved and Miriam.

> The reward for Yocheved's sacrifice was the ability to do more mitzvos.

Why was the reward of the midwives a larger Jewish nation? As the nation increased, the midwives were placed into more danger as they had to continually defy Pharaoh's command and provide food and shelter for all the newborns being delivered.

Hashem saw that the midwives' sole motivation for saving the children was *yiras Shamayim*, fear of Heaven. Hashem wanted these women to receive the most reward possible for their altruistically motivated actions and prepared them more opportunities to perform mitzvos by creating more babies to save. Thus, their primary reward was the chance to save even more babies than would have otherwise been born. As a result of Yocheved and Miriam's actions, a whole nation was born, and they received much reward for their roles.

In a short time, the whole nation existed only because of the actions of two women, Yocheved and her daughter. As the adult and primary motivator behind the plan, Yocheved's reward was more significant than Miriam's. Yocheved's sons, Moshe and Aharon, merited leading the whole nation. Since the nation was alive only because of the choices of Yocheved, it was only fitting that her sons, Moshe and Aharon, should be the leaders of the Jewish People. The Ohr HaChaim continues that Moshe was unique in the history of the Jewish People. His soul encompassed the souls of every Jew. Each Jew in the Jewish nation is a piece of the soul of Moshe Rabbeinu. Since Yocheved saved all these Jews, her son's soul encompassed all of theirs.

Getting Practical: Vision in Marriage

Yocheved and the *eishes chayil* had the same goal that drove all of their decisions: a desire to serve Hashem. When making a choice, they considered the correct path to take and then did it with enthusiasm and purpose. Hashem rewards the *eishes chayil*, like He rewarded Yocheved, by giving her more opportunities to do mitzvos. These new mitzvos lead to the greatest reward possible.

How did the *eishes chayil* and Yocheved remain so focused and committed to do what is right? Most of us know how we would like to act in an ideal world, but knowing is not enough. How did they translate their desire into action?

The answer is that Yocheved and the *eishes chayil* had defined their goals for themselves in a concrete way. They knew what they wanted from life and were constantly reevaluating their current life work in light of this vision.

How do we get the same clarity and focus as described in *Eishes Chayil*?

Defining Our Goals

We need a vision that is not vague and subject to the whims of our daily stresses, and we must define and clarify this vision for ourselves. A woman wears many different hats in her many roles. She is an individual, a mother, a wife, a daughter, a sibling, a friend, and a professional. These roles can become confused unless she defines what her vision is for each.

My friend is a doctor who specializes in heart transplants. She also volunteers her time at her children's school. Depite pressure to increase her hours, she worked part-time rather than full-time when her children were growing up, and she is a good friend to the many women who know her. I asked her how she manages to balance everything and prioritize what to do and when to do it. She showed me the key to her success: a list. In this list, she had defined her mission for each area of her life. She had described in a few sentences what she wanted her home to feel like, the quality of her marriage, her professional goals, and her goals as a mother. She knows how she wants her life to look, and she has set up a system to make sure her ideals and her daily life correspond to each other.

My friend challenged me to do this exercise for myself. It was quite difficult.

For days, I walked around in a daze thinking, "What is it I want to accomplish as a mother? What should my home feel like? Look like? What does my marriage mean to me? What are my goals when I work?"

My mission statement had to be different from that of my friend. I had to reflect on my strengths, my values, and what I wanted for my life. I wrote a few sentences, revised them, talked to my husband and friends, and edited some more. In the end, I had an understanding of my vision for myself as an individual, a wife, a mother, a daughter, a relative, a friend, and a professional. Through the writing, editing, and thinking I came to a clarity that I wouldn't have had without the process. Having a mission statement written on paper makes us focus on what our main goals are. It helps us express who we want to be and become.

After we have a few sentences summarizing our vision, we need to be able to put that vision into practice. The next step is to write long-term objectives and short-term goals. I want my home to be warm and inviting, what does that mean? What is a long-term objective I can set to make that happen? Perhaps over the long-term, I want to create an atmosphere where people can relax. A short-term goal to make this happen would be to have furniture that is budget-friendly so my children can play with their friends without it making me nervous.

What is it I want to accomplish as a mother? What should my home feel like? Look like? What does my marriage mean to me? What are my goals when I work?

When I make long-term objectives and short-term goals, I am setting my priorities for my life. I am making decisions of what I am willing to sacrifice and what cannot be compromised. Making my long-term objectives was intimidating. I had goals that could not be achieved for many years. Years later, as I complete a project, I realize how powerful writing these seemingly impossible objectives and goals had been for me.

There is a famous parable that is told by many *mussar* masters that explains this concept:

Imagine you are traveling in Manhattan and you want to go uptown to visit friends. You see the Number Six train pull into the station, and in a panic, you rush to board the train. As you are traveling, you realize, to your dismay, that the train is going downtown. You do not want to waste any more time on this mistake. While you are still standing on the downtown train, you turn to face uptown.

This trick does not work. You are still going downtown!

You need to get off the downtown train before you can go uptown.

Defining our vision for our lives gets us off the downtown train of doing things that are taking us in the wrong direction. Sometimes, we are doing things that we do not even realize are taking us to places that we do not want to go. If we stop and consider whether we are on the right train in the first place, we can turn things around for ourselves.

Every day, we have so many conflicting demands on our time and focus. We must be like Yocheved and the *eishes chayil* and define what our priorities are. With that clarity, when new opportunities arise, we can make decisions that enhance our mission rather than missing opportunities that are all around us but that, in our haste, we may miss. Our reward will be the opportunity to do many more beneficial things and create a future filled with positivity and joy.

Summary

"She considers a field and takes it."   זָמְמָה שָׂדֶה וַתִּקָּחֵהוּ
               Yocheved   יוֹכֶבֶד

From the Pasuk We Learn

The *eishes chayil* has a clear understanding of her priorities and can make changes as opportunities arise.

From the Midrash We Learn

Yocheved risked her life to save and nurture Jewish babies because of her values and spiritual compass. She teaches us that the reward for making decisions based on our spiritual priorities is the opportunity to do more mitzvos and to have children who carry on our legacy.

Practical Steps

1. Setting a vision
    A. Define your strengths and values.
    B. Craft a written vision for each area of importance in life: As an individual (spiritual, emotional, financial, physical) and as a wife, parent, friend, and professional.
    C. Set a few measurable long-term objectives for each area of importance.
    D. Define concrete action steps to reach the long-term objective.

2. Making a choice when both seem equal
    A. Pray.
    B. Seek spiritual guidance.
    C. Do your best — don't be scared to act, and don't wait due to fear. Act with faith that Hashem will help.

Questions

Self-Growth

1. What roles am I playing now in my life?
2. What strengths do I bring to each of these roles?
3. What is my mission statement for myself as an individual? What is my mission statement for my other three most important roles?
4. What are my highest priorities?
5. Does my daily life match my vision?
6. What are some long-term objectives and short-term goals I am implementing so that my life reflects my mission statement?
7. How do I determine what is *ratzon Hashem*, the will of G-d, and what is driven by peer pressure, ego, or desires?
8. Are there any changes I would like to make in my life to help me serve Hashem better?
9. How have I made decisions in the past when the choices were not clear? Have I been comfortable with the outcome?

As Wives and Mothers

10. What is my mission statement for myself as a wife? As a mother?
11. What are some long-term objectives and short-term goals I am implementing so my life reflects my mission statement?

Teaching Our Daughters

12. How do I help my daughter find her own unique mission in life?

CHAPTER 10

Strength

חָגְרָה בְעוֹז מָתְנֶיהָ וַתְּאַמֵּץ זְרוֹעֹתֶיהָ.

She girds her loins with strength and makes strong her arms.

Peshat

Reading about the *eishes chayil* could make someone tired. After all, she works and cares for her children and somehow still has time to be a loving wife and mother. How does she do it all, and why should we not resent her for being "too perfect?"

Doing It All

The *eishes chayil* has a simple tactic for how she does it all. She takes care of herself. She takes the long view and recognizes that unless she is healthy and strong, she will never be able to achieve what she wants. She wants to be able to be calm, kind, active, and loving. To do so, she needs to be healthy. And so, the *eishes chayil* girds her loins — a term associated with men — to be strong. Her constitution is not naturally physically powerful; she must work to make it so. The Meiri explains that she makes her arms strong by regularly and consistently exercising and caring for her body so that it can continue to serve her.[145]

Exercising, and specifically strength-training as mentioned in the *pasuk*, has myriad short-term and long-term benefits. Lifting weights cuts a woman's risk of obesity, diabetes, and osteoporosis. It helps a woman have stronger muscles and bones, which leads to a far better quality of life. Women who strength-train have more endurance, less fatigue, and less risk of injury doing regular household tasks. It also reduces the chances of depression and anxiety. The increased muscle mass from weight-lifting even helps with weight loss and counteracts the muscle loss that happens to women over forty.

With all these obvious benefits to our daily lives and long-term health, why is it so hard to find time to exercise? Why is it so hard to get away and make the time for ourselves?

The reason is we magnify the voices of people who are requesting our time and attention. We hear in their requests that without us, they will fall apart. From children, husbands, friends, and school, from morning until her head hits the pillow, a woman is bound to hear: "But I NEED you! I cannot do it without you!" The chorus and subsequent guilt often reaches a feverish pitch just as she is about to walk out the door and do something for herself. Indeed, a woman may even begin to believe that she is indispensable and cannot ever get away. Slowly, without realizing it, she starts to neglect herself. She skips the gym, eats one too many instant soups, and forgets to drink enough water. She rationalizes her neglect by feeling proud of how giving and kind she is. Then, the woman wonders why she feels so run-down, overwhelmed, and cannot hold it together.

> With all these obvious benefits to our daily lives and long-term health, why is it so hard to to get away and make the time for ourselves?

---

145   Meiri, *Mishlei* 31:17.

The *eishes chayil* recognizes that without her health she will be useless to everyone. And so, she pauses and takes care of her needs. She ignores the requests/demands/guilt from the people she wants to help and takes care of herself first.

Self-Care vs. Self-Absorption

There are some women who prioritize themselves, and it makes us uncomfortable to do the same because they seem so self-centered; they ignore their kids' cries for help as they text or chat with their friends, or they are constantly engaged in self-care and seem oblivious to the needs of others.

What differentiates the *eishes chayil* from women who are over-indulgent is their focus on themselves. Women who are self-centered are thinking about what they want to do to enjoy themselves more. Their wants are the highest priority because they haven't expanded their world to include the needs and wants of others. The *eishes chayil* is not putting her needs first because she thinks she is more important than everyone else. Her needs are merely a measured part of the mix of priorities.

> The difference between the *eishes chayil* and women who are self-absorbed is their focus on themselves.

Other women at the opposite extreme are not much better, even though they appear selfless. They make other people's needs the center of their universe, be it the needs of their children, their husband, or their community. They neglect themselves so that another person's wants are always fulfilled. They go to sleep late, eat poorly, schedule dentist appointments for everyone except themselves, and don't exercise. Inevitably their kindness is marked with anger, frustration, and resentment — as only they are aware of what has been sacrificed to help others.

The *eishes chayil* is different. She is not living to fill her wants, her children's wants, or her husband's wants. She is only acting based on what Hashem wants. This awareness lets her make decisions without guilt, as she is certain that Hashem knows her limits and her abilities. Hashem gave her the body she has, as well as her responsibilities, and she can only do what she is physically able to do. Without the guilt, the *eishes chayil* can care for herself just as she cares for her family because both stem from the same source: her desire to fulfill the will of Hashem.

> Without the guilt, the *eishes chayil* can care for herself just as she cares for her family because both stem from the same source — her desire to fulfill the will of Hashem.

The simple meaning of this *pasuk* is that the *eishes chayil* must keep herself physically strong and not succumb to pressures to forget her needs. There is equal pressure when it comes to maintaining one's spiritual strength. The Midrash highlights a woman who teaches us how to exercise our spiritual muscles to achieve against great odds to do what is right.

Midrash – Miriam

"She girds her loins with strength." This is Miriam, whom, before Moshe was born, she said, "In the future my mother will bear a son who will save Yisroel." When he was born and the tyranny of the government intensified for them, her father stood and struck her on her head. He told her, "Where are your predictions?" and he stood and spit in her face. And with all that, she maintained her prophecy, as it is written, "His sister guarded from afar" *(Shemos 2:4).*	חָגְרָה בְעוֹז מָתְנֶיהָ זוֹ מִרְיָם שֶׁקֹּדֶם שֶׁנּוֹלַד מֹשֶׁה אָמְרָה "עֲתִידָה אִמִּי שֶׁתֵּלֵד בֵּן שֶׁמּוֹשִׁיעַ אֶת יִשְׂרָאֵל" כֵּיוָן שֶׁנּוֹלַד וְכָבֵד עֲלֵיהֶם עוֹל מַלְכוּת עָמַד אָבִיהָ וְסָפְתָהּ עַל רֹאשָׁהּ אָמַר לָהּ הֵיכָן נְבוּאָתֵיךְ וְעָמַד וְיָרַק בְּפָנֶיהָ וְעִם כָּל זֹאת הִיא מִתְאַמֶּצֶת בִּנְבוּאָתָהּ דִּכְתִיב "וַתֵּתַצַּב אֲחוֹתוֹ מֵרָחוֹק" (שמות ב:ד)

The Midrash tells us that Miriam is the one who strengthened herself to do what needed to be done, despite pressures to abandon her efforts — when she was doubted and shamed by her father. She maintained her commitment to her prophecy and grew to be a leader of the Jewish People.

> Miriam strengthened herself to do what needed to be done, despite pressures to abandon her efforts.

Miriam was born at the worst point of the slavery in Egypt.[146] Around the time of her birth, Pharaoh increased the torture of the Jewish slaves. Her parents named her Miriam from the root *mar* (bitter) to commemorate this time of transition to a more bitter exile. The only life she knew was one of witnessing her fellow Jews being beaten.

Miriam's Prophecy

When Miriam was five years old, life for the Jews took an even more dramatic turn for the worse.[147] Pharaoh decreed that all baby boys be thrown into the river. As the spiritual leader of the Jewish People, Miriam's father, Amram, divorced her mother and thus set a precedent that all Jewish couples should separate rather than have their newborn sons killed.

It was at this time that Miriam had a prophecy. She learned that a brother yet to be born would lead the Jewish People from the exile. She turned to her father and said, "Your decree is worse than Pharaoh's. His decree only concerns the boys — your decree applies to both boys and girls!"[148] Her father, upon hearing her prophecy, remarried Yocheved, Miriam's mother. Six months later (three months prematurely), a boy was born whose face shone with light and who promised to be the savior that Miriam had predicted. Amram kissed his daughter Miriam for bringing salvation to the Jewish nation.

---

146 *Seder Olam*, chapter 3.
147 *Talmud Bavli*, *Sotah* 11b.
148 *Talmud Bavli*, *Sotah* 12a.

Three months later, all hope seemed to be lost. The Egyptians began to search for the child when the baby should have been full-term. It was no longer safe to keep this wondrous child at home, and Yocheved had to place her infant in a basket in the river. According to the Midrash, Amram slapped Miriam and spat, "Where is your prophecy?" He questioned her and all that she had promised.

Miriam's Strength

Our parents' opinions of us count. Whether at six or sixty, most children are stung by parental criticism. Yet Miriam persevered. She showed a strength and resolve despite the seeming futility of her prophecy.

חָגְרָה בְעוֹז מָתְנֶיהָ.
She girded her loins with strength.

She strengthened herself with the knowledge that her prophecy was true. The *pasuk* quoted by the Midrash tells us that she went to the water's edge where her mother placed the basket in the reeds. She stood from afar to watch what would happen to the baby.

The word used to describe her standing at her post was וַתֵּתַצַּב. The word וַתֵּתַצַּב is different from עָמַד, the general verb that means "to stand." וַתֵּתַצַּב denotes standing with determination and confidence, much like an officer or guard.[149] Miriam stood with confidence at the river's edge to learn what would happen to the child and how, not if, her prophecy would be fulfilled.

> Miriam stood with confidence at the river's edge to learn what would happen to the child and how, not if, her prophecy would be fulfilled.

When Basya found Moshe, it was Miriam who suggested that a Jewish woman be called to nurse Moshe. Chazal tell us that Moshe refused to nurse from a non-Jewish nursemaid because he did not want to taint the mouth that was destined to talk to Hashem. It was

---

149 Rav Hirsch, *Devarim* 29:9.

Miriam who came up with a solution that ensured that Moshe did not allow the milk of a pagan into his mouth by suggesting that Yocheved fill the role of nursemaid.[150] By standing with confidence by the river's edge, Miriam helped shepherd her prophecy to fruition. She set into motion the events that led to the redemption of her nation by maintaining her resolve and not succumbing to self-doubt because of those who doubted her.

Getting Practical: Strength in Marriage

Miriam comes to teach us that we need to prioritize and have confidence in our decision to take care of both our spiritual and physical wellbeing.

Rabbeinu Bachaya makes a fascinating point:[151]

> כִּי הַדְּבָרִים הַשִּׂכְלִיִּים בְּדִמְיוֹן הַדְּבָרִים הַטִּבְעִיִּים, כִּי יִקְרֶה לַשֵּׂכֶל כְּמִקְרֶה הַחוּשִׁים, וְכֹחוֹת הַנֶּפֶשׁ הֲלֹא הֵם קְשׁוּרִים עִם כֹּחוֹת הַגּוּף.[152]
>
> *Spiritual things are comparable to physical things. What happens to a person's intellect (spiritual capacity) is similar to what happens with his senses. Aren't the powers of the soul tied to the powers of the body?*

Rabbeinu Bachaya teaches us that we must analyze how we care for our bodies to learn how we should treat our souls. He continues with the following example:

> *A man was imprisoned in a dungeon for many years with no access to sunlight. One day, he was pardoned and told he was free to leave. If he would have just walked out the door to freedom, he would likely have been blinded as his eyes would not have been able to cope with the sudden change from complete darkness to light. Instead, the man had to*

---

150 *Likutei Sichos*, vol. 18, p. 132.
151 *Rabbeinu Bachaya, Shemos* 3:1.
152 Ibid.

gradually transition to the light so his eyes could have time to adjust.

Similarly, Rabbeinu Bachaya explains, a soul cannot change from darkness to light in "one fell swoop." It needs to move slowly and carefully so as not be overwhelmed and lose all hope of lasting change.

Spiritual Health

Rabbeinu Bachaya's simple advice can help us understand our soul and how to care for it as much as the *eishes chayil* cared for her body. There is a certain regimen that our bodies need in order to function in good health. We need to eat right, exercise regularly, and get enough sleep.

What does a proper diet and exercise look like for our soul? What does our soul need to maintain its spiritual health?

In our daily diet, we have to eat a balance of proteins, vegetables, fruit, fat, and carbohydrates. If we want our bodies to be healthy, we cannot skip any food group. A healthy spiritual diet consists of regular doses of other building blocks:

- prayer
- learning Torah
- performing mitzvos
- doing acts of *chessed*
- having quiet time to think

> A healthy spiritual diet consists of regular doses of these building blocks: prayer, learning Torah, performing mitzvos, doing acts of *chessed*, having quiet time to think.

Every person can find time for these essential parts of her spiritual diet. The amount we have of each and how they look may be different at different stages of life. A new mother may find herself saying a few heartfelt words of request while an older woman may daven *Shacharis*, *Minchah*, and *Maariv* — but both make sure to pray every day.[153]

---

153 Consult with your own rabbinical authority for guidance as to basic halachic requirements in each area.

Strength Exercises for the Soul

A diet must be combined with exercise. Spiritual exercises include engaging in activities that stretch us to do more than we thought we were able to do. We need to implement what we learn and work on all areas of our spiritual world. There are areas that involve our interactions with man, those that address our interaction with Hashem, and those that deal with how we relate to and view ourselves. Recently, I did a thirty-day exercise challenge. On my first day, I struggled to complete five repetitions and doubted I would ever be able to do the 125 repetitions they would be asking of me on the thirtieth day. The first few days, I was sorer than I have ever been. Unbelievably, by the last day, the 125 repetitions were easier than the first five I did on the first day. My body got stronger with each day of exercise.

> A diet must be combined with exercise. Doing a little more every day builds up our spirit and allows us to achieve heights we never would have considered possible.

Spiritual goals follow the same rule. At first, it may feel like it is impossible to create a new habit. Doing a little more every day builds up our spirit and allows us to achieve impossible heights that could never have been considered when we began.

Just like laziness and guilt can prevent us from doing the right exercises physically, that same laziness and guilt can stop us from getting the spiritual diet and exercise we need as well. We may be so concerned about helping our children get to shul that we forget to daven ourselves, or we may be devoted to the learning of our spouse and our children, but we ourselves have not learned any *Torah* in a long time.

Habits are powerful. After a while, instead of seizing an opportunity, we use our few spare moments to immerse ourselves in sensational articles or chat about recipes and home decorating ideas rather than taking a moment to say *Tehillim* or learn something new. We may think it is no big deal, but just like our bodies will eventually get fat and weak from neglect, our souls will have a similar fate.

Miriam and the *eishes chayil* come to teach all women a very important lesson: We need to push ourselves to do more for ourselves — both physically and spiritually. We know what we should do. We instinctively know what is right and what is wrong. We know when we do not need that extra piece of cake, that we need to exercise, and that we should go to sleep and forget about our never-ending to-do lists. We know that learning what *Tehillim* means or studying the *parashah* is important, but we rationalize.

Just like our bodies will eventually get fat and weak from neglect, our souls will have a similar fate.

Most of us succumb to pressures not to listen to our better judgment. Physically, we rationalize that it is too cold to leave the house, that we are not in control of what we eat, or that someone else needs our time more. We figure it will not hurt us much if we skip the gym one day, then two. After all, our kids need (fill in the blank), which no one else can provide.

Spiritually, we succumb to the voice in our head that tells us we are under too much pressure, and others need us to be available so we cannot go to a *shiur*, listen to one on an MP3, daven, or sit quietly and think.

Both the *eishes chayil* and Miriam have taught us that we are stronger than we think. As women, we all have the capacity to be strong and stand up to the pressure. We are doing the best we can do based on what Hashem wants. Keeping ourselves physically and spiritually healthy allows everything else to fall into place. We can do what is right and quiet those voices that are shouting that we cannot.

Summary

"She girds her loins with strength."   חָגְרָה בְעוֹז מָתְנֶיהָ
Miriam   מִרְיָם

From the Pasuk We Learn

The *eishes chayil* prioritizes keeping herself physically healthy among her other responsibilities.

From the Midrash We Learn

Miriam helped shepherd her prophecy — that Moshe would save the Jewish People — to fruition and never lost confidence in it. From her we learn that the *eishes chayil* does not let doubt of others translate into her own self-doubt when she knows the correct thing to do.

Practical Steps

1. Schedule physically healthy living habits such as exercise, healthy meal preparation, appropriate sleep times, and doctors' appointments.
2. Schedule spiritually healthy habits such as prayer, Torah learning, mitzvos, and reflection time.
3. Adopt small changes to ensure long-term results.
4. Identify areas of positive growth to improve in our relationship with Hashem, with others, and with ourselves.

Questions

Self-Growth

1. Am I aware of what my body needs at my age, given my body type?
2. What exercises do I enjoy? Are they a regular part of my schedule?
3. What nutritional diet do I need to be healthy and have energy? Is my attitude to my diet driven by health or by popular culture?
4. Do I visit my doctor for all recommended health screenings and checkups?
5. Are my spiritual needs — prayer, learning, and *chessed* — part of my daily and weekly schedule?
6. Am I aware of what types of learning and *chessed* I enjoy so that I can more easily incorporate them into my life?
7. What is keeping me from caring for myself as I need to (people? messages?)?

As Wives and Mothers

8. How do I balance caring for the physical and emotional needs of my husband with my own?
9. What happens to my relationships when I neglect self-care as opposed to when I practice self-care?

Teaching Our Daughters

10. How do I teach my daughter to exercise and eat properly without having her become hyper-focused on looks and diet?
11. How do I encourage my daughter to have a healthy body image?
12. How do I teach my daughter to self-care in an appropriate manner so she doesn't neglect herself or become self-absorbed?
13. How do I help my daughter develop spiritual tools that she can use for life?

CHAPTER 11

Self-Actualization

טָעֲמָה כִּי טוֹב סַחְרָהּ לֹא יִכְבֶּה בַלַּיְלָה נֵרָהּ.

*She perceives that her merchandise is good;
her candle is not extinguished at night.*

Peshat

We have already seen the *eishes chayil*'s diligence in the early hours and during the day. This *pasuk* describes the world of the *eishes chayil* at night.

In this line, the *eishes chayil* is טָעֲמָה (*taamah*) that she has a good product and as a result does not extinguish a candle at night. What does the word טָעֲמָה (*taamah*) mean? What is her merchandise that she has evaluated? And what does this have to do with her evening activities?

טָעֲמָה Defined

The word טַעַם (*taam*) can have two meanings in *Tanach*. The first meaning is "to taste,"[154] the second is "to understand."[155] The *Daas Mikra* explains that in this case, it means to understand with one's intellect and common sense.[156] Here, the *eishes chayil* understands the value of her merchandise.

The Eishes Chayil's Merchandise

What is the *eishes chayil*'s merchandise that she understands to be valuable? Is it a bushel of wheat or a scarf she has knitted? Is this the value system that we are extolling — that a woman be caught up with her business and property?

The merchandise of the *eishes chayil* encompasses far more than what she owns; it includes all that she is: her talents, her property, her opportunities, and her family. The *eishes chayil* values what makes her a unique commodity in the world. She does so, according to the Meiri, by recognizing her strengths and her capabilities.[157] The *eishes chayil* recognizes that she is a talented writer, has quality merchandise to sell, or is skilled at parenting.

There are many people who shy away from being confident in their own abilities. They reason that to do so would be arrogant. According to this *pasuk*, it is the very knowledge of her gifts itself that allows a woman to become an *eishes chayil*. Without this self-awareness, the *eishes chayil* would never reach her potential; without this knowledge, a person may never know herself or truly understand what she can achieve.

> The merchandise of the *eishes chayil* encompasses all that she is and includes her talents, property, opportunities, and family.

In contrast, the *eishes chayil* has a sense of her potential that allows her to chart how she can best develop herself. When she acknowledges and draws from her strengths, she is happier and more successful.

---

154 *Metzudas Tzion, Shmuel I* 14:24.
155 *Metzudas Tzion, Tehillim* 34:9.
156 *Daas Mikra, Mishlei* 31:18.
157 Meiri, ibid.

Humility with Self-Awareness

How does the *eishes chayil* not allow her self-regard to color her behavior negatively? The *pasuk* continues:

לֹא יִכְבֶּה בַלַּיְלָה נֵרָהּ.

Her candle does not go out at night.

Even with the *eishes chayil*'s knowledge of her gifts, she does not take them for granted or have a false sense of entitlement. When the *eishes chayil* understands her strengths, she views them as obligations rather than a cause for praise. She works hard at night to actualize her potential in whatever area she may be so blessed.

> The *eishes chayil* views her strengths as obligations rather than a cause for praise.

Interestingly, the *pasuk* does not say, "She does not extinguish her candle"; rather, it says that her candle is not extinguished.

Why is this part of the *pasuk* written in the passive tense, unlike the first half of the *pasuk*, which is written in active tense?

Simply put, the *eishes chayil* has a husband and children. She has lit the candle and encourages them to use it as long as they are able. Despite her great strengths, she does not lord her needs over her husband, claiming her efforts are more important or that she needs his attention. Instead, she actively encourages her husband to continue his studies by candlelight. She encourages him to devote himself to the actualization of his own potential in Torah learning. Through her efforts, her family benefits from her light and carries on with her work in their own lives.

Midrash – Channah

This *pasuk* is painting a picture of a confident woman who has high expectations for herself and her family. The Midrash tells us that Channah is the woman who represents this thoughtful determination to realize her potential and the potential of her son, Shmuel.

Channah knew that she had a gift and did not rest until it bore fruit. She not only pushed herself to use her gift, but she sacrificed her relationship with her son so that he could use his own gifts and help the Jewish People.

The Midrash relates:

"She perceives that her merchandise is good."	טָעֲמָה כִּי טוֹב סַחְרָהּ
This is Channah,	זוֹ חַנָּה
who understood the meaning of prayer,	שֶׁטָּעֲמָה טַעַם תְּפִלָּה
as it is said, "And Channah prayed	שֶׁנֶּאֱמַר "וַתִּתְפַּלֵּל חַנָּה
and she said, 'My soul rejoiced with Hashem'"	וַתֹּאמַר עָלַץ לִבִּי בַּה'"
(Shmuel I 2:1).	(ש"א ב:א)
Accordingly, she merited a son from her	לְפִיכָךְ זָכְתָה וְיָצָא מִמֶּנָּה בֵן
who was a match to Moshe and Aharon	שֶׁהָיָה בֶּן זוּג לְמֹשֶׁה וְאַהֲרֹן
[in] that they lit up Yisroel like candles,	שֶׁהָיוּ מְאִירִין לְיִשְׂרָאֵל כְּנֵרוֹת
as it is written, "Moshe and Aharon	דִּכְתִיב "מֹשֶׁה וְאַהֲרֹן
among His priests,	בְּכֹהֲנָיו
and Shmuel among them	וּשְׁמוּאֵל
that call upon His name"	בְּקֹרְאֵי שְׁמוֹ"
(Tehillim 99:7).	(תהלים צט:ז)
And it is written about Shmuel,	וּכְתִיב בֵּיהּ בִּשְׁמוּאֵל
"And the lamp of G-d had not yet gone out,	"וְנֵר אֱלֹהִים טֶרֶם יִכְבֶּה
and Shmuel laid down to sleep	וּשְׁמוּאֵל שֹׁכֵב
in the temple of Hashem"	בְּהֵיכַל ה'"
(Shmuel I 3:3).	(ש"א ג:ג)

The Midrash states that Channah understood prayer, and this understanding, as demonstrated by her prayer in *Sefer Shmuel I* 2:2, caused her to have a child who was on par with Moshe and Aharon. Shmuel's light was not extinguished, just as the *eishes chayil*'s light was not extinguished.

The Midrash needs to be examined so that we can know how Channah's understanding of prayer caused her to have such an illustrious child and how Channah's actions help us understand the message of this *pasuk* more profoundly.

Channah's Life

The book of Shmuel begins with the story of Elkanah, a communal leader from the tribe of Ephraim.[158] Every year, he and his two wives, Channah and Peninah, would travel to the Mishkan (Tabernacle) in Shiloh for the holidays. The two wives had very different experiences on the journey: Channah was childless and despondent over her lack of children, while Peninah was a mother of ten, caring for her rambunctious brood. Each year, Elkanah would bring *korbanos*, sacrifices, in the Mishkan and distribute the portions of meat from the *korbanos* to his wives and to his and Peninah's children. Each year, Peninah taunted Channah about her barren state.[159] Each year, Channah would be left shattered by Peninah's remarks, unable to eat and drink or celebrate her time in the holy Mishkan.

After many years, Elkanah was distraught by Channah's depression and begged her to appreciate their relationship.[160]

> Channah realized that prayer was the key to everything in the world. She committed to use her gift of prayer to its maximum.

"Am I not better to you than ten children?" he asked. Channah considered her husband's words and agreed to participate in the festivities. Channah then considered how she could ease her suffering and deal with her inner pain. She realized that there was only one way to solve her problems and came to Hashem with a broken heart, unable to bear the torment of Peninah any longer. Shattered by her lack of children and her inability to fulfill her role as a Jewish mother, she turned over her emotions to Hashem and asked for His help. She made a commitment that her firstborn child would be devoted to a life of spirituality and service of Hashem.

The next year, Channah bore a son whom she called Shmuel.[161] His miraculous birth made her realize that prayer was the key to everything

---

158 *Shmuel I* 1:1–7.
159 Rashi, *Shmuel I* 1:6.
160 *Shmuel I* 1:8–11.
161 *Shmuel I* 1:20.

in the world. Channah recognized she had a gift for prayer and committed to use it to its maximum.

Channah's Gift of Prayer

When Shmuel was weaned, Channah was ready to fulfill her commitment by devoting her son's life to the service of Hashem.[162] The family brought Shmuel to Shiloh to be educated and raised by the leader of the generation, Eli.

At this joyous event, Channah realized that she once again had an opportunity to use her powerful emotions to pray to Hashem.[163] This is the prayer to which the Midrash is referring.

The prayer of thanksgiving and joy that Channah said on this occasion did not only focus on her own gratitude and thanks. In her prayer, she recognized the strength of Hashem to change fortunes and bestow blessings. As she thanked Hashem for her own miracle, she beseeched Him to change the fortunes of the Jewish People. She concluded her prayer:

וְיִתֶּן עֹז לְמַלְכּוֹ וְיָרֵם קֶרֶן מְשִׁיחוֹ.[164]
*May He give strength to His king and raise
the pride of His Mashiach.*

Channah asked that Hashem give strength to the Jewish king who represents Him and bring His Mashiach, the nation's ultimate savior.

Channah had learned that anything could be accomplished through prayer. She decided to apply her prayers to the good of the whole nation. Channah knew that the world should have a clear recognition of Hashem. She tried to play her part by devoting a son to this goal.

---

162 *Shmuel I* 1:24.
163 *Shmuel I* 2:1–10.
164 *Shmuel I* 2:10.

טָעֲמָה כִּי טוֹב סַחְרָהּ.
She perceives that her merchandise is good.

Channah, who understood the power of *tefillah*, now requested an even larger miracle. She asked that the whole world be united under the powerful leadership of Mashiach.

Shmuel's Greatness

> Channah had learned that anything could be accomplished through prayer. She applied her prayers to the good of the whole nation.
>
>

The Midrash continues that because Channah davened to Hashem, asking for the maximum, she merited a son who is compared to Moshe and Aharon. The Midrash quotes a *pasuk* in *Tehillim*:

מֹשֶׁה וְאַהֲרֹן בְּכֹהֲנָיו וּשְׁמוּאֵל בְּקֹרְאֵי שְׁמוֹ.[165]
Moshe and Aharon were among His priests and Shmuel among those who invoke His name.

The comparison between Moshe and Shmuel is strange. In *Bamidbar* 12:6–8, the Torah states that the prophecy of Moshe is incomparable to any other prophecy that preceded or followed it. In fact, the uniqueness of Moshe's prophecy is one of the thirteen fundamental principles of our faith.[166] How, then, could Shmuel be compared to Moshe — isn't this in direct contradiction to the Torah?

The *Metzudas Dovid* explains that just as Moshe was the ultimate leader and prophet, Shmuel was the ultimate man of prayer.[167] The Ramban singles out an episode from the life of Shmuel to describe his greatness in prayer:[168]

Shmuel had led the Jewish People faithfully for many years when

---

165 *Tehillim* 99:6.
166 Rambam, Introduction to *Perek Chelek*.
167 *Metzudas Dovid, Tehillim* 99:6.
168 Ramban, *Bamidbar* 12:6.

they approached him with a complaint.¹⁶⁹ They wanted a king who would lead them in battle and provide them with a stable government. Shmuel rebuked them for asking for a king, as he had been an honest and righteous leader and did not deserve their rejection. In contrast, the Jewish People had served idols and lost faith in Hashem time after time. Shmuel told them that if they would listen to Hashem's commandments, life would be tranquil, but if they did not, having a king would not ease their lives.

> Just as Moshe was the ultimate leader and prophet, Shmuel was the ultimate man of prayer.

Shmuel continues (*Shmuel I* 12:16–18):

טז גַּם עַתָּה הִתְיַצְּבוּ וּרְאוּ, אֶת הַדָּבָר הַגָּדוֹל הַזֶּה, אֲשֶׁר ה׳, עֹשֶׂה לְעֵינֵיכֶם.
יז הֲלוֹא קְצִיר חִטִּים, הַיּוֹם אֶקְרָא אֶל ה׳, וְיִתֵּן קֹלוֹת וּמָטָר; וּדְעוּ וּרְאוּ, כִּי רָעַתְכֶם רַבָּה אֲשֶׁר עֲשִׂיתֶם בְּעֵינֵי ה׳, לִשְׁאוֹל לָכֶם, מֶלֶךְ.
יח וַיִּקְרָא שְׁמוּאֵל אֶל ה׳, וַיִּתֵּן ה׳ קֹלֹת וּמָטָר בַּיּוֹם הַהוּא; וַיִּירָא כָל הָעָם מְאֹד אֶת ה׳, וְאֶת שְׁמוּאֵל.
יט וַיֹּאמְרוּ כָל הָעָם אֶל שְׁמוּאֵל, הִתְפַּלֵּל בְּעַד עֲבָדֶיךָ אֶל ה׳ אֱלֹקֶיךָ וְאַל נָמוּת: כִּי יָסַפְנוּ עַל כָּל חַטֹּאתֵינוּ רָעָה, לִשְׁאֹל לָנוּ מֶלֶךְ.

> **16** Now, therefore, stand still and see this great thing, which Hashem is doing before your eyes.
> **17** Is it not wheat harvest today? I will call to Hashem, that He may send thunder and rain; and you shall know and see that your wickedness is great, which you have done in the sight of Hashem, in asking for you a king.
> **18** So Shmuel called to Hashem; and Hashem sent thunder and rain that day; and all the people greatly feared Hashem and Shmuel.
> **19** And all the people said to Shmuel: "Pray for your servants to Hashem, your G-d, that we do not die, for we have added onto all our sins this evil, to ask for us a king."

---

169 *Shmuel I* 12:1–15a.

Shmuel davened to Hashem that rain should fall during the wheat harvest so that the Jewish People would learn a lesson. In modern times, when rain falls during a harvest, we use dryers to prevent our grain from becoming moldy. In Biblical times, wet grain was a significant threat to the food supply.

According to Rashi, Shmuel was demonstrating that the Jewish People had underestimated the power of prayer.[170] They had thought they needed a king to help fight their battles. Shmuel, the living proof of the power of prayer, demonstrated to the nation assembled before him that nothing is beyond that power. Just as he had been born to a barren woman and he was able to make rain fall at a time when there should naturally be no rain, the Jewish People would have been able to conquer their worst enemies without a king. All they had needed to do was pray.

The Jewish People recognized their error.[171] They had insulted Shmuel and betrayed Hashem by asking for a king. They turned to Shmuel and asked him to daven that the rain should stop. He answered that he would pray for them as he always had. He had only prayed for the rain to help them do *teshuvah*. He would now pray again to help them and strengthen them.

Shmuel, the Light

The Midrash concludes that Shmuel was a light for the Jewish People. It quotes a *pasuk* from the time when Shmuel received his first prophecy and began his years of service to Hashem and his people:

וְנֵר אֱלֹהִים טֶרֶם יִכְבֶּה וּשְׁמוּאֵל שֹׁכֵב בְּהֵיכַל ה'.[172]

And the lamp of G-d had not yet gone out, and Shmuel laid down to sleep in the temple of Hashem.

---

170   *Shmuel I* 12:16.
171   *Shmuel I* 12:19–25.
172   *Shmuel I* 3:3.

Chazal note that the candle mentioned cannot only refer to a candle that lit up the room where Shmuel rested because that would be an extraneous detail.[173] This candle also refers to the allegorical light that guided the Jewish People. When Shmuel received his first prophecy, the Jewish People were being led by Eli, a great *Kohen*, whose vitality and guidance were waning. Before Eli died, Shmuel's light and leadership began to shine brightly. His leadership climaxed with his anointment of Dovid HaMelech, the ancestor of Mashiach.

Indeed, Shmuel's rise as a leader was the answer to Channah's prayer. She had concluded her prayer by beseeching Hashem to establish a strong king and bring Mashiach. Hashem fulfilled Channah's prayer by giving her a son who was the conduit for her prayers to be realized. Her son was the light and the leader who directed the Jewish People to fulfill their mission.

Shmuel, Channah's Son

We can now understand the Midrash completely. Channah understood that she had something powerful:

טָעֲמָה כִּי טוֹב סַחְרָהּ.
She perceives that her merchandise is good.

She had the power of prayer. Even in her darkest moments, she held onto this power to give her strength and to access Hashem's blessings.

לֹא יִכְבֶּה בַלַּיְלָה נֵרָהּ.
Her candle is not extinguished at night.

Channah encouraged her son to fulfill his potential in the same area so that he could use the tremendous spiritual power that lay within him as well.

---

173 *Talmud Bavli, Kiddushin* 72b.

Shmuel inherited his understanding of the power of prayer from his mother. He was able to use this awareness to direct the entire nation to the service of Hashem. His prayers, like Channah's, did not focus on bringing himself comfort; they focused on helping the Jewish People fulfill their potential. Thus, he was able to daven for complete miracles because he knew that prayer can do anything and should be used to further Hashem's will in the world. The prayers of both Channah and Shmuel have helped guide and protect the Jewish People and will ultimately help the world reach its highest potential.

> The prayers of both Channah and Shmuel have helped guide and protect the Jewish People and will ultimately help the world reach its highest potential.

Getting Practical: Self-Actualization in Marriage

Channah's self-awareness of her power brought salvation to everyone in the world. Had she dismissed her great gifts, the whole world would have suffered.

This *pasuk* from *Eishes Chayil* teaches us that we must also look at our strengths honestly and embrace them. Are we creative? Organized? Warm? We must be comfortable labeling our positive attributes and thinking of how to maximize our potential. If we do, the world at large benefits. If we do not, the world suffers.

By identifying our strengths, we become prepared to use them. When we use our gifts, we succeed; when we succeed, we are more likely to continue to work hard and contribute to society. We are energized by our accomplishments, which pushes us to continue accomplishing. The positive energy our successes generate gives us the ability to do more. It also gives us the strength and confidence to look at our weaknesses with less shame and fear so that we can change ourselves in a positive and uplifting way.

Every woman is different. My strengths will be quite different from yours. I will never be as tall as my sister or as responsible as my neighbor. How I parent, cook, and set up my home will look very different from how anyone else does. When I celebrate my strengths rather than focus on my weaknesses, I will have more patience with myself. I will be able to notice other people's strengths and celebrate their uniqueness because I will not feel as judged and defensive. Instead of criticizing and judging, I will appreciate others and try to work with them so their strengths can complement my own.

The Power of Our Prayers

Channah taught us that in the realm of the spirit, we also all have access to remarkable strengths. We can all access the power of prayer if we so choose. Every year on Rosh Hashanah we shout:

תְּשׁוּבָה וּתְפִילָה וּצְדָקָה מַעֲבִירִין אֶת רוֹעַ הַגְזֵירָה!
Prayer, repentance, and charity make tragedies pass over us!

What happens during the days between Rosh Hashanah and the next year? Do we pray with the same passion and intensity as we do on Rosh Hashanah?

A few generations ago, most women recognized their power of prayer. Grandmothers would spend spare minutes saying *Tehillim*, and their *siddurim* would be soaked with tears even though they could hardly read Hebrew and probably did not understand the meaning of the words. What they understood is that their prayers had an impact. Health, marriage, and happiness were acknowledged to be outside of their control, and they knew that Hashem was their Father and King and that only He could help them.

In our generation, as we believe that we have more control over our health, fertility, and finances, we have lost sight of how little we actually control. We don't realize that every aspect of our life is tenuous and how much we actually rely on Hashem for anything that happens during our day. If we have a small problem, we think it is too insignificant to ask for help from Hashem. If we have a big challenge, we label it a crisis and start solution-shopping and bemoaning our fate. Both approaches ignore that Hashem is the כָּל יָכוֹל — Omnipotent — completely able.

He is able to deal with the minor issues and the major issues; He can solve anything. There is no such thing as a small issue or a big crisis — every moment is an opportunity to increase our connection to Him.

> There is no such thing as a small issue or a big crisis — every moment is an opportunity to increase our connection to Him.

This awareness is difficult to develop and maintain. It is challenging to build our trust in Hashem's availability to help with any problem to the point that we turn to Him for all our large and small issues. One way to foster this trust is to give Hashem a small task for which to be "responsible." When we see that Hashem has that base covered, we will appreciate His great power and turn to Him more frequently and for bigger issues.

Before Pesach, I desperately needed shoes. I wanted fashionable shoes, but generally the ones that fit are the sensible kind that my grandmother would say are too old-looking for her. The problem is that without proper shoes, I end up injuring my feet. I had already been to five or six stores and through one mall. Nothing fit, not even the sensible ones, and I envisioned myself wearing sneakers on Yom Tov. I sat outside a small store in my car and thought about my options. It occurred to me that this situation was truly outside my control. I was making Pesach and only had a limited time available to shop. The more time I spent shopping, the more chaotic my Pesach preparations would be. I could take risks with my attitude because not having new shoes for Yom Tov would be annoying but not life-threatening. I consciously turned the situation over to Hashem and said a prayer, unsure of what would happen next. Feeling somewhat foolish, I walked into the store and immediately found not one, but two pairs of shoes!

The "old me" would have cynically dismissed finding the shoes as a coincidence. After learning about the power of prayer, this was a wake-up call: I could ask Hashem to help me and He is always available. I could talk to Hashem more about bigger things, too. Raising children, marriage, my job — Hashem could solve all of my problems, causing me less stress than if I tried to solve them myself. I started asking for help, guidance, and support from Hashem much more frequently.

Turning to Hashem in prayer is only half of what Channah taught us about the power we have lying dormant within us. Channah also taught us that we can help the whole nation with our prayers. Channah did not just pray for herself, she universalized her prayer. She wanted the whole world to experience the joy and redemption she felt. She knew she could make it happen through her prayers, and she was able to teach this lesson to her children so they believed it too.

Channah taught us that our prayers can solve problems big and small and can help others as well.

Three Mothers

In June 2014, the Jewish world was introduced to three women who, like Channah, recognized the power of prayer and faith and used it to bring the whole Jewish nation closer to Hashem. These three women looked like ordinary Jewish mothers, but their strength and courage were remarkable. Their three teenage sons Gilad Shaer, Eyal Yifrach, and Naftali Fraenkel, *Hy"d*, were kidnapped on their way home from school.

These mothers took their most powerful emotions and led the Jewish People, teaching them how to respond to this crisis. They announced publicly that the only solution to this calamity was to turn to Hashem in prayer. The mothers did not limit their prayers to their own communities. They organized prayer and unity events across the world, bringing countless Jews closer to Hashem and His mitzvos. The nation became united for eighteen days of prayer and introspection. On day seventeen of the prayer vigil, the families organized a rally of one hundred thousand Israelis who joined them in prayer and solidarity. The next day, the three boys' bodies were found and brought to a Jewish burial.

The story of these three mothers does not end at the funeral. Almost immediately, a war broke out between Gaza and Israel. Hamas retaliated for arrests made during the eighteen-day ordeal by firing missiles into cities populated by millions of people. While missiles landed and caused damage, the loss of life and property could have been far worse. Israel was forced to begin a ground invasion to stop the missile attacks whereupon they discovered an extensive network of tunnels that had been dug to be used in a mass terrorist attack planned for a few months later, on Rosh Hashanah. The kidnapping of the three boys had resulted in a war that saved hundreds, if not thousands, of lives. The prayers of so many Jews did not go unheard, and we merited to see open miracles every day.

These three mothers were the daughters of Channah. They recognized the power of prayer — and their own power. They used their strength to transform a nation from one that was broken and angry to a prayerful and united one. They did this by remembering the power they had to positively impact the direction of their nation. They embraced their potential to make positive changes and did not shy away from the mantle of leadership when it was presented to them.

> In June 2014, three mothers became the daughters of Channah. They used their strength to transform a nation from one that was broken and angry to a prayerful and united one.

We, too, have this power. When we know our strengths, we will be able to call upon them when the opportunity arises. We will be able to use our emotions, our prayers, and our skills to save our family and our nation. When we pray or do good deeds, we wield tremendous power. We can include all of the hopes and dreams of our nation. If we do not value our power, we may limit our prayers and thus render them much less effective. If we discount our strengths, we cannot change our nation for the better.

Hashem is willing to listen to all our *tefillos*; He is willing to help us use our strengths. We need to believe enough in ourselves to merit His help.

Hashem believes in our greatness. We must believe in ourselves, as well.

Summary

"She perceives that her merchandise is good." טָעֲמָה כִּי טוֹב סַחְרָהּ
Channah חַנָּה

From the Pasuk We Learn

The *eishes chayil* knows her strengths and uses them to accomplish great things. She encourages her husband and her children to use their strengths as well.

From the Midrash We Learn

Channah knew that one of her greatest assets was her power of prayer. She included her nation in her prayers to bring Mashiach and also taught her son to use his power of prayer to achieve greatness and lead the Jewish nation.

Practical Steps

1. Be aware of our strengths and talents.
2. Encourage our husbands and children to use their strengths and talents.
3. Actively seek help from Hashem through prayer.
4. Include others in our prayers to help them as well.

Questions

Self-Growth

1. What are the talents, strengths, and gifts Hashem has given me?
2. How can I bring myself to actualize my potential to the fullest?
3. How can I give those around me the opportunity to fulfill their potential?
4. What are some of my needs that I thought were too big to ask Hashem?
5. What are some of my needs that I thought were too small to ask Hashem?
6. How can I use my prayers to help others?
7. How do I become aware of what other people need so that I may pray for them?

As Wives and Mothers

8. How do I balance my intellectual, spiritual, and emotional strengths with the responsibilities of caring for my family? How do I know what skills to use and when to use them?
9. What are the talents, strengths, and gifts Hashem has given my husband? How can I help him find opportunities to fulfill his potential?
10. What are the talents, strengths, and gifts Hashem has given my children? How can I give them the opportunity to fulfill their potential?

Teaching Our Daughters

11. How do I help my daughter discover her strengths so she can use them to make life choices?
12. How do I help my daughter learn the power of prayer?

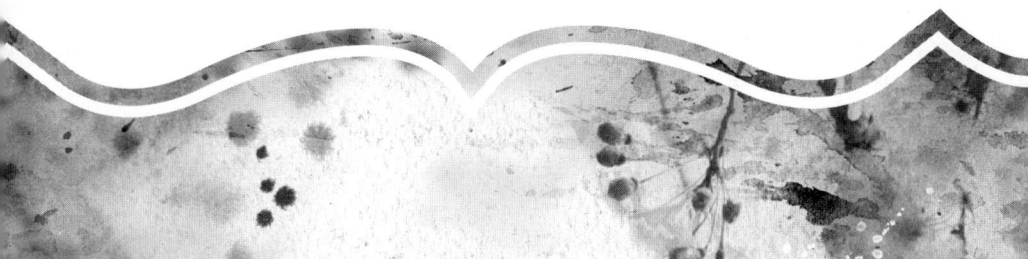

CHAPTER 12

Creative Femininity

יָדֶיהָ שִׁלְּחָה בַכִּישׁוֹר וְכַפֶּיהָ תָּמְכוּ פָלֶךְ׃

*She lays her hands to the distaff,
and her palms hold the spindle.*

Peshat

This *pasuk* tells us that the *eishes chayil* spins using her hands. This seems redundant, as we had already learned this in an earlier *pasuk*:

דָּרְשָׁה צֶמֶר וּפִשְׁתִּים׃
She seeks wool and flax.

Furthermore, that *pasuk* seems far more praiseworthy than this one. There, the *eishes chayil* was being proactive and showing initiative to collect the raw materials. Here, she is simply involved in the mundane, domestic task of spinning.

This *pasuk* comes at the end of the second section of *Eishes Chayil*. The first section, comprised of the first three *pesukim*, was an introduction to the greatness of the woman of valor. The second section begins with דָּרְשָׁה צֶמֶר וּפִשְׁתִּים and ends with יָדֶיהָ שִׁלְּחָה בַכִּישׁוֹר, and primarily deals with the *eishes chayil*'s daily tasks and involvement in financial and managerial matters. The parallel beginning and ending of the section serve to underscore how important spinning is within this framework. The question remains: Why is this domestic chore so important in the life of the *eishes chayil*?

> Why does this section end with the domestic chores of a successful woman, the same way it began the section?

Building the Mishkan

The answer to this question can be found by looking at the role of spinning in the Torah. After the sin of the Golden Calf, the Jews built the Mishkan to reconnect to Hashem.[174] Each individual donated his resources and talents toward its construction.[175] When discussing the contributors to the Mishkan, the *pasuk* tells us that the women volunteered to spin and craft the necessary cloth for the Mishkan coverings.[176]

> וְכָל אִשָּׁה חַכְמַת לֵב בְּיָדֶיהָ טָווּ וַיָּבִיאוּ מַטְוֶה אֶת הַתְּכֵלֶת וְאֶת הָאַרְגָּמָן אֶת תּוֹלַעַת הַשָּׁנִי וְאֶת הַשֵּׁשׁ: וְכָל הַנָּשִׁים אֲשֶׁר נָשָׂא לִבָּן אֹתָנָה בְּחָכְמָה טָווּ אֶת הָעִזִּים:[177]
>
> *And all the women who were wise-hearted did spin with their hands and brought that which they had spun, the blue, and the purple, the scarlet, and the fine linen. And all the women whose heart stirred them up in wisdom spun the goats' hair.*

Every woman came and spun fibers into thread. Like the *eishes chayil*, each woman spun בְּיָדֶיהָ (with her hands). Both the Torah and

---

174 *Shemos Rabbah* 48:6.
175 *Shemos* 35:5–24.
176 *Shemos* 35:25.
177 *Shemos* 35:25–26.

Shlomo HaMelech felt it was necessary to mention that the women were spinning with their hands. Is this not obvious? Should they have been spinning with their toes?

The *Ksav V'Kabbalah* answers that the Torah and Shlomo use the word יָדֶיהָ, her hands, meaning "her own hands" — to indicate that each woman did the work herself, neither hiring a servant nor buying ready-made thread.[178] Each woman did this work because of her love of the mitzvah.

Women's Unique Wisdom

The Torah mentions there that the wisest women spun the goats' hair with wisdom. Chazal considered this event so important that Rabbi Eliezer learned from it:

אֵין חָכְמָה לְאִשָּׁה אֶלָּא בַּפֶּלֶךְ.[179]

A woman's wisdom is only at the spindle.

This *pasuk* and Chazal's interpretation seem at odds. The Torah describes the women's devotion to the construction of the Mishkan. The wisest women chose to spin the most complex threads; yet Chazal interpret the *pesukim* to mean that the extent of a woman's intellect is that she can spin. Why would Chazal diminish the meaning of the story by interpreting it to limit women's abilities rather than focusing on the extent of the women's devotion?

As a modern woman who does not spin, understanding this contradiction is even harder. As was explained earlier, in the section דָּרְשָׁה צֶמֶר וּפִשְׁתִּים (she seeks wool and flax), spinning had a different importance during the time of Chazal. Before the Industrial Revolution, spinning was essential to the functioning of a home, as fabric had to be produced by hand, first spinning fibers into thread, and then weaving those threads into cloth. It was laborious and time consuming — yet essential if a family wanted to have bedding and

---

178   *Ksav V'Kabbalah, Shemos* 35:25.
179   *Talmud Bavli, Yoma* 66b.

clothing. This *pasuk* is highlighting that the *eishes chayil* was constantly involved in providing for her home's most basic needs. The Torah is recounting how the women provided the basic materials for the construction of the Mishkan, which was covered in the layers of woven fabric.

Yet it still seems rather mundane to claim that a woman's prowess at spinning is the greatest evidence of her talent. This seems to contradict the tremendous respect with which women have been treated up until this point in the poem.

Chazal are noticing the deeper implications of what spinning represents and how the women who spun for the Mishkan are described in the *pesukim*. The *pasuk* calls them חַכְמַת לֵב, possessing wisdom of the heart. In Biblical language, *chochmas lev* has a specific connotation that is high praise indeed.

> *Chochmas lev* is a wisdom that is driven by a passion to fulfill Hashem's will and comes from the depths of one's heart. It is rewarded by intelligence that is divinely inspired.

When Shlomo HaMelech first became king, Hashem asked him what he wanted more than anything in the world. He responded that he wanted wisdom. As a reward for his altruistic request, Hashem bestowed upon him *chochmas lev* — wisdom of the heart.[180] Betzalel (the chief designer of the Mishkan) and all the men who volunteered to build and design vessels for the Mishkan were also described by the Torah as having *chochmas lev*.[181] *Chochmas lev* is a wisdom that is driven by a passion to fulfill Hashem's will.[182] It comes from the depths of one's heart and is rewarded by intelligence that is divinely inspired.

The *chochmas lev* of a woman has an added dimension. It is connected to her hands: Her passion and wisdom find expression through that which she creates.

---

180   *Melachim I* 3:5–12.
181   *Shemos* 36:1.
182   Rav Chaim Shmuelevitz, *Sichos Mussar*, Book 1, p. 31.

Rav Tzadok HaKohen explains that a woman's strength, her *chochmas lev* — as depicted by her ability to spin with her hands — is her mastery of all matters that are emotional and practical.[183]

In the Mishkan, there were two groups of women who had *chochmas lev*. The first spun the most beautiful wall hangings, and the second spun, from goat hair, a large covering for the structure that formed the roof and walls of the Mishkan. This second group is the one that is praised more by Chazal. Rav Samson Raphael Hirsch explains that the second group chose to spin a more basic fabric because it was a key component in erecting the Mishkan.[184] They understood the value of what they were doing. The beautiful fabrics made by the first group were adornments that beautified the Mishkan, but the piece made by the second group was the primary item that created the Mishkan itself. The smartest women focused on building the home for the *Shechinah* rather than on making its decorations.

> The smartest women focused on building the home for the *Shechinah* rather than making its decorations.

The actions of spinning and choosing what to create represent the wisdom Chazal are extolling. Spinning begins with a pile of unprocessed fiber, where each fiber on its own is weak and purposeless. By spinning, the spinner takes the fibers and intertwines them, creating an object that has great strength and potential beauty. The praise of the woman is not just that she can spin. It is that she can take the raw materials in her home, most notably her children, and through her attention, wisdom, and creativity she makes them stronger, united, and capable of great things.

Spinning represents more than a chore — it symbolizes the role a woman can choose to play in her home. For this reason, her dedication to spinning is highly praiseworthy. We have already learned about the other exceptional qualities of the *eishes chayil*. She is industrious and

---

183 Rav Tzadok HaKohen, *Sefer Likutei Amarim* Letter 16.
184 Rav Samson Raphael Hirsch, *Shemos* 35:25.

prosperous, she manages her workers and plans for the next day, and she executes astute business deals and has an understanding of multiple industries.

It is difficult to accomplish so much in areas that are publicly praised and still devote oneself fully to those things that are tedious and often go unnoticed. No one will know if a mother sings a lullaby to each of her children, but they do know if she chairs the school fundraiser that raises thousands of dollars.

> The *eishes chayil* is praised for taking the raw materials in her home — most notably her children — and through her wisdom and creativity, strengthening and uniting them.

The *eishes chayil* is living in this world of expectations and productivity but does not lose sight of what she needs to do to create her home. She recognizes her gift of *chochmas lev*, wisdom of the heart, and she understands that despite her success in business and management, her most significant contribution to the world is her ability to create a home for her family. Despite her professional successes, the *eishes chayil* continues to spin. She continues to take all the disparate pieces in her world — her children, their needs, their personalities — and she spins these forces into something strong and everlasting. She creates a family life in her home that weaves her love, traditions, and joy together to build up her children so they can fulfill their potential. They will take the tools their mother has given them and weave them into a meaningful life.

Midrash Yael

The Midrash discusses one woman who focused on her goals as a wife and mother even when she was forced to act in an aggressive role to save the Jewish People. The Midrash describes Yael, who chose to kill a general with an unconventional weapon so as not to violate the Torah prohibition of a woman acting like a man.

"She lays her hands to the distaff."	יָדֶיהָ שִׁלְחָה בַכִּישׁוֹר
This is Yael,	זוֹ יָעֵל
who did not kill Sisera	שֶׁלֹּא הָרְגָה אֶת סִיסְרָא
with a weapon	בִּכְלִי זַיִן
but with a peg with the force of her hands.	אֶלָּא בְּיָתֵד בְּכֹחַ יָדֶיהָ
And why did she not kill him with a weapon?	וּמִפְּנֵי מַה לֹּא הֲרָגַתּוּ בִּכְלִי זַיִן
To fulfill that which is written,	לְקַיֵּם מַה שֶּׁנֶּאֱמַר
"A woman shall not wear the clothing of a man"	"לֹא יִהְיֶה כְלִי גֶבֶר עַל אִשָּׁה"
(Devarim 22:5).	(דברים כב:ה)

To understand how killing can become an example of femininity, we must learn about Yael and how her act was considered praiseworthy and necessary — even though she killed a man in cold blood.

Yael lived during the period that followed the conquest of the Land of Israel by Yehoshua. The three hundred years following the death of Yehoshua until the anointment of the first king was called the time of the *Shoftim*, the Judges. During the time of Yehoshua, the whole nation worked as a unit to conquer the land from the Canaanites. After his death, some enemies remained, but each of the twelve tribes was now individually responsible for securing its own land. There was only a loose confederacy between the tribes, as there was no central political leadership.

The time period of the *Shoftim* was marked by political instability and turmoil, based on the nation's varying religious observance.[185] When the Jews followed Hashem, the twelve tribes had peace and security. When the nation abandoned Hashem and the Torah, Hashem sent a foreign nation to oppress them. A leader, a *shofet*, would arise who would lead the Jewish People back to Hashem and help them conquer the foreign invaders. Under the *shofet's* leadership, peace and security returned to Eretz Yisroel's borders. The leader would die, and the process would start again.

Yael, the woman mentioned in the Midrash, lived during a transition period between two judges, Ehud and Devorah.[186] The tribes began to

---

185 *Shoftim* 2:11–20.
186 *Shoftim* 3:1–4.

abandon their commitment to Torah. As a result, Hashem empowered the Canaanite king, Yavin, together with his general, Sisera, to oppress the Jewish People. Sisera waged a guerilla war against them in never-ending attacks and pillage.

וַיֹּסִפוּ בְּנֵי יִשְׂרָאֵל לַעֲשׂוֹת הָרַע בְּעֵינֵי ה'; וְאֵהוּד מֵת.
וַיִּמְכְּרֵם ה' בְּיַד יָבִין מֶלֶךְ כְּנַעַן אֲשֶׁר מָלַךְ בְּחָצוֹר;
וְשַׂר צְבָאוֹ סִיסְרָא, וְהוּא יוֹשֵׁב בַּחֲרֹשֶׁת הַגּוֹיִם.[187]

And the children of Israel again did that which was evil in the sight of Hashem, when Ehud died. And Hashem gave them over into the hand of Yavin king of Canaan, who reigned in Chatzor; the captain of his army was Sisera, who dwelt in Charosheth-Goyim.

Yael's husband was a Keini, a descendant of Yisro, who moved away from the rest of his clan to the North.[188] As a descendant of a convert and not of one of the Jewish twelve tribes, he was able to negotiate terms so that he could live in peace.[189] His presence in the area was divinely orchestrated to allow the events that were to unfold between his wife, Yael, and the general Sisera.[190]

Yael and Sisera

As Canaan's oppression worsened, the Jewish people did *teshuvah*. Devorah, a female judge, together with the general, Barak, waged a war against Yavin and his general, Sisera. During the war, Hashem caused the army of Canaan to panic — a clear harbinger of defeat. As the battle ensued, Sisera escaped from the battlefield on foot and ran toward Yael's tent, knowing she was an ally.[191] As he ran toward her tent, he hesitated: Yael was an ally, but she was also a

---

187 *Shoftim* 4:1–2.
188 Radak, *Shoftim* 3:11.
189 Ralbag, ibid.
190 Malbim, ibid.
191 *Shoftim* 4:17–18.

Jew.[192] He questioned whether he could escape safely into her home. Yael came out of the tent and encouraged him to rest as he fled the Jewish armies.

Sisera entered the tent parched and exhausted. Instead of giving Sisera water as he requested,[193] Yael gave him warm milk to induce drowsiness.[194] When Sisera reached the point of exhaustion and fell asleep,[195] Yael took a peg used to hold down the tent walls and drove it into Sisera's skull with a hammer.[196] She ran to tell Barak, the Jewish general, that Sisera was dead. Sisera's death was a decisive step that contributed to the defeat of King Yavin and Canaan on that very day.

Yael's actions helped solidify the Jewish People's victory over its enemy. She hastened the end of murder and pillage and unending battles. Given the importance of killing Sisera, why did Yael choose to use a tent peg? A sword or even a knife would have done the job in a much faster, neater, and easier way. Also, Sisera could have awakened as Yael fumbled with the tent peg while trying to kill him.

Preserving the Jewish Home

Chazal explain Yael's rationale.[197] There is a halachic prohibition for women to use standard weaponry that is used on the battlefield. Doing so violates the prohibition of wearing men's clothing. When Sisera entered her tent, Yael knew she had an opportunity to decisively end the war and save the Jewish People, and she needed to act quickly and aggressively and enter the battlefield. Yet she refused to do so in a way that compromised this halachah, because doing otherwise would have

---

192 *Metzudas Dovid, Shoftim* 4:18.
193 *Shoftim* 4:19.
194 Rashi, ibid.
195 Chazal (*Talmud Bavli, Nazir* 23b) discuss how Yael seduced Sisera to save the Jewish People and how her decision was considered an *aveirah lishmah* — an appropriate sin. A discussion of what this means is outside the scope of this chapter.
196 *Shoftim* 4:21–24.
197 Midrash, *Mishlei* 31:19.

compromised her own identity as a nurturer and a woman. She would remain a woman even as she needed to kill.

Why did Yael specifically use a tent peg? Even though Yael was preserving the Jewish People, she would not do so at the expense of the Jewish home. The Jewish home is the most fundamental unit of the Jewish People; without it, all Jewish life ceases to exist. Winning a war was less important than preserving her identity as the protector of her home. The *yased* — the peg — holds down the tent and keeps it from blowing away. Yael was reminding herself that building her home preserved the Jewish nation as much as the execution of an enemy combatant and the methods she needed to employ to accomplish that end.

Getting Practical: Creative Femininity

Both the *eishes chayil* and Yael recognize the centrality and importance of the Jewish home and a woman's role in making that home. A woman's *chochmas lev*, her creative wisdom, can generate an environment that enlivens and enriches her husband and her children. A woman can use all of her intellect and wisdom to create a home that prepares her children for a brilliant future.

> A woman's *chochmas lev*, her creative wisdom, can create an environment that enlivens and enriches herself as well as her husband and her children.

Both the *pasuk* and the Midrash about Yael are needed to understand this lesson. The *pasuk* teaches us that a woman needs to use all of her intellect and creativity to help her children become who they can be. The Midrash teaches us that this job is far more important than anything else a woman can do for the world.

Bringing the Abstract to Life

On a personal level, when I first learned this *pasuk*, I was resistant to the implications it held. I am an intellectual and a professional, and I found it hard to believe (and perhaps a little insulting!) that my ability to spin was my most valuable asset. When I discovered that this *pasuk* was talking about using my creativity and intelligence to help bring out my children's gifts, I decided to put this notion to the test in a very pragmatic way.

I love to learn Torah, and I wanted my young children to appreciate it as well. I knew that I needed to pique their interest and hold their attention. What is more attention-grabbing for kids than food? I committed myself to make a weekly cake for Shabbos based on the events of that week's *parashah*. I do not enjoy baking, but I figured that if the *pasuk* said that my most valuable asset was my creativity, I needed to jump in with both feet. I did not satisfy myself by making a simple cake. This was an opportunity to teach my children abstract concepts they might have difficulty learning otherwise. I made a reconstruction of the Mishkan based on its dimensions, I made a pair of *tefillin* that showed the difference in the construction of the *tefillin* worn on the hand and the head, and I made a scale model of the spies returning from Eretz Yisroel to Moshe and the nation waiting in the desert.

Sure enough, the lesson of this *pasuk* held true. I was able to turn the abstract into reality for my family. I used all of my talents, and my children grew as a result. My three-year-old was more conversant in the clothing of the *Kohanim* and the service in the Mishkan than most adults. I also enjoyed myself and found it gratifying to combine all my skills and responsibilities to build up my children in such a creative way.

> Our creativity cannot be limited to artistry and crafts. It takes tremendous creativity to figure out our children's talents and help them fulfill their potential.

Bringing out a child's potential takes creativity and *chochmas lev*. This creativity can show itself in art projects, Purim costumes, or family trips — but it cannot be limited to artistry and crafts.

It takes tremendous creativity to figure out a child's talents and help him fulfill his potential. It takes intuition and intelligence to recognize a child's needs and meet them. A teacher calls up with a report that your child is acting out in class. Figuring out the story behind the story and how to help better the situation takes *chochmas lev*. Does he need more positive attention at home? Is she struggling with the schoolwork? Figuring out the problem and then helping arrange solutions calls upon all the intelligence and creativity that we possess. Your teenager is bored in the summer. Finding an appropriate and affordable outlet that fosters his confidence requires *chochmas lev*.

The Importance of Creativity

I have a friend who has taught art to high school girls for many years. Her students often tell her, "I'm not artistic" and "I can't think of anything." She told me her real job is to help every student unlock the "out-of-the-box-thinker" within them. Every girl will one day grow up to be a mother, and every mother will have at least one child who is not like her at all. One child, and often more, will be completely different in his thoughts, behavior, and personality. A mother needs to adapt to each child and craft a childhood for him that will bring out his best and teach him the lessons he needs to learn on his journey. The more kids in the family, the more of a three-ring circus the act will need to be.

> A mother needs to adapt to each child and craft a childhood for him that will bring out his best and teach him the lessons he needs to learn on his journey.

Creativity is far more than planning day trips or cute, themed *mishlo'ach manos*. It is making a home where everyone feels valued and loved as an individual. Being able to think outside the box and beyond our own conceptions is critical for both parents — but more so for the mother because she is most present when the children are young and foundations are being laid.

I bring this *pasuk* to life at the most unlikely times. When I apply an article on parenting to a child refusing to go to bed, I am living this *pasuk*. When I get off the phone and focus on my spouse because I "read" his signals, I do so as well.

On *erev Shavuos*, my children asked me to turn my challah into flowers, my cake into a mountain, and my hot dogs into mini Torahs. By combining my creativity and passion with the abstract knowledge they are learning at school, I am creating strong and committed Jews just like someone who spins creates a strong thread by combining the best qualities of different fibers.

The Irreplaceable Role of a Mother

The story of Yael in the Midrash explains why this *pasuk* concludes the section that describes the professional accomplishments of the *eishes chayil*. This *pasuk* reminds us that no matter what she may be doing at any given time, the *eishes chayil* is always focused on building a home. There will always be other businesswomen, merchants, and scholars to take her place. In her home, though, a mother is irreplaceable. Yael reminds us that only an *eishes chayil* can use her unique gifts to bring creativity and warmth to her home and the life she has with her family and friends.

> There will always be other businesswomen, merchants, and scholars to take her place, but in her home, a mother is irreplaceable.

Every family has only one wife and one mother. Our wisdom will never be measured by our success at work or our social circles. It will be measured by how we choose to build our home and educate and nurture our families.

This idea was played out over the course of two weeks on social media. There is a photographer who takes portraits of random strangers and posts the portraits and an accompanying quote online. One of his portraits was of a middle school African-American boy named Vidal from one of the toughest sections of Brooklyn. Vidal mentioned that his principal, Ms. Lopez, was his inspiration to do well in school. This post and Vidal's admiration for his principal led the photographer to start a fundraiser to help the boy's school raise money to take field trips and have programming after school hours in safe quarters.

Within a few hours, hundreds of thousands of dollars were raised by individuals who were inspired by this young boy and his principal. The next series of photographs tracked the school, the principal, the fundraiser, and the publicity. The photographer posted a speech the principal gave to her students. In it, she said how the week before, she had been broken, felt her work in her school was wasted, and had been ready to quit. She called her mother, who refused to allow her to give up so easily. Her mother asked her daughter to pray for help and told her that G-d put her in this job for a reason, and as a principal she was making a difference. That Sunday, Ms. Lopez prayed. On Monday, she saw Vidal's praise online.

Everything snowballed from there. Within a week, the photographer raised over a million dollars for the school. The principal and Vidal were invited to multiple television news programs to explain the fundraiser, Target outfitted every classroom in the school and neighborhood with the latest technology, and the principal, the photographer, and Vidal met with President Barack Obama in the White House.

> Yael reminded herself and all of us that we are indispensable. She needed us to know that our job as mothers makes everyone else's job in life possible.

There were many prominent people who became part of the narrative of this story. There was the intrepid photographer, the famous television personalities, a dedicated principal, and the esteemed President of the United States. Each was making a huge contribution to the betterment of society because of his involvement with this story. Behind them all stands Ms. Lopez's mother: the true heroine of the story. The mother was the one who gave her daughter the confidence and faith she needed to persevere in challenging times. She was the one who recognized her daughter's talents and encouraged her when no one else would. She reminded her of her gifts and used the dark moments to teach her daughter to pray. The mother in this story received almost no attention from the media — but without her, none of this would have happened.

This is why Yael cared to use a tent peg. She needed to remind herself and all of us that we are indispensable. She needed us to know that our job as mothers makes everyone else's job in life possible.

Summary

"She lays her hands to the distaff."   יָדֶיהָ שִׁלְּחָה בַכִּישׁוֹר
Yael   יָעֵל

From the Pasuk We Learn

The *eishes chayil* is constantly involved in providing for her household's most basic needs with passion to fulfill Hashem's will. She understands, with all of her successes in her professional and social life, that her most significant contribution is her ability to create a home for her family to help her children lead meaningful lives. All of her intellect and creativity are needed to help her children become the best they can be.

From the Midrash We Learn

Yael killed Sisera with a tent peg to show that her top priority was her home. Her devotion to her home was essential, and its integrity was something she would never risk. She teaches us that a mother's influence on her children has tremendous impact.

Practical Steps

1. Incorporate creativity into our lives so we can use "out-of-the-box" thinking when parenting.
2. Think of creative and practical ways to teach abstract lessons.
3. Celebrate the important role of the mother and recognize its value.

Questions

Self-Growth

1. How do I develop my *chochmas lev* — my creative and practical intelligence?
2. How do I learn to trust my *chochmas lev* and intuition?
3. To which situations can I bring my *chochmas lev*?

As Wives and Mothers

4. How can I use my wisdom and talents to better improve my family's practical and emotional life?
5. How can I remind myself of the value of what I do for my family in the face of a society that does not value this role?
6. What situations with my children and family might be helped with some "out-of-the-box" thinking?
7. How can I bring fulfillment and joy to my chores and job as a mother by tapping into my creativity?

Teaching Our Daughters

8. How do I help my daughter develop her creativity?
9. How can I help my daughter appreciate the role she will play in the development of her home?

CHAPTER 13

As a Charitable Woman (Kindness)

כַּפָּהּ פָּרְשָׂה לֶעָנִי וְיָדֶיהָ שִׁלְּחָה לָאֶבְיוֹן.

*She stretches out her hand to the poor;
she reaches forth her hands to the needy.*

Peshat

This *pasuk* begins the third section of *eishes chayil*. The previous section dealt with the concrete accomplishments of a woman in her home and at work. This section deals with something much harder to quantify; it explores the spiritual greatness of the *eishes chayil* by examining how she acts in each of her roles and in her different relationships.

A person can be judged by what she says or the image she projects, but that is not a true measure of her character. A person's actions and how she treats those around her is the true indication of who she really is. The *eishes chayil* interacts with many people every day; she is at once a mother, a wife, a community member, and a professional. This section deals with how she approaches each relationship and role in a way that makes her the woman who deserves such praise.

כַּפָּהּ פָּרְשָׂה לֶעָנִי.
She stretches out her hand to the poor.

The *pasuk* describing the *eishes chayil*'s relationship with the poor and needy is the first in this new section. How a woman deals with the poor and indigent is the most fitting introduction to the many hats she wears on a daily basis. It reflects on all the roles that she plays throughout her life.

Shlomo HaMelech highlights this connection by associating the *eishes chayil*'s charitable acts with her work in the home as a mother and wage earner. Both this *pasuk*, which discusses her charity, and the previous one, which discussed her work in the home, mention the *eishes chayil*'s palm and hand. The repetition of the words in the two verses show that Shlomo HaMelech is purposely trying to connect the work the *eishes chayil* does for her family with the kindness she does for strangers.

> The *eishes chayil* helps her family and the poor with the same motivation. She does for others because she is a *baalas chessed*, a doer of kind deeds.

The Motivation behind It All

The *eishes chayil* acts with the same motivation in both cases. She does for others because she is a *baalas chessed*, a doer of kind deeds. In her home, the *eishes chayil* performs the physical, mundane tasks because she is doing *chessed*, and in this verse, she gives charity because she is doing *chessed*. She is driven by a spiritual goal whether she is acting as a benefactress, a mother, or a wife. It is fitting to begin the discussion of her many roles with the awareness that all these roles are predicated on her being a *baalas chessed*, a doer of kindness.

This *pasuk* is used as an introduction to the rest of the spiritual accomplishments because it encapsulates the essence of every woman's greatness. In almost every role that the *eishes chayil* has, she is helping another person, even if that person is herself. Even her relationship with Hashem depends on her heightened sense of kindness. A generous person trains herself to consider how her actions impact others. Once she trains herself to fulfill other people's needs, she will become conscious of how to fulfill Hashem's will. In this way, she will become the best possible servant of Hashem. The ability to do for others becomes the cornerstone of all spiritual greatness.

Attitude toward Chessed

This *pasuk* and the previous one are the middle verses of the poem. Not only do they highlight the importance of *chessed*, they also involve individuals whose relationships with the *eishes chayil* are vastly different: her family is the closest to her, while the poor are strangers to her. With her family, the *eishes chayil* could potentially feel comfortable treating them poorly because they will not abandon her. The *eishes chayil* could likewise treat the poor rudely because the poor person is the most vulnerable of all people. Few friends and fewer advocates would complain. It is

> The *eishes chayil* acts in a manner consistent with her values at all times: to her family and to the poor, she gives with kindness and joy.

also possible that the poor person has behavioral issues and is abrasive or imbalanced, and the *eishes chayil* could be tempted to be nasty and off-putting as she gives *tzedakah*. Instead, the *eishes chayil* acts in a manner consistent with her values at all times: to her family and to the poor, she gives with kindness and joy.

Priorities

The repetition of the words in the *pasuk* describing the *eishes chayil*'s workday and her giving *tzedakah* connect the two in a different way as well.[198] The *eishes chayil* works long hours to help her family. As she labors, wondering how she will sell her work and how much money she needs to keep her lights burning, there is a knock at the door. It is a

---

198 Meiri, *Mishlei* 31:20.

poor man, down on his luck and asking for help. The *eishes chayil* takes her palm — the palm that was expertly plying her craft — and takes some money to give to the man. She takes some money and food that she had set aside for her family and sends it to the beggar down the street. Most people would be flustered by having to transition between these two very different activities, work and charity.

The *eishes chayil* is able to redirect her efforts without getting annoyed because she views all she does as *chessed*. She can quickly change activities because her goal is always the same. She understands that one of her primary roles is to be a woman of *chessed*. She is not so overly focused on her daily chores that she forgets why she is doing them. Her mind is occupied with how to help others rather than on finishing the next spool of thread at the spinning wheel.

How a person does *chessed*, then, is a barometer of her spirituality and sensitivity. With this understanding of why this *pasuk* begins the next section, we must examine it more closely. The *pasuk* itself seems rather redundant. It says that the *eishes chayil* "stretches out her palm to the poor" and then that "she sends forth her hands." Why does the *pasuk* repeat that the woman is giving charity to the poor, with two parts of her hand? Wouldn't it have been enough to state this once?

> How a person does *chessed* is a barometer of a her spirituality and sensitivity.

How to Give Tzedakah

The commentaries explain that the different words in the *pasuk* emphasize the sensitivity of the *eishes chayil* in how she does her *chessed*. The *eishes chayil* does different types of *chessed* for each person she meets:[199]

- An *ani* is a poor man whose needs change as his circumstances change. He will ask for help when needed.
- An *evyon* is a helpless person, an extraordinarily needy individual whose basic needs seem endless. He may be a rich man

---

199 *Keren L'Dovid*, quoted in *Sefer Eishes Chayil*, p. 169.

who has lost all he had or a person who is overwhelmed by hardship. He is embarrassed to ask and may not even know where to begin.[200]

To the *ani*, the verse says, the *eishes chayil* stretches out her palm. To this person, she is generous when asked. She allows him the dignity of trying to solve his own problems but helps when approached. This is why she stretches out her palm rather than her hand. The palm is hidden when fingers close over it.[201] The *ani* is still embarrassed to take money in public. The *eishes chayil* gives him money discreetly and sensitively, from her palm to his. No one knows what is hidden in her palm and she preserves his honor at all costs.

In contrast, the *eishes chayil* is far more direct and sends funds and necessary items to the *evyon* with both of her hands. The *evyon* can never have enough help and may not even come to ask.[202]

The *evyon* is so poor that he is:

תָּאֵב לְכָל דָּבָר.
He desires everything.

With this person she "sends forth" both her hands. She evaluates what the *evyon* needs and proactively does *chessed* before being asked.[203] If she were not to do so, the *evyon* could suffer irreparable harm because he might never ask or he may be overwhelmed by the enormity of his troubles. The *eishes chayil* sends the gifts with both her hands, aware of the extreme need that requires her to initiate the help.

This *pasuk* shows how *chessed* and *tzedakah* must be done eagerly, promptly, and with sensitivity. There is no specific right way to do *chessed*. Each instance requires a different attitude and a different approach.

---

200 Rav Kalev Feivel Shlezinger, *Toras Bar Nash*, quoted in *Sefer Eishes Chayil*, p. 163.
201 Rabbi Aharon Yosef Templer, *Revid Yosef*, quoted in *Sefer Eishes Chayil*, p. 160.
202 *Meam Loez*, *Mishlei* 31:21.
203 Rav Meir Tannenbaum, *Imrei Meir*.

The Midrash teaches about one woman who epitomized what it meant to be a woman of *chessed* and the great reward she experienced as a result.

Midrash – The Widow from Tzarfas

"She stretches out her hand to the poor."	כַּפָּהּ פָּרְשָׂה לֶעָנִי
This is the woman who was the widow	זוֹ אִשָּׁה אַלְמָנָה
of Tzarfas,	הַצָּרְפִית
who supported Eliyahu	שֶׁכִּלְכְּלָה לְאֵלִיָּהוּ
with bread and water.	בְּלֶחֶם וּבְמַיִם

The story of this woman of *chessed* begins during a time of crisis for the Jewish People. The Jewish nation had already achieved sovereignty. They had been ruled by Dovid and Shlomo who achieved peace for the nation and constructed the Holy Temple in Jerusalem. During the rule of Shlomo's son Rechavam, the nation was split into two kingdoms: *Malchus Yehudah* (the kingdom of Judah) ruled by the descendants of Dovid, and *Malchus Yisroel* (the kingdom of Yisroel) ruled by a succession of kings who rose to power through greed and violence.

The kings of Yisroel dissuaded the Jews under their leadership from worshipping Hashem and encouraged the service of idols to help consolidate their power. One particularly evil ruler in the kingdom of Yisroel was a king named Achav, who tried to create a culture of paganism in his kingdom.

A Famine Begins

During Achav's reign, there was a prophet named Eliyahu who was charged primarily with rebuking the kingdom of Yisroel so that they would repent from their evil ways. One day, Achav met Eliyahu at a shivah house of a person named Chiel, who had just buried his tenth child.²⁰⁴ The father had insisted on reconstructing Yericho even though Yehoshua had warned that whoever did so would lose his children as a punishment.²⁰⁵ Just as he had been forewarned, Chiel's children died one after another, and both Achav and Eliyahu were at the final shivah for these sons. Achav spitefully mocked Hashem by noting that G-d had not yet punished him or his kingdom with drought as the Torah predicted for idolaters in the Land of Israel, and yet, the words of Yehoshua, His prophet, had been fulfilled.²⁰⁶

Eliyahu proclaimed that from then on there would be no rain in the kingdom of Israel.²⁰⁷ A paralyzing drought began. Fearing for his life from the evil king Achav, Eliyahu hid in a cave. Ravens brought him bread and meat to eat, and he was able to obtain water from a nearby brook. Eventually, the brook dried up from the drought. Hashem commanded Eliyahu to go to Tzarfas where he would encounter a woman who would feed him.

Testing for Kindness

Eliyahu went to the city of Tzarfas. At the entrance to the city, he met a widow collecting wood for kindling.²⁰⁸ Replicating the experiment of Eliezer trying to locate Rivkah, he asked this stranger for water to drink.²⁰⁹ The woman acted much like Rivkah and graciously offered Eliyahu water. This woman, a widow living during a famine, was happy to share water with a stranger who requested help.

As if this request for water was not enough, Eliyahu then asked the widow for bread.²¹⁰ The widow hesitated at this second request and explained that she only had enough flour to make a final supper for

---

204   Rashi, *Melachim I* 17:1.
205   *Melachim I* 6:34.
206   Rashi, *Melachim I* 17:1.
207   *Melachim I* 17:1–9.
208   *Melachim I* 17:10.
209   Rashi, ibid.
210   *Melachim I* 17:11–12.

herself and her child. After this final meal, the two of them would have nothing left to eat and would most likely die from starvation.[211]

Eliyahu assured the widow that by doing the act of kindness of feeding him bread first and then taking for herself and her son, her food supplies to make more bread would never run out.[212] The widow did as Eliyahu asked, and a miracle occurred. The widow had a constant supply of flour and oil and never wanted for more food. Although the woman thought she was doing a *chessed* that would leave her with less, she ended up with much more than she originally had.

> Although the widow thought she was doing a *chessed* that would leave her with less, she ended up with much more than she originally had.

The widow's reward for her *chessed* did not end with having food during a drought. A while later, the widow's only son fell ill and died. The widow complained to Eliyahu about her son's death, and Eliyahu restored him to life.

The Midrash explains why this vulnerable woman merited to survive a famine and to have her son brought back to life. When she gave Eliyahu water in the midst of a drought, she had done so with no ulterior motive, despite the hardship it imposed on her. Even when she said no because she feared the request would endanger her and her child, she spoke to Eliyahu with empathy and warmth. The kindness she did for another was what saved her and her child.

A Role Model for Chessed

We can now understand why the widow of Tzarfas was chosen to be the role model of a woman of *chessed*. This woman was living in a time of famine. She was a widow — a single mother — with no resources and no hope. Her near future would see herself and her son die a slow, painful death. The widow had every excuse to be curt and self-involved, but she chose differently: she chose to focus on what others needed.

---

211 *Metzudas Dovid, Melachim I* 17:12.
212 *Melachim I* 17:13 –23.

The widow from Tzarfas teaches us that there is no excuse not to do kindness for another and that it needs to be done with grace. She also teaches us that our prosperity comes from giving to another and not worrying about ourselves. In the end, the widow was saved because of her self-sacrifice. She taught us that when we do *chessed* for others, the one we are helping is really ourselves.

Getting Practical: Chessed in the Home

A woman is involved in multiple acts of *chessed* every day. When a woman feeds her children breakfast, does laundry for her husband, picks up some food at the grocery for her parents, or drives carpool, she is doing *chessed*. Every day we are inundated with requests for favors from individuals and institutions. The question, then, is not *if* we do *chessed* but *how* we do *chessed*.

> Every day, all day, we are involved with giving to individuals and institutions. The question is not *if* we do *chessed* but *how* we do *chessed*.

We have a choice whether to stay focused on ourselves and our needs or to transform our actions into a source of merit.

This *pasuk* teaches us that changing our attitude changes the quality of how we do things for others. We can choose to help with a positive attitude or with resentment. In addition to changing the quality of our *chessed*, our attitude toward doing the *chessed* can change the quality of our own lives.

Chessed and the Quality of Our Lives

I knew of an elderly woman who had two daughters. She lived closer to one of them, and as she aged, she would ask that daughter to buy her a small bunch of grapes a few times a week. The daughter, who normally went shopping once a week, usually fulfilled this request with a sense of annoyance. She complained to her sister on a regular basis and it became a source of tension in the whole family. The woman felt taken advantage of that her mother sent her running to the store for an inconsequential errand after a long day of work! The mother felt hurt that this simple joy in life was such a problem, and the other sister grew frustrated at hearing about grapes on a regular basis.

A few years went by, and the woman needed more help. She moved into her other daughter's home in a different city. This daughter and her family were delighted to have her in their home. She needed nursing staff in the home, and she often repeated herself. When the woman died after a few years of care in her daughter's home, the second daughter expressed how lucky she was to host her mother and how much the children had learned from her. Her children had fond memories of their grandmother and laughed about her quirky nature and interesting habits.

> When we are feeling put upon, we should ask ourselves if we are making an issue over grapes.

Which daughter ended up with a life we would want? Which woman was happier? The one who savored her relationships and her chance to be of service or the one who protected "her rights" and needs against unwanted intrusion?

Which daughter has a happier life and which daughter are we?

Perhaps, when we are feeling put upon, we should ask ourselves if we are making an issue over grapes.

How to Do Chessed

The *eishes chayil* teaches us more about *chessed* than the importance of having a good attitude. She shows us how to do *chessed* and that we need to treat each person differently based on his needs and sensitivities.

When someone requires our help, we should give him what he needs rather than just what comes easily to us. Sometimes, this is obvious. A person needs a meal, so we cook a meal. There are times, though, when we need to think about how we fill the need. In many communities, when a family has a member who is sick, the community will pitch in and arrange for dinners to be brought. This is a great service and should be continued and encouraged. One community looked at this *chessed* and thought about how they could improve it. They realized that families might have to wait for the nightly meals at inconvenient times. It takes away some of the independence of the family and the family's sense of predictability. This community started a new *chessed*. When a family needed dinners due to illness, friends delivered a freezer stocked with microwaveable dinners. The family could decide when and what they wanted to eat. That was a sensitive *chessed*!

When someone needs our help, we need to give him what he needs rather than what we want.

When a Chessed Is Not a Chessed

Sometimes, the question is whether helping is a *chessed* or not. A child forgets her homework. Do we bring it to school for her or let her experience the consequence of her actions? Which one would help her learn and grow in the long run? A gambling addict does not have money for tuition. Do we lend him cash or not? A person wants to go to shul. His doctor says that he needs to walk so his muscles do not atrophy, but he wants to be pushed in a wheelchair. How do we help him? At times, *chessed* is complex and needs thought and analysis.

Quiet Chessed

The *chessed* of the *eishes chayil* is not driven by ego. Neither family members nor the impoverished will publicize her acts of kindness. Rebbetzin Chaya Mushka Schneerson, the wife of the Lubavitcher Rebbe, *zt"l*, epitomized this kind of egoless, selfless kindness. Whenever she did *chessed* or interacted with anyone in public, she introduced herself simply as "Mrs. Schneerson from President Street." She did not do her *chessed* to receive accolades, to advance her husband's reputation, or to gain a reputation as a woman of action. She **did her** *chessed* because it was the right thing to do.

Who Benefits from Chessed

The widow from Tzarfas added a new and final dimension to our understanding of *chessed*. She taught us that it is we who are helped the most from the *chessed* we do. We may think that we are helping the other person by doing *chessed*, but when we do *chessed* properly, our whole day is transformed.

We never know when the merit of our *chessed* will be to our own benefit. When I was in eighth grade, I would stop by a neighbor's home so that I could walk her daughter to the bus stop. It wasn't a big inconvenience for me, and it was a favor that my parents encouraged and expected me to do. At the end of the year, the neighbor moved away, and I soon forgot about my daily favor.

> We never know when the merit of our *chessed* will be to our own benefit.

A decade later, I was looking for a job and wanted to try teaching. I applied for a substitute position in a prominent New York school, anticipating that a more qualified candidate would be hired. I walked into the interview and discovered that the principal was my former neighbor whom I had last seen so many years before. She commented how she knew that I was responsible from how I had acted with her daughter so many years earlier, and she would give me a chance as a long-term substitute. I ended up teaching in the school for four more years until I moved to a different city. When I was thirteen, I thought that I was the one doing the *chessed*. I learned firsthand that when we do *chessed*, the one who we are truly helping is ourselves.

The Centrality of Chessed

Chessed is the theme of the two central *pesukim* of the *Eishes Chayil* poem. It is the basis for all that we achieve and do in our day and in every role that we play in our lives. When we do *chessed* with thought and care, as the *eishes chayil* and the widow from Tzarfas have taught us, our day and all of our activities become infused with spirituality and meaning. We end up with a life where we are the ones who have gained the most.

Summary

"She stretches out her hand to the poor."
The widow of Tzarfas

כַּפָּהּ פָּרְשָׂה לֶעָנִי
אִשָּׁה אַלְמָנָה הַצָּרְפִית

From the Pasuk We Learn

The essence and driving force behind all that the *eishes chayil* does is her desire to help others. She treats everyone — family or not, rich or poor — with respect. She tailors her help to the needs and sensitivities of the recipients and treats them all with dignity.

From the Midrash We Learn

The widow from Tzarfas gave Eliyahu bread and water during a famine even though it was difficult for her. When she had to say no, she did so with warmth and kindness. She teaches us that we should try to do kindness for others with grace. She also teaches us that our prosperity comes from giving to another and not worrying about ourselves. In the end, the widow was saved because of her self-sacrifice. When we do *chessed* for others, we are really helping ourselves.

Practical Steps

1. Focus on helping others with a positive attitude.
2. Think about the goal of our work so that we can transition to other tasks with less stress.
3. Allow others the dignity of working things out on their own. Help as discreetly and minimally as possible to preserve the other person's sense of independence.
4. Look for people who won't, or can't, ask for help. Step in to get them back to the point where they can ask for help when needed.
5. When help is requested, say yes or no with warmth and empathy.
6. Try to give creatively, and base our actions on what is needed.
7. Evaluate whether a *chessed* is helping or harming.

 Questions

Self-Growth

1. How do I stop myself from judging those I am helping? How can I treat everyone warmly and kindly?
2. How do I stay calm when I need to multitask and am bombarded with many requests at once? How do I do *chessed* and meet many different people's needs without coldness and stress?
3. Sometimes it is important to say no to requests even if we would like to be able to help. How do I say no in a polite manner and without being defensive?
4. How can I perform acts of kindness so that my contribution is kept private and I remain anonymous?
5. How do I determine what kind of *chessed* I need to do for an individual? How do I meet his needs rather than make assumptions based on my own opinions?
6. How do I determine what *chessed* needs to be done without engaging in gossip to make me feel important?
7. How can I balance the Jewish value of doing *chessed* with the need to give others the chance to solve their problems on their own so that their independence and dignity are preserved?
8. How can I help people who cannot or will not ask for help even though they may need it? How do I know when to be forthcoming and when to wait?
9. It is natural to want to help people and organizations that are more popular. How can I ensure that my *chessed* and *tzedakah* are based on what is needed rather than on what is most popular?

As Wives and Mothers

10. How can I appreciate that the work I do for my family and my community is *chessed* while I am doing it?

11. How can I treat my family with the same kindness and patience as I show people I consider important? What changes do I need to make in my life to act with integrity to all?

Teaching Our Daughters

12. How do I teach my daughter to love to do *chessed*?
13. How can I encourage my daughter to view what she does for the family as *chessed* and not to resent it?

CHAPTER 14

As a Homemaker (Preparation/ Responsibility)

לֹא תִירָא לְבֵיתָהּ מִשָּׁלֶג כִּי כָל בֵּיתָהּ לָבֻשׁ שָׁנִים.

She is not afraid of the snow for her household, for all her household are clothed with scarlet.

Peshat

This *pasuk* deals with the *eishes chayil* in her role as a homemaker and as the outfitter of the family wardrobe.

It seems a strange thing about which to praise a woman. I know many women who will take pride in their jobs, their involvement with *chessed*, their learning, or in their children's accomplishments, but would never brag about how well they mop the floor or shop. Mundane activities that keep a household running seem so...mundane. This *pasuk* is here to reveal the deeper implications of being a homemaker and to explain the importance of the role.

Interestingly, this *pasuk* begins with an emotion when none were attached to any of the previous *pesukim*. It tells us that the *eishes chayil* is not afraid because her family has clothing. Why is there an emotion connected to this job? Should we be praising a woman for staying calm because she shopped for clothes? How does the lack of fear reflect the importance of this role?

Through a Child's Eyes

Imagine a five-year-old is late for the bus and cannot find his coat. He knows that come 10:15, there will be outdoor recess. As a new kindergartener, he hardly knows his teacher's name and does not know what he will do if he does not have his coat. He imagines freezing on the playground with no one to help him. He is afraid.

A six-year-old is hungry. Her mother is not around, and she does not know how to work the microwave to warm up the pizza that is in the freezer. That child is afraid that she will starve.

Children are too young to care for their basic needs of survival. Any lack in their physical needs can truly lead to their death. They can't judge when they are in danger and when they are just missing a snack. Any break in their care will then bring up powerful emotions that those of us who have control over getting food and shelter never feel.

> Any break in a child's care will bring up powerful emotions that those of us who have control over getting food and shelter never feel.

This *pasuk* teaches that the *eishes chayil* is sensitive that her children not feel vulnerable because she has been irresponsible. She is never concerned that her family will be caught unprepared.

Moreover, children's emotions reflect how their mother is thinking and feeling. When a

mother is feeling chaotic because her children do not have the right clothing to wear or the proper food in the house, it is not only she who feels anxious. This chaos and anxiety is absorbed and mirrored by the children as well. However, if the mother has the child's basic needs of clothing and food met with calm and serenity, her children will mirror this calm in their own lives and in meeting their own responsibilities.

> The chaos and anxiety or calm and serenity that we as mothers feel is absorbed and mirrored by our children.

Chessed in the Home

This *pasuk* comes after a *pasuk* that focused on *chessed* for a very important reason. Doing *chessed* for nonfamily members results in accolades. There are dinners held in the benefactor's honor, plaques to go on the wall, and admiration from friends and family.

Doing the laundry does not quite get the same reaction. A mother is lucky to get a passing thank-you from her child as she runs out the door.

The *pasuk* is telling us that providing for our family's basic needs must be the first *chessed* we do, despite the reactions to it or the lack thereof. The Malbim explains that the *eishes chayil* is the woman who is devoted to the poor while still taking care of her main priority: her family.[213] She only gives to the poor as long as she can provide *chessed* in a timely and calm fashion for those who are her primary responsibility.

The *pasuk* further develops this idea by describing how the *eishes chayil* cares for her family by describing the clothing she gives them. She gives her family clothes of scarlet. Our stores do not have a scarlet section, so it is difficult to relate to this statement. The *Metzudas Dovid* explains that clothes of scarlet means that she chooses the best clothes possible for her family.[214] The *shani* fabric described in this *pasuk* was a heavy wool that was dyed red to indicate its warmth.[215] The *eishes chayil*

---

213 Malbim, *Mishlei* 31:21.
214 *Metzudas Dovid*, ibid.
215 *Daas Mikra*, ibid.

ensures that her family has clothing appropriate for the season before it is needed.[216]

In a play on words, *shanim* also hints to the fact that the *eishes chayil* buys clothing for family members based on their *shanim*, their years. The old need warmer clothes while the young require fewer layers, and the *eishes chayil* makes sure everyone gets what they need based on who they are. She takes care of things for each of her family members with thought and care.

The Importance of Chores

Caring for our family's needs helps our children feel secure and grow to become self-sufficient adults. A good friend of mine has a child with constant medical needs who needs round-the-clock nursing care. Despite all the medical crises, she has made it a priority to have clean laundry in the closets and healthy food in the cupboards. Despite the chaos that arises from the constant care that their sibling requires, the other children feel nurtured and cared for. As the siblings have become adults, they are confident, warm, and filled with compassion and love for their younger brother who is very much a part of their family and their hearts. Their confidence is no accident. Their mother has been concerned that they have what they need since they were small, and she always made it a priority, so they have grown up knowing they are important.

> Caring for our family's needs helps our children feel secure and grow into self-sufficient adults.

The ordinary tasks that no one appreciates are the very things that allow our children to feel loved and grow to fulfill their potential. They grow up with a sense of self-worth since they were worthy of having their basic needs met happily. This in turn frees them to prepare for a brilliant future of accomplishment. While it is true that a sterile household is stifling for children, a dirty one is equally problematic. Children who have healthy meals, regular bedtimes, and clean clothes

---

216 Meiri, *Mishlei* 31:21.

appropriate for each season grow up with the foundation necessary to achieve great heights.

An Enthusiastic Life

The *pasuk* can also be interpreted to mean that the *eishes chayil* prepares for her family's spiritual needs. The *pasuk* says that the *eishes chayil*'s home is not afraid of snow, a symbol of the winter. The Malbim explains that we can examine this phrase as an allegory: winter is a symbol of death. The *pasuk* is teaching us that the *eishes chayil* has provided for her family spiritually so that they are unafraid to face their Creator after death. She has prepared them for a life full of meaning, with mitzvos and values, so they can fulfill their potential as Jews and servants of Hashem.²¹⁷

> The *eishes chayil* has prepared her family for a life full of meaning, with mitzvos and values, so they can fulfill their potential as Jews and servants of Hashem.

We often think that the punishment in the World to Come is one of heat. This punishment is only for people who succumb to their passions. There is another kind of punishment: one of cold, of snow.²¹⁸ The punishment of snow mentioned here comes from a lack of passion — from apathy — where a person lives his life based on what is easiest. The *eishes chayil* prevents her children from falling prey to this kind of life. She imbues within them an enthusiasm to learn Torah and do good deeds with a fire that melts any complacency.

Teaching Independence

For this reason, the *pasuk* first says that the *eishes chayil* is not afraid of the snow and then adds that her family is dressed in warm clothes. The *pasuk* is teaching that not only has the *eishes chayil* helped her family deal with the challenge of apathy, but the family is prepared

---

217 Malbim, *Mishlei* 31:21.
218 *Zohar, Bereishis* 298b.

to confront these issues independently in life. She has cared for them as well as taught them how to care for themselves.[219]

By teaching her children the skills to live a full life, the *eishes chayil* has prepared her household for the best possible life. She has given her children what they need, and these priorities have become her children's own. Her whole household, independently, wears *shanim*.

This *pasuk* is emphasizing how important the job of homemaker is to a family both physically and spiritually. The Midrash focuses on one woman, Rachav, so we can understand how transformative a woman's efforts are for her family and for all of her future generations.

Midrash – Rachav

"She is not afraid of the snow for her household,	לֹא תִירָא לְבֵיתָהּ מִשָּׁלֶג
for all her household are clothed with scarlet."	כִּי כָל־בֵּיתָהּ לָבֻשׁ שָׁנִים
This is Rachav, the harlot.	זוֹ רָחָב הַזּוֹנָה
When Yisroel came	בְּשָׁעָה שֶׁבָּאוּ יִשְׂרָאֵל
to destroy Yericho,	לְהַחֲרִיב יְרִיחוֹ
she wasn't afraid of them	לֹא נִתְיָרְאָה מֵהֶם
because they gave her a sign,	מִפְּנֵי שֶׁנָּתְנוּ לָהּ סִימָן
"This line of scarlet thread"	"אֶת תִּקְוַת חוּט הַשָּׁנִי"
(Yehoshua 2:18).	(יהושע ב:יח)

The Midrash talks about Rachav, who lived during a period of great turmoil and transition in the Land of Israel.[220] We are introduced to Rachav in the book of *Yehoshua* just as the Jewish People were about to settle the Land after having wandered in the desert for forty years. Moshe had died, and Yehoshua bin Nun, his preeminent student, was appointed the Jewish leader. The Jews were encamped on the plains of Moav next to the Jordan River, ready to begin their conquest.

---

219 Rabbi Eliyahu Hakohen of Izmir, *Midrash Eliyahu*, quoted in *Sefer Eishes Chayil*, p. 116.
220 *Yehoshua*, chapter 1.

In the book of *Yehoshua*, we learn how Yehoshua sent two spies to scout the land to determine which location should be conquered first.[221] These spies found their way into the city of Yericho, which was surrounded by impenetrable walls, and into the home of Rachav, whose home was located next to the wall of the city. Somehow, the king of Yericho learned of the spies' presence and sent a retinue to capture them in Rachav's home. Instead of complying with the king's demands, Rachav hid the two spies on her roof, using wood scraps to conceal them from the searching guards.

As the guards searched her home, Rachav sent them on a wild goose chase to give the spies time to escape from her home. Rachav assured the spies that they could emerge from their hiding place after the guards had departed, and she had one favor to ask from these men who were now indebted to her for their lives. Rachav knew that the Jews would successfully conquer the land of Canaan. She wanted assurance that she and her family would be spared from the carnage that was to come.

> Rachav put out a red string during the siege of Yericho, so she and her family had no reason to fear.

The spies agreed to this request on one condition. When the Jews were attacking, any of Rachav's family who wanted to be saved would have to be in her home. She was instructed to put a red string, which is the string mentioned by the Midrash, out of the window so the Jews would know which home to spare from attack. Yehoshua kept the spies' promise, and on the day of the attack he told the spies to go into Rachav's home and save her family and all her possessions. With the red string, the *shani*, Rachav, her parents, and siblings had no reason to fear.

Rachav's Spiritual Legacy

Rachav's story does not end with her physical salvation. While Rachav provided for her extended family's safety, she provided a

---

221 *Yehoshua*, chapter 2.

different kind of future for herself and her children. Chazal tell us that after the Jewish nation entered the land of Canaan, Rachav converted to Judaism and married Yehoshua, the leader of the Jewish People.[222] The Gemara in *Megillah* 14b states that eight of their descendants were both prophets and *Kohanim*, including the great prophet Yirmiyahu. Rachav's actions to save the spies and to negotiate with them did not just save herself and her family physically; she established herself as the matriarch and wife of a prominent and spiritually rich Jewish family.

Like the *eishes chayil*, Rachav did not fear for her family's security. She had prepared for them provisions that would help them during the chaos of battle. Her efforts to provide for her family's material needs did not just help them physically. These actions provided her with a spiritual legacy that impacted the entire Jewish nation.

The Midrash is teaching us that the consequences of a woman providing for her family's physical needs are far-reaching. Providing for one's family creates a spiritual legacy.

While there are other women in the Torah who took care of their families, the lesson about its impact is best learned through Rachav. Rachav was a *zonah*, a famous prostitute,[223] yet she ended up marrying Yehoshua, who was the spiritual heir of Moshe, the ultimate prophet and Jewish leader.

Providing for one's family creates a spiritual legacy.

Despite the years she spent living a life of sin, Rachav did complete *teshuvah* and transformed her life. She knew that no matter her

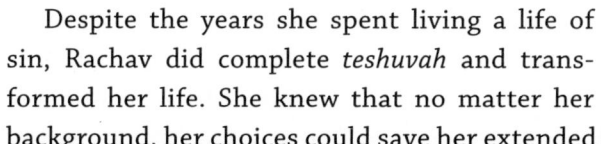

background, her choices could save her extended family from certain death, and she did not hesitate to act. This awareness helped Rachav become the appropriate wife for Yehoshua. Yehoshua was the leader and general of the Jewish People, who were about to engage in battles and land allocation for the following fourteen years. His wife would have to be a woman who recognized her far-reaching impact.

---

222 *Talmud Bavli, Megillah* 14b.
223 Malbim, *Yehoshua* 2:5.

The descendants of this marriage, who included the great Yirmiyahu, learned this lesson well. They inherited a spiritual legacy from their ancestor Rachav: their actions would have consequences and could better their world.

Yirmiyahu took this lesson to the next level. He was the prophet who was given the mission to inform the Jewish People that the Holy Temple in Jerusalem would be destroyed because of their sins. He made dramatic declarations, and he suffered imprisonment and torture when relaying this message, yet he had the strength and confidence to continue to transmit his message of prophecy despite his unpopularity because his ancestor Rachav had bequeathed him an awareness that doing for others, even when unappreciated, is valuable.

> Yirmiyahu had the strength to transmit his unpopular prophecies because of the lessons of his ancestor Rachav.

Getting Practical: Preparation for Success

The *eishes chayil* teaches us the importance of providing for our family's material needs. The Midrash teaches us the long-range impact our efforts can have.

As mothers, we care for people who are completely dependent on us. How we embrace this responsibility is a barometer of our broader relationship with Hashem and our attitude toward serving Him. When we prioritize taking care of the people who depend on us, we emulate Hashem Himself, who provides for our every need.[224] If we regard our home responsibilities as unimportant, we are minimizing the importance of "private" good deeds.

The act of being a mother will never be repaid. It is a *chessed* that is (largely) thankless despite the fact that it is more important than what we do for others publicly. Being involved in these activities may mean that we are limited in the more prestigious things we can do. However, the short-term investment is well worth the long-term benefit.

---

224   *Tehillim* 145:16.

A few years ago, one of my kids was angry at my husband and me. He was on the stairs pouting when I asked him, "You know I love you, right?" His response was so insightful. "Of course you love me. You cook me all the foods I love." My son summed up what caring for a child feels like to him. It feels like love.

I have met adults who did not have their needs met happily as children. Some children were made to feel like burdens, while others had responsibility that went beyond their capability at a given age. These people are stunted as adults and have difficulty taking care of themselves in a healthy way. Often their adult relationships are unequal, and they do not feel worthy of success. They sabotage their best efforts and continue the chaotic lives they learned as children.

> My son summed up what caring for a child feels like to him. It feels like love.

Rachav seized the opportunity to save her family because their physical well-being was foremost on her mind. Her care and concern for her family's physical needs resulted in children who themselves achieved great spiritual heights. Likewise, the *eishes chayil*'s care of her family infuses them with passion for living a meaningful life and a drive to do for others as well.

Fostering Independence

As mothers, helping our children inculcate our values as their own requires planning on our part. As we do our chores and provide for our children's spiritual and emotional needs, we have an ever-present audience. We can use the opportunity to train the next generation to fill our roles whenever we are with them.

I bake cookies for my children, and I'd like them to do the same for their children. If I want my children to bake cookies themselves, I need to teach them how to do so. If I read books about baking with the kids and read recipes aloud at bedtime, they probably won't end up baking. Nor will they learn to bake if I simply wait until they are adults and expect them to have learned to bake by themselves. I guarantee that they will bake by having them bake with me now. The toddlers add a few ingredients that I have measured. As I make decisions, I speak aloud what I am doing so that they learn along with me. As they get older, they measure the ingredients, and finally, under my supervision, my children read the recipe and pick out the ingredients themselves. The result is often batches of lopsided sugar cookies with thumbprints and too many sprinkles, but that's okay. It isn't important if the end result is pretty, or even edible. The goal is for my children to become my apprentices in the kitchen until they learn the tricks of baking and can do so by themselves.

Baking with children often results in batches of lopsided sugar cookies with thumbprints and too many sprinkles, but that's okay.

Our children need similar training for their spiritual lives. If I want my children to become giving people, I cannot leave it to the schools to teach them or assume they will learn this by watching me or listening to me talk about *chessed*. They need to be a part of the *chessed* I do, just like I include them when baking cookies. They can join me on visits to the elderly, help host and entertain guests, and be given responsibilities commensurate to their age and ability. The key is not having them do too much so they are frustrated or excluding them entirely from the process.

If I want my children to feel passionate about Judaism, I need to teach them how to do so. If it is important to me to appreciate every day and to express gratitude for what I have, I need to figure out how I am going to introduce these practices to my children and involve them when I am doing so. They need to celebrate my spiritual achievements — and theirs — with me on a regular basis. They need to feel that they are like Rachav's children — important and valuable — no matter what. They will then have the passion to create the life that we hope and pray they will.

Apprentices, Not Students

Viewing my children as my apprentices does not mean that I am monitoring and assessing every action that my children do; I am not the teacher grading their performances. Having an apprentice means that I am providing guidance while simultaneously trying to improve my own practice and master my own skills. The difference between treating children as students as opposed to apprentices, is powerful. We all want our children to learn how to pray. It is tempting to turn times of prayer into a time of intense focus on the child, making sure she is looking inside the *siddur*, checking her attention, and nagging her to participate. Viewing our children as apprentices means that our main focus during prayer is on improving our own prayers while still making sure our children have the age-appropriate tools to participate.

Children are our apprentices, not our students.

Living this *pasuk* requires us to be both confident and humble at the same time. We must be confident in our ability to influence and impact our children while humble enough to do the seemingly menial tasks that being a wife and mother requires. On the same day, we can be on a high from seeing our kids include an unpopular classmate because of the morals and values we have taught them, and we can feel the tedium of changing the clothes in the closets from one season to another. Rachav and the *eishes chayil* have taught us that both are important and that you can't do one without the other. All of our work on behalf of our family has a long-reaching impact on our future, both spiritually and physically. While it may not make our chores less boring, the knowledge of what our work means can transform it from the mundane to the sublime.

Summary

"She is not afraid of the snow for her household." לֹא תִירָא לְבֵיתָהּ מִשָּׁלֶג
Rachav, the harlot רָחָב הַזּוֹנָה

From the Pasuk We Learn

The *eishes chayil* is a woman who knows that before helping others, she must first help her family. She provides for each member of her family based on his individual needs. Her care is both physical and spiritual and imbues within the members of her family a passion to live a life of Torah. Moreover, she helps her children make her values their own.

From the Midrash We Learn

When the Jewish People were conquering her city in the land of Canaan, Rachav did not fear for her family's security. She had prepared for them a way to be safe. Likewise, she also prepared for her family's spiritual future. These preparations impacted the entire Jewish nation. When a woman provides for her family's physical and spiritual needs, she is ensuring her own spiritual legacy.

Practical Steps

1. Set priorities for choosing the order of whom to help. Those who depend on us or are in our home get taken care of first.
2. Educate children to be independent by giving them increasing levels of responsibility alongside us as we together complete a task. Give them responsibilities commensurate to their age and ability. They should not do so much that they become frustrated, nor should they be excluded from the process.
3. Set aside time to express daily gratitude and celebrate spiritual achievements with our children to help them learn to be

passionate about their spiritual lives and their connection to Hashem.
4. View children as apprentices. Our main focus is on our own growth while we teach them, not force them, to comply with our expectations.

Questions

Self-Growth

1. How can I infuse my household chores and responsibilities with joy so that I can take pleasure in them?
2. Who are the people in my life that I need to care for first, before caring for strangers?

As Wives and Mothers

3. What do I anticipate my family will need in the next few months?
4. What work do I need to do now to make sure they have it?
5. Are my family's needs being cared for as I do *chessed* for those outside my family?
6. What kind of life preparation do I need to provide for my family?
7. How can I involve my family in my work so that my children learn how to do it on their own?
8. How do I balance giving my children responsibility without spoiling them or overburdening them?
9. What are my spiritual goals that I would like to pass on to my children? How can I help them learn to feel enthusiastic about their Torah learning, their mitzvah observance, and their spiritual lives?

Teaching Our Daughters

10. How can I help my daughter feel positive about household tasks and infuse joy into the process of caring for her home?
11. How can I involve my daughter in spiritual goals so she learns these values from me in addition to practical goals?

CHAPTER 15

As an Individual (Self-Respect)

מַרְבַדִּים עָשְׂתָה לָּהּ שֵׁשׁ וְאַרְגָּמָן לְבוּשָׁהּ.

*She makes for herself linens;
her clothes are fine linen and purple.*

Peshat

The last *pasuk* discussed the clothing the *eishes chayil* provides for her family and how she ensures that every member of her household has what he or she needs. This *pasuk* contrasts what she does for others with what she makes for herself. It discusses how she makes bed linens and clothing for herself and the fabrics she uses for them.

The first things that the *eishes chayil* makes for herself are *marvadim*, bed linens.[225] Bed linens are not used to decorate the public areas of the home.

---

225 Rashi, *Mishlei* 31:22.

Generally, only a woman and her husband will notice the sheets that are used in the privacy of her bedroom. Yet the *eishes chayil* concerns herself that her private space be beautiful. In this *pasuk*, she is not praised for the curtains in the living room or the tablecloths in the dining room; she is praised because her first priority when making linens is to honor and beautify the room that reflects the intimate bond that she and her husband share.

Dignity in Dress

Next, the *pasuk* describes her clothing as *shesh v'argaman* — linen and purple thread, in contrast to the red fabric that she used to make her family's clothes. Purple dye and linen were the fabrics used to make the clothes of the *Kohanim* and the clothes of royalty.[226] The *eishes chayil* chooses for herself clothes that exude dignity. According to the Ralbag, these clothes look majestic and are both clean and well-fitting.[227] The *eishes chayil* spends her days caring for her family but does not look like a maid. She dresses with dignity and refuses to appear before others dirty and disheveled.

> The *eishes chayil*'s clothing exudes dignity. She may spend her days caring for her family, but she does not look like a maid.

These two phrases (that describe a woman's bedroom linen and her refined clothing) paint a picture of a woman who has self-respect. In her choice of clothing and home furnishings, she is not trying to impress others with her worth. Her efforts are invested in decorating a room no one outside her closest family will see, and despite her hard work on behalf of her family, she continues to dress with pride. She has not lost sight of who she is, despite all that she does for others.

This *pasuk* is teaching a twofold lesson.

Priorities and Choices

The first lesson is that a person's priorities can be seen by her choices. There are always options about what comes first and what follows.

---

226 *Daas Mikra, Mishlei* 31:22.
227 Ralbag, ibid.

Assume that in our budget, we have a certain amount of money to be used to decorate. Do we choose the room our friends frequent or the one that only we and our husbands share? The decision becomes even harder when we realize that our husbands may not even appreciate the small touches that we add to a room, while our friends are thrilled by our choice of throw pillows. The question boils down to this: For whom are we decorating; is it for others or for ourselves?

These choices extend beyond home decorating to other choices that arise when we have limited time and resources. In what do we invest? Do we set up a date night with our husband or with our friends? Do we talk on the phone with our friends when our husband comes home from work? Do we get dressed up to go out with our friends or when we are home alone with our husband? Are we more concerned about what our friends (and strangers) will say or what our husband needs? *Eishes Chayil* is teaching that our first priority should be to put our efforts into our most important relationship, our marriage. The goal is not to do what will make our husband happy, although of course that is very important. These statements of priority may never be noticed by our husband. Rather, the goal is to help us to develop a sense of respect for our marriage and help us hold it sacred.

> Our primary role is to be the matriarch, the nobility of our home. We don't get dressed to impress others but to remind us of our most important role.

When we prioritize our marriage and make efforts to make it special, we reinforce to ourselves how central our marriage is to our life.

The Importance of Self-Respect

The second lesson this *pasuk* is teaching us is that we need to respect ourselves. As we have more children and our responsibilities grow, it is very easy to stop taking care of ourselves. The *pasuk* wants us to remember that our primary role is to be the matriarch, the nobility of our home. When we get dressed every day, it is not to impress others. When we choose to treat ourselves properly, even when no one else is around, we are reminding ourselves of who we truly are and how vital we are to our family. When we neglect ourselves, we are broadcasting to ourselves and to our family that we do not think we are very important.

 Midrash – BasSheva

The Midrash highlights a woman who understood her greatness as a wife and mother and used it appropriately within the privacy of her home:

"She makes for herself linens."	מַרְבַדִּים עָשְׂתָה לָּהּ
This is BasSheva,	זוֹ בַּת שֶׁבַע
who had Shlomo come from her,	שֶׁיָּצָא מִמֶּנָּה שְׁלֹמֹה
who was clothed in linen and purple wool	שֶׁהָיָה מְרֻקָּם בְּשֵׁשׁ וְאַרְגָּמָן
and ruled the world from end to end.	וּמָלַךְ מִסּוֹף הָעוֹלָם וְעַד סוֹפוֹ

After the period of the Judges, the era of the Kings began. The first king was Shaul, who was anointed by the prophet Shmuel and was a member of the tribe of Binyamin. The next major king was Dovid, a descendant of the tribe of Yehudah. Dovid united all twelve tribes, conquered the invading enemies who had been attacking the Jewish nation for the previous three hundred years, and brought peace to the land. His son Shlomo continued his legacy and built the Holy Temple, the Beis Hamikdash. Shlomo was even more powerful than his father Dovid — with international alliances and extraordinary wealth.

> BasSheva chose to influence her family within the privacy of her home and never wielded her potential power as she could have.

BasSheva was the wife of Dovid and the mother of Shlomo. In her role as the queen and mother of the heir to the throne, BasSheva could have wielded tremendous influence and swayed the political and economic life in the kingdom to her benefit. Despite her position, we do not read much about her in *Navi*. We only read about her when her story is important in the life of Dovid and when she intervened because she felt the spiritual state of her family and nation was at risk. From the few times BasSheva is mentioned in the text of the *Navi*, we learn that she knew how powerful she could be but chose not to wield her influence. She decided to influence her family within the privacy of her home, which is the lesson we are meant to learn from BasSheva's story that is highlighted by the Midrash.

BasSheva's Influence

The first time we hear of BasSheva's advocacy and political involvement comes at the end of the life of her husband, Dovid HaMelech.[228] Dovid's son from another wife, Adoniah, decided that he should be declared king — even while his father was alive! The primary prophet for the kingdom, Nosson HaNavi, approached BasSheva and advised her to inform the king of Adoniah's arrogant grab for power. When BasSheva entered Dovid's throne room and bowed to him, Dovid, aware that BasSheva was not a regular visitor who asked for favors, immediately asked, "What's wrong?"[229] BasSheva informed Dovid of Adoniah's quest to be king and reminded Dovid of his earlier promise to her that Shlomo, their child, would inherit the throne. Nosson HaNavi presented Dovid with similar information, and Dovid immediately anointed Shlomo as the next king. In this unassuming manner, BasSheva assured her son of his rightful position as the next ruler.

The next time that BasSheva used her influence to steer the course of the nation was on the day that Shlomo dedicated the Beis Hamikdash. The Midrash recounts events that are not mentioned in the *Navi* but are hinted at in the *pesukim* immediately preceding the poem of *Eishes Chayil* in *Mishlei*.

The *pasuk* in *Mishlei* says:

דִּבְרֵי לְמוּאֵל מֶלֶךְ מַשָּׂא אֲשֶׁר יִסְּרַתּוּ אִמּוֹ.[230]

The words of King Lemuel. The theme [is the rebuke with] which his mother admonished him:

---

228 *Melachim I* 1.
229 *Metzudas Dovid, Melachim I* 1:16.
230 *Mishlei* 31:1.

When did this rebuke take place? The *Midrash Rabbah* fills in the details.²³¹

Shlomo had just completed building the Beis Hamikdash in Yerushalayim. Everything was in place to begin the daily service to Hashem in a permanent home filled with grandeur. Every day, for hundreds of years, the *Kohanim* would offer a morning sacrifice as early in the day as possible. No other sacrifices could be offered before the initial daily offering was brought.²³² It was the fourth hour, and the king, who held the keys to the Temple under his pillow, had still not arrived at the inaugural day.²³³

The previous evening, Shlomo had gotten married to the daughter of the Pharaoh of Egypt. His new wife arranged that he should oversleep so that he would not begin the service in the Holy Temple with the proper respect.²³⁴ The whole nation waited to begin service in the new Temple as their king slept, unaware of their turmoil. They were afraid to wake Shlomo since it could be perceived as disrespectful, and they approached BasSheva, the king's mother, for help.

Like she had done with Dovid, BasSheva took matters into her own hands, but only in private. She entered Shlomo's bedroom, woke him up, and chastised him:

מַה בְּרִי וּמַה בַּר בִּטְנִי וּמֶה בַּר נְדָרָי.²³⁵

What, my son? What, O son of my womb?
And what O son of my vows?

BasSheva said to him, "You are my son; I nurtured you, educated you, and prayed for your success. I did everything I could so that you would lead a life of holiness and service to Hashem, before you were born and after. Your behavior reflects on me as a mother, since everyone knows you are my son, and they also know that Dovid, your father, was a righteous man."²³⁶

---

231 Bamidbar Rabbah 10:4.
232 Rambam, *Mishneh Torah, Temidim and Musafim* 1:1, 3.
233 Rashi, *Mishlei* 31:1.
234 *Bamidbar Rabbah* 10:4.
235 Ibid. 31:2.
236 Rashi, *Mishlei* 31:2.

BasSheva continued her rebuke, telling her son Shlomo the dangers of overindulging in alcohol and of marrying too many wives. Both would prevent him from having the clarity needed to judge and lead the nation based on Torah values.

Shlomo awoke and took his mother's words to heart. He recounted her approach and words in *Mishlei* immediately before the poem of *Eishes Chayil* to teach everyone a mother's power.[237]

Privacy and Dignity

With both her husband and her son, BasSheva used her influence in private. She understood her status but used it only when it was necessary. Her manner in both cases was refined, respectful, and confidential. No one in the nation needed to know what had been said or done. The *Navi* shared with us the story of her conversation with Dovid, and Shlomo recalled her conversation with him to help us learn from her words. BasSheva herself kept her relationships discreet and dignified.

The result of BasSheva acting with dignity in these interactions was that her son wore the clothing of royalty, a sign of the honorable station that he inherited from her.

Getting Practical: Dignity in Marriage

The *eishes chayil* teaches us that we must have self-respect and reinforce our self-respect by according ourselves and our marriage honor. We need to dress ourselves in a manner that reflects our dignity and honor our marriage through acts that demonstrate that we respect its holiness. Although it is tempting to focus on our children or others at the expense of caring for ourselves and our marriage, it is dangerous to do so. When we do, we forget what we can accomplish in those very roles for which we are sacrificing.

BasSheva adds to this lesson that we must respect our power as wives and mothers and the influence we hold in our homes. I was once

---

237 Malbim, *Mishlei* 31:10.

talking to a mother who was complaining about how her teenagers did not understand her values. I asked, as a young mother of only younger children, why the mother did not tell her children about her values. The mother thought I was crazy. At this point, she claimed, her teens listen to their friends not their parents.

Research disagrees.[238] In the long-term, the primary influence on adolescents' values and later-life decisions is from their parents. If we do not recognize the great power we hold in influencing them, we will ignore the opportunities when they arise.

The Importance of Privacy

BasSheva also taught us how to influence our family. The goal is not for others to think that we are good educators, wives, and parents. The goal is that our children should incorporate our values as their own and make changes when necessary. If we are constantly critical over meaningless issues, or we choose to make our disagreements public, we squander our chance to influence our spouse and children.

> Our goal is not for others to think that we are good educators, wives, and parents, but to be good educators, wives and parents. This can only happen if we keep our interactions private.

A young boy was playing with his friends. In their fun, the boys destroyed a neighbor's fence. A group of adults gathered around waiting to see how the parents would take care of the problem. The first father who came home saw what happened, dragged his son off by his ear, and screamed at him all the way to his home. The second father came, picked up his son dramatically, and carted off the screaming, scared child while threatening him. The third parent came, looked at the crowd waiting expectantly, looked at his cowering son, and silently went home and returned with his hammer, some wood, and nails. He proceeded to work to fix the fence, handing his son the tools to help rebuild the damage, all the while ignoring the crowd who waited for a dramatic scene.

---

238 Steinberg, L., *Age of Opportunity, Lessons from the New Science of Adolescence.*

Which father taught his son the lesson that needed to be learned? The ones who performed for the crowd or the one who wanted to teach his son the meaning of making amends?

As wives and mothers, we need to decide which kind of parent and wife we want to be and what we are trying to accomplish when we talk to our husband and kids. If we are trying to placate someone else, be it our parents, our siblings, or our friends, we will not influence our families. But if we keep our influence to the privacy of our relationship, we have a chance. Our husband and children will sense the great respect we have for our role and come to respect it as well.

This *pasuk* reminds us that our children and husband are not there to serve us by impressing others. How we dress is not to impress others. The cars we buy, our home furnishings — nothing we do is to impress others. The main person we need to impress is ourselves so we understand the potential that lies within us. With this awareness, we can focus our efforts on being the best woman, wife, and mother we can be to serve Hashem and do His will.

Summary

"She makes for herself linens." מַרְבַדִּים עָשְׂתָה לָּהּ
BasSheva בַּת שֶׁבַע

From the Pasuk We Learn

The *eishes chayil* respects her marriage and herself even as her family grows and her responsibilities increase. She prioritizes her marriage and takes steps to emphasize its specialness to reinforce how central it is in her life. She also expends effort to dress in a manner that reflects her role as a matriarch. She dresses in clothing that is clean and well-fitting, and that reminds her of the essential role she plays in the home beyond her homemaking chores.

From the Midrash We Learn

BasSheva influenced the decisions of her husband, Dovid HaMelech, and her son, Shlomo HaMelech, privately and respectfully. We learn from her choices that our advice and guidance to our family is not a public affair but should be said privately and only with the involved family member.

Practical Steps

1. Invest time and attention in the areas of our home that we share with our husband before investing in areas that we share with the public.
2. Choose a wardrobe that is dignified, clean, and well-fitting to remind us of our status in the home.
3. Make time with our spouse a priority.
4. Communicate our values and thoughts with our children so that they learn our value system.
5. Share criticism and guidance in private when it is needed.

Questions

Self-Growth

1. How do I balance creating a wardrobe that is dignified and refined while maintaining a spiritual mind-set?
2. What should I wear for each of my different roles? How do I preserve my clothing so it doesn't get ruined when doing chores?
3. How do I set my priorities so they are based on my needs rather than on trying to please people?

As Wives and Mothers

4. How can I create a beautiful, private home life?
5. When I need to guide my children, what time and place is most appropriate to do so? What should be done if others are around so that I can balance privacy and parenting?
6. What is the ratio of positive, nurturing interactions I have with my children compared to corrective interactions?
7. How do my interactions with my children and parenting style need to change based on their age?

Teaching Our Daughters

8. How do I teach my daughter to value the privacy of marriage?
9. How do I teach my daughter to think about privacy and dignity when educating and teaching others?

CHAPTER 16

As a Wife (Supportiveness)

נוֹדָע בַּשְּׁעָרִים בַּעְלָהּ בְּשִׁבְתּוֹ עִם זִקְנֵי אָרֶץ.

*Her husband is known in the gates,
when he sits among the elders of the land.*

Peshat

After focusing on the priorities of the *eishes chayil* and how she interacts with others, the poem shifts to talk about the *eishes chayil*'s husband and how famous he is within the community. This seems strange.

After all, modesty is a core Jewish virtue. Why is the emphasis on how well-known a man is rather than on his righteousness? One of the greatest rabbis of the twentieth century, the Chazon Ish, tried to remain anonymous and even published his initial writings under a pseudonym so as not to draw attention to himself. He only publicly undertook the mantle of leadership when it was necessary to save the life of Mendel Beilus, a Jew accused of ritual murder in the Russian Empire.[239] Clearly, fame was not something the Chazon Ish was pursuing. Why would this be a value of the *eishes chayil* or her husband?

> Why is the emphasis on how well-known a man is rather than on his righteousness?

Moreover, why is this line about a man's social position placed in a poem about his great wife? Every other *pasuk* in the poem talks about the *eishes chayil*'s accomplishments, while this *pasuk* does not mention her at all.

With the help of commentaries to this *pasuk*, we can understand how each word of the *pasuk* that discusses her husband also adds to the praise of the *eishes chayil*.

The Gates of Wisdom

The *pasuk* stresses that the *eishes chayil*'s husband sits at the gates of the city with the elders. In the language of *Tanach*, the "gates of the city" was not the "local hangout" for unemployed men. Rather, it was the center of scholarship. The most distinguished and respected elders of the city would congregate there and discuss Jewish Law and Torah.[240] The *pasuk* is not discussing how famous the *eishes chayil*'s husband is, rather, it is discussing how learned her husband is and how much he is sought after for religious and spiritual guidance.

The *pasuk* is also pointing out that a man's greatness in Torah, and his ability to sit at the gates as a respected elder, stems from the support of the *eishes chayil*. While a husband has free will, his choices — positive or negative — are also a reflection of how the *eishes chayil* acts in her role as a wife and partner.[241] The *eishes chayil* was a key factor in her husband gaining his reputation as a scholar. Perhaps she encouraged him or gave him the time and opportunity

---

239 Rav Avrohom Yeshaya Karelitz, *Kovetz Igaros*, Book 2, Letter 1:73.
240 Meiri, *Mishlei* 31:23.
241 Rav Hirsch, ibid.

to study Torah. She may have assumed additional household and financial responsibilities, or she may have sacrificed leisure time with her husband to increase his opportunity to learn with the elders.

Sacrifices for Torah

In our generation, we had a man whose wife epitomized the idea expressed in this *pasuk*. Rav Yosef Sholom Elyashiv, *zt"l*, was known to learn eighteen hours a day until he was well into his nineties. His halachic decisions were followed without question, and he was known as the *posek hador*, the halachic decisor of the generation. His ability to attain this level of commitment was, in some part, thanks to his wife. After their marriage, Rebbetzin Sheina Chaya agreed to allow Rav Elyashiv to learn for one thousand consecutive days while assuming all the household responsibilities. When she was on her deathbed, she crawled out to the porch to cough rather than disturb Rav Elyashiv's sleep so as not to impair his concentration the following day.[242] Rav Elyashiv had a partner who was equally devoted to his goals in learning.

Initially, when I learned this *pasuk* and read these stories, I found them disheartening. I knew myself, and I knew I could never achieve that commitment to my husband's learning. Rebbetzin Elyashiv was the daughter of the sainted Rav Aryeh Levin, the subject of the book *A Tzaddik in Our Time* (Feldheim). She was raised in a different generation and in a different environment. What could this *pasuk* and these stories say to me?

> I am not expected to be Rebbetzin Elyashiv, much like my husband is not expected to be Rav Elyashiv.

With more thought, I realized that I was not expected to be Rebbetzin Elyashiv, much like my husband is not expected to be Rav Elyashiv. I could, however, take the example and make some sacrifices to help my husband learn. To begin with, I could limit the number of times I interrupt his learning, and I could also assume some household duties that I would rather he do so that learning

---

242   Naftali and Naomi Weinberger, *Rebbetzin Kanievsky*, p. 71.

could be a priority in my home. Being willing to assume more responsibility and becoming more self-sufficient in order to make my husband's spiritual growth a priority of mine is a small price to pay for the benefit of having a spiritual force in my home.

Where to Study

The *pasuk* adds another point about how the *eishes chayil* helped her husband achieve greatness in Torah learning. The *pasuk* specifically notes that her husband sits and talks with the elders at the gates. It would have been easier for the *eishes chayil* had her husband stayed home to learn. In this way, she could have more opportunity to go out herself without worrying about finding a babysitter to watch her children. Instead, the *eishes chayil* encouraged her husband to go out of the house and to the gates where Torah scholars would be found so he could grow by learning from them.[243]

Many of us have workout equipment at home. The most popular use for home treadmills is as a spare closet. Most treadmills are covered with clutter and are used only a few times after they are purchased. More people keep their commitment to exercise by joining a gym or attending group classes. Going to a place where there are other like-minded people helps us fight the laziness that sets in after the work gets hard. Being with other motivated people is a strong motivator to keep working and learning.

The gates of learning that we have nowadays are the *batei midrash* and *batei knesios* — the yeshiva study halls and the synagogues. A man will find it more difficult to leave the house to learn without the approval and encouragement of his wife. Without it, the comfort of home and the responsibilities that lie there will draw him more strongly than the hard work of the yeshiva or shul study hall. While I cannot force my husband to learn, and I can't ignore my true needs, I can work on being flexible and positive about the time my husband spends outside the house learning.

---

243 Rabbi Mordechai Shlesinger, *Bigdei Mordechai* quoted in *Sefer Eishes Chayil*, p. 192.

This *pasuk* is teaching us that when a man marries, he is full of potential. As a young man, though, there are many directions his life may lead. A wife who encourages and prioritizes a focus on Torah learning helps direct her husband's efforts and enables him to fulfill that potential.

This explains why a woman's greatness is tied to her husband. His achievements and his Torah learning are a reflection of her devotion to this goal.

Midrash – Michal

"Her husband is known at the gates."	נוֹדָע בַּשְּׁעָרִים בַּעְלָהּ
This is Michal,	זוֹ מִיכַל
who saved Dovid from death.	שֶׁהִצִּילָה דָּוִד מִן הַמִּיתָה

How devoted should a woman be to her husband's growth? How much should it be her priority and concern?

The Midrash states that Michal was a woman who brought this trait to life by saving her husband's life. The story of this act came early in her marriage. Michal was the daughter of Shaul, the first king of the Jewish nation. Michal was given to Dovid in marriage as a reward for his service to the king, but soon afterward Shaul HaMelech decided that Dovid deserved to be killed.[244] Shaul knew that he would lose his kingdom to a rival as a punishment for ignoring Hashem's command to kill out the nation of Amalek, and he feared that Dovid was this rival.[245]

Initially, Dovid had been respected by Shaul HaMelech. The two were introduced because Shaul's kingdom was beset by problems and was being attacked by the Plishtim.[246] Dovid became a key figure in the battle against the Plishtim and became beloved to the whole nation.

---

244   *Shmuel I*, 18:21–29.
245   Ralbag, *Shmuel I*, 18:28.
246   *Shmuel I*, 17:31–58; 18:1–30.

Michal, Shaul's daughter, recognized Dovid's sterling character and loved him. Shaul agreed to allow her to marry him on the condition that Dovid would first kill a large number of Plishti soldiers, hoping that Dovid would be killed in the pursuit of marrying his daughter.[247] Dovid was successful in this impossible quest, and Michal and Dovid were married. Soon after, Shaul HaMelech decided to kill Dovid.[248] Shaul sent soldiers to the home of Dovid and Michal at night to ensure that Dovid could be captured and killed in the morning. Michal heard about the plot and helped Dovid escape through a back window. She then set up the bed so that it looked like Dovid was still lying in it. In the morning, when the soldiers arrived, she pointed to the bed and told them that Dovid was sick and could not come, giving Dovid even more time to flee.

Michal made a clear decision to support her husband over her father.

Shaul discovered this ploy and asked Michal why she had deceived her father. Michal claimed that Dovid had forced her to help him flee, and she was merely a pawn in his plot. In this manner, she saved both her life and that of her husband.

It was this act that earned Michal the praise of Chazal. Michal had a choice: She could support her father, she could support her new husband, or she could remain a passive viewer of the drama unfolding between them. Michal made a clear decision to support her husband over her father. She enabled Dovid to live, thereby ensuring his rise to prominence, and ensured that her brothers and father lost their power.

Dovid HaMelech's Growth

After a long series of trials, Dovid was finally anointed as the rightful king of the Jewish nation. He was not only the sovereign leader of the Jewish People, he was also their spiritual leader. The Rambam lists the

---

247 *Shmuel I*, 18:21.
248 *Shmuel I*, 19:10–17.

individuals who were responsible for the transmission of the Oral Torah from the time of Moshe Rabbeinu until the codification of the Gemara.[249] These men were also the leaders of the Sanhedrin, the seventy elders who made all halachic decisions. Dovid was the sixth person in the transmission of the Oral Torah after Moshe. Without Dovid, Jewish learning and scholarship would have floundered. Dovid was not only known as a king; he was also known at the gates of scholarship where the Sanhedrin gathered under his leadership.

Dovid HaMelech also became known because of other gates: the gates of the Beis Hamikdash. Dovid HaMelech had been told by Hashem that he could not build the Beis Hamikdash because he had been involved in too much bloodshed, even though the bloodshed was warranted.[250] Dovid spent his final years collecting all the materials needed for the Holy Temple's construction. Shlomo HaMelech, his son, was given permission to build the Holy Temple. When it was completed, Shlomo tried to bring the *Aron* into the Beis Hamikdash, but the gates would not open. Shlomo prayed and praised Hashem, but they still would not open. Finally, Shlomo proclaimed that Hashem should remember the kindness of Dovid.[251] At that moment, the gates of the Beis Hamikdash opened and the Jewish People knew that Dovid was a righteous man who had been forgiven for all of his sins.

Thus, we can see that Michal's decision to save Dovid's life had far-reaching consequences. Her husband became the king, he became the leader of all Jewish scholars, and the service in the Beis Hamikdash began in his merit. Michal's efforts to support Dovid over all other familial ties allowed him to become the person who was "known in the gates" — the gates of scholarship and at the gates of the Beis Hamikdash.

---

249 Rambam, Introduction to *Mishneh Torah*.
250 *Divrei HaYamim I*, 22:8.
251 *Talmud Bavli, Shabbos* 30a.

Getting Practical: Supportiveness in Marriage

How does Michal's saving her husband's life relate to helping our husband become a great scholar? What are we meant to learn from Michal's choices?

Michal is teaching us how large a role we play in our husband's spiritual development and what sacrifice we are encouraged to make.

On the surface, this *pasuk* is challenging for some and not so for others. When we look at the Midrash, the *pasuk* becomes demanding for everyone.

On the surface, this *pasuk* is about sacrificing time so that our husband may learn. This devotion to learning Torah has always been the source of the Jewish community's strength and a priority for generations of Jewish women. In the *shtetl*, the Jewish family was subject to harsh poverty as Jews were restricted from easy professions and land ownership. The men were forced into menial labor that broke their bodies. After they finished their long hours of chopping wood, hauling stones, or carrying water, the Jewish men found a place to rejuvenate and find their inner core. They could go to the *beis midrash* and reconnect with their bigger selves. There were different shuls for different professions and groups learning a variety of subjects: The *Chevrah Mishnayos*, *Chevrah Shas*, *Chevrah Ein Yaakov*; each group learned up to its potential. This learning infused the people in the Jewish community and their homes with the sacred values of the Torah despite the coarse environment in which the men spent their workdays.

> Torah learning infused the Jewish home with sacred values despite the coarse environment in which the men spent their workdays.

In our generation, our communities have learning opportunities for men and women. In some ways, while it is popular, it is not as easy as in days past. There are many distractions that can pull us or our spouses away from making this a priority. Work is no longer sunup to sundown but continues as long as the smartphone has a charge. We are different and our marriages are different; we need more time with our husband to talk about our day. We are also exhausted and harried from being in the workforce. Finally, even if our husband gets out of the house, he is only a phone call away from a crisis that can bring him home. Finding time for our husband to learn in a *beis midrash* requires concentration and commitment from both the husband and wife to use this time well. The challenge grows as the years pass and the responsibilities at home increase.

> Even if our husband gets out of the house, he is only a phone call away from a crisis that can bring him home.

Our husband's greatness in Torah will not be based on what he learns when he is newly married. It will be based on how we steal moments after he gets more work responsibilities, our workload increases, and we have children who need our time and attention. It will be determined by a mutual commitment to find time for our husband to frequent the *beis midrash*.

Becoming a Couple

The Midrash adds an additional challenge to the commitment we must make to our husband. Michal had to choose between supporting her husband or her father when there could only be one winner. She chose her husband.

That was a brave choice. Her father was a *tzaddik*, he was the king, he was anointed by Shmuel HaNavi, and he raised her. Still, she chose to be loyal to Dovid. How did this choice help Dovid become a great scholar, and how will following Michal's example impact our husband's greatness in Torah learning?

Most of us marry young men. When we get married, our husband might seem immature and unimportant in comparison to the men whom we respect. We might have a father, a rabbi, or a teacher from high school who we feel is important. Our husband seems unaccomplished. What can he offer us in spiritual guidance that we cannot get from our parents or teachers? What happens when the choice is even starker and we need to choose between what our spouse needs from us and what our parents and siblings need from us?

Michal was faced with such a decision: her father's kingdom or her husband's life? Which was more important to this newlywed?

It is very tempting to side with our parents and give their views more weight than that of our spouse. Until recently, we were supposed to defend and respect our family of origin above all else. But now we are married. We have another person to consider: our husband. We need to realize that at these pivotal moments, we can create a respected man, a scholar. We are giving him a position that he needs to strive to earn: that of the leader of his new family.

At pivotal moments, we can create a respected man and a scholar based on how we treat our husband.

Part of this commitment to our husband includes respecting him as the spiritual leader of our new family. Our husband can become the one who decides halachah for our family if we give him the respect and confidence to do so.

When I first got engaged, I was faced with this challenge. My husband already had *semichah* and could decide halachic questions himself. I called up a seminary teacher and told her how horrified I was that my fiancé was disagreeing with the rabbis from whom I had learned in school. She told me that my soon-to-be-husband was now the rabbi of my house. If he said I couldn't use tea bags on Shabbos and my parents did — or vice versa — I needed to follow him. It took getting used to, and I needed to learn to bite my tongue, but it changed our home. That respect gave him a foundation upon which to build.

Rabbi Akiva and Rochel

There is a famous couple, Rabbi Akiva and Rochel, who lived by this ideal. Rochel was the daughter of Kalba Savua, a learned and wealthy man. Her father disinherited her when she chose to marry Akiva, an illiterate shepherd, rather than suitors who were learned and accomplished.[252]

---

252 *Talmud Bavli Nedarim* 50a.

Rochel saw Akiva's potential and chose to encourage her husband even though it meant sacrificing her relationship with her father. In the end, Akiva became the leader of the whole generation. Rabbi Akiva told his students quite plainly:

שֶׁלִּי וְשֶׁלָּכֶם שֶׁלָּהּ הוּא.²⁵³

[The Torah learning and achievements that are] mine and yours come from her.

Rochel's devotion paid off. The students of Rabbi Akiva are responsible for all the Torah we have today.

The Lesson of Devorah

Let's assume though, that our husbands are never going to be scholars. What then? How does a wife position her husband as the spiritual leader of her home and help him develop this aspiration?

Another woman in *Tanach* shows us how to encourage our husband's growth and aspirations in a healthy way.

> Devorah shows us how to encourage our husband's growth and aspirations in a healthy way.

Devorah was a prophetess who decided halachah for the Jews of her area.²⁵⁴ She would sit under a date palm, and men and women would approach her to render halachic judgment. The *Navi* introduces her as *eishes lapidos* — the wife of the wicks.

Rashi fills in the backstory.²⁵⁵ Devorah was married to a man who did not have the background to be a scholar. Yet she wanted him to fulfill his potential and came up with an idea. She fashioned wicks and asked her husband to deliver them to the Mishkan to be used in service of the Menorah.

---

253 *Talmud Bavli, Kesubos* 63a.
254 *Shoftim* 4:4–5.
255 Rashi, *Shoftim* 4:4.

The Midrash states:[256]

> Devorah's husband was unlearned (an am ha'aretz).
> She said to him, "Let me make you wicks and you'll take them to the Mishkan in Shilo; your portion will be among righteous people there and you'll merit the World to Come."
> He made thick wicks to increase their light, and that's why his name was Lapidot (torches).
> And G-d said to Devorah, "You both intended to light up the Tabernacle; I, too, will make your light shine in Yisroel and Judah and among all the twelve tribes."

The Mishkan was the center of Jewish scholarship. Devorah hoped that her husband's exposure to greatness would propel him to greater heights. Indeed, this tactic worked, as her husband expanded on her idea and made bigger wicks to provide more light to the sanctuary. Through Devorah's subtle encouragement — encouragement that was never tainted with sarcasm or contempt — she built her husband.

Why is Devorah not the woman chosen to highlight this *pasuk*? Both she and Michal encouraged their husbands to increase their spiritual pursuits. Devorah seems to have an even larger role in her husband becoming known as a spiritual man while we don't hear of Michal's involvement in Dovid's learning and scholarship. Perhaps Devorah was not chosen because there is no antagonist or threat in her story. She encouraged her husband, and

If we choose to support our husband, we are choosing a life that has eternal significance.

he was excited by her idea. True support is learned from Michal, who sacrificed her relationship with her family when it was necessary to support her husband.

We wives may be asked to choose sides between our spouse and our original family, our spouse and our siblings, or our spouse and our

---

256 *Eliyahu Rabbah*, chapter 9.

children. This *pasuk* in *Eishes Chayil* and the life of Michal should serve as a reminder of what is at stake in our choice. If we choose to support our husband, we are choosing a life that has eternal significance. If we choose to act as an individual rather than as a team, we lose so much more than just the consequences of the immediate decision. We may make other people happy for a few days, but we are losing out on greatness for the rest of our life.

Summary

"Her husband is known in the gates."   נוֹדָע בַּשְּׁעָרִים בַּעְלָהּ
Michal   מִיכַל

From the Pasuk We Learn

The *eishes chayil* helped her husband become a scholar and acquire a respected reputation. She encouraged him to devote time to his studies and to spend time with other scholars even when it was difficult for her. Her encouragement and priorities to focus on Torah learning helped direct her husband's efforts and enabled him to become the person he was capable of becoming.

From the Midrash We Learn

Michal supported and protected her husband Dovid HaMelech even when doing so was at odds with her father's desires. We learn from her that when there is a difficult choice between siding with her original family or her husband, the *eishes chayil* chooses to support her husband. This helps him gain the confidence to be the spiritual leader of the family.

Practical Steps

1. Work with our husband to come up with a plan that works for both of us to allow him time to learn.
2. Limit the number of times we interrupt our husband's learning to true emergencies. Agree on what constitutes an emergency for both of us.
3. Assume some household responsibilities that are not overwhelming to free up time for our husband to learn.
4. Provide the opportunity for our husband to learn in a shul or beis midrash.
5. When forced to choose between our parent's needs or our husband's needs, give more weight to our primary family — our husband.

6. Give our husband respect as the spiritual leader of our new family.
7. To help build our husband's potential as the spiritual leader of our home, provide positive encouragement that is never tainted with sarcasm, contempt, or manipulation.

Questions

Self-Growth

1. How do I develop self-sufficiency so that I can take care of things that I am capable of doing but do not yet know how to do?
2. How do I encourage and support the study of Torah?
3. Am I sensitive not to make a friend or family member choose between her spouse and me?

As Wives and Mothers

4. What system do my husband and I have in our house to encourage his Torah learning?
5. Is there a place where he finds he gets more encouragement and support?
6. What constitutes an emergency to intrude on his learning time?
7. How do I balance conflicting needs from my original family (and friends) and my husband? How does this balance with my own needs?
8. How do I encourage my husband to develop his religious leadership in the family, like Devorah and Michal did for their husbands?
9. What are some of my husband's priorities and goals for his religious self? How can I best help support those goals without being maternal or nagging?

Teaching Our Daughters

10. How can I help my daughter develop a sense of loyalty to her husband while creating a strong sense of family?
11. How can I help my daughter appreciate the importance of Torah learning in the home and her role in creating this reality?

CHAPTER 17

As a Professional (Self-Sacrifice)

סָדִין עָשְׂתָה וַתִּמְכֹּר וַחֲגוֹר נָתְנָה לַכְּנַעֲנִי.

She makes linen garments and sells them and delivers belts to the merchant.

Peshat

This *pasuk* tells us that the *eishes chayil* **makes** linen garments that she sells and that she gives **woven belts** to a merchant. Once again, the *pasuk* is talking about the *eishes chayil*'s business and her work to produce garments.

It seems that we are rehashing a subject that we have already discussed a number of times. We know the *eishes chayil* weaves, we know she spins, and we also know that she is involved in business. What does this *pasuk* add to our understanding of this great woman? What new information is included here that was not included in a previous *pasuk*?

The Malbim explains that the *eishes chayil* is not merely selling her merchandise to provide for her family.²⁵⁷ Her family already has more than it needs. She has bought them the most practical clothes for each season and has dressed herself in a manner that is tasteful and dignified. She has decorated her home as she sees fit, and her husband has enough free time to become a scholar. This *pasuk* is describing how the *eishes chayil* uses her leisure time. She has many options of what she could do. She has already spent much time devoted to others. She could use her free time to do something nice for herself or to make more money. Instead, the Malbim tells us, she works on projects to raise additional funds for *tzedakah*.

This *pasuk* describes how the *eishes chayil* uses her leisure time to help others.

Rav Hirsch notes that the two parts of the *pasuk* are similar but not synonymous.²⁵⁸ First, the *eishes chayil* makes linen cloth to sell for charity. She also gives away her belts to a merchant (for free). Why is she giving away belts if she is selling her cloth for *tzedakah*, as the Malbim suggests?

Both the first and second half of the *pasuk* are talking about her charity. In the first half of the *pasuk*, it discusses how she raises money to give to *tzedakah* by working hard and donating the profits to charity; the second half of the *pasuk* discusses how the *eishes chayil* is involved in an even greater form of *tzedakah*: giving a person a job.

Contributing Talents

As we described, in earlier times, every woman spent time spinning. Periodically, the *eishes chayil* had leftover thread from her sewing projects. Rather than giving this thread away or selling it for a profit, the *eishes chayil* fashioned the thread into belts. She then gave these belts to a poor merchant to sell, thereby increasing the merchant's wares. As a result, more people would come to look at his merchandise. The *eishes*

---

257   Malbim, *Mishlei* 31:24.
258   Rav Hirsch, ibid.

chayil thus set into motion a more hopeful future for a downtrodden man. She allowed the unfortunate merchant to now earn a livelihood with dignity.

The Meiri comments that the *eishes chayil* could choose to make trinkets and accessories for her own wardrobe.[259] She chooses differently; she chooses to use her skills and talents to help a poor person. This way, she acquires something lasting and meaningful with her possessions: eternal reward.

The work that is highlighted in the *pasuk* is different from the work discussed in the previous section. Here the *eishes chayil* is working for the sake of someone else. She has no hope of benefitting from the product of her labors. She is focused on helping others with the satisfaction of knowing that in the next world she will get her reward.

Leisure Time Option

The *eishes chayil* is involved in an activity that is relatable to all of us. We will have times in our lives when we have leisure time. How do we use that time? Can we use some of that time to help someone else? Equally important is understanding what our talents are and how we can use them to benefit others. Once our basic responsibilities are fulfilled, we can find ways to make our free moments more meaningful by being of service.

> We all have talents, and we can often make more money by using them. Once we have enough money for our needs, we can choose to invest in our spiritual future rather than just in our financial one.

The *eishes chayil* founded a charity with the profits of a side business. We can also look for **ways to do** *chessed* with what we **know how to do**. One woman I know used her extensive knowledge of computers to systemize food distribution to poor families for Shabbos. Another friend is an artist who spent her time decorating a shul's *sukkah* to enhance the mitzvah for all who came. There are doctors who volunteer to provide

---

259   Meiri, *Mishlei* 31:24.

medical know-how to organizations that help sick children, and lawyers who help advocate for schools on a pro bono basis. We all have talents, and we can often make more money by selling our expertise. However, once we have enough money for our needs, we can choose to invest in our spiritual future rather than just in our financial one.

Creative Giving

The second half of the *pasuk* is highlighting how to use out-of-the-box thinking to give charity. The *eishes chayil* used her creativity to expand a poor man's business. She did not take over his business; instead, she found ways to easily increase his profits.

We can also look for creative solutions to communal problems. We do not have to be the ones who get the credit for the solution. We can be the facilitator by bringing two people together who otherwise would not have met.

Chessed includes facilitating bringing two people together who otherwise would not have met.

Last year, I told a friend about my interest in educational technology. Every once in a while, she sends an email with the name of a new contact who might be able to help me professionally. That is this *eishes chayil*'s method of helping someone out: creatively, modestly, and respectfully.

Another friend of mine also looks for creative ways to help organizations and people thrive. She is a creative woman and is full of energy and drive. She noticed that many communal organizations were expending countless man-hours on fundraisers that duplicated the efforts of other fundraisers being held in the community. Rather than sitting on the sidelines in frustration, she helped coordinate a fundraiser that included nineteen different organizations in different cities to raise money on one day. Her goal was to raise a million dollars. On the day of the event, the goal was reached, and there was much celebration. People paid attention to the organization and its mission rather than to the coordinator of the event. The fundraiser not only gave them money, it gave them positive attention and a time to celebrate their mission. Like the *eishes chayil* giving away her belts to help the poor man increase his business, my friend's help allowed the organizations to become more self-sufficient because of her efforts.

We all have potential to effect great change for others. Once we realize that our efforts will be noticed and repaid in a better way, we are free to devote and contribute our energies without thinking about needing more money and more recognition.

Midrash – Shimshon's Mother

"She makes linen garments and sells them."	סָדִין עָשְׂתָה וַתִּמְכֹּר
This is the mother of Shimshon	זוֹ אִמּוֹ שֶׁל שִׁמְשׁוֹן
through whom Yisroel was saved.	שֶׁנּוֹשְׁעוּ יִשְׂרָאֵל עַל יָדוֹ

Shimshon was a man who fought the Jewish People's enemy, the Plishtim, to save his people — and he eventually died doing so. His mother and her role in his success is relatively unknown, yet the Midrash chooses to highlight her as the example for this *pasuk* to help us understand how much we are capable of sacrificing to be of service to our community.

Shimshon's mother lived during a particularly difficult time in Jewish history — the time of the *Shoftim* — the Judges.[260] There was a neighboring tribe, the Plishtim, who attacked the Jews mercilessly, and there was no leader to unite the people to withstand their attacks. The Jewish tribes suffered from the persecution.

The mother of Shimshon, who is known in another Midrash as Tzalphonis, had her own personal pain as well.[261] She was barren for many years and longed for a child.[262] One day Tzalphonis was working in a field when an angel approached her and informed her that she was pregnant. The angel told her that the son she would bear would be

---

260 *Shoftim* 13:1.
261 *Bamidbar Rabbah* 10:5.
262 *Shoftim* 13:2–5.

different from all other children. He was destined to save the Jewish People from the Plishtim. However, her son's success would depend on how Tzalphonis raised him. Her son, Shimshon, needed to live based on the Nazirite laws in the Torah. He would never be allowed to drink wine, eat grapes, or cut his hair. These restrictions were to begin during the pregnancy, which meant that his mother had to abstain from drinking wine and eating grapes. From the day he was born, Shimshon's mother had to be careful to avoid serving her son these foods and to never cut his hair to preserve his *nazir* status. In the merit of these restrictions, the angel guaranteed her that Shimshon would hamper the Philistine enemy and help protect the Jewish tribes.

Shimshon's success would depend on how Tzalphonis raised him.

A Child's Choice

Shimshon's mother bore a son, raised him, and then protected him from all things that would make him spiritually unfit. Yet she did not see her son follow in the path that had been predicted for him. As an adult, Shimshon made choices that betrayed all she held dear and seemed to undo everything for which she had strived.[263] Shimshon came to his parents and asked to marry a Plishti women. His parents did not know that this was part of the divine plan to help him exact revenge against the Plishtim for their constant oppression of the Jews. Shimshon's parents begged him to reconsider and made a strong case as to why marrying a Plishti went against all that they and he valued. Shimshon remained unconvinced and married the woman.

This marriage provided him with the opportunity to attack the Plishtim. As a result of his relationship with his first wife, and other women thereafter, he was able to fight using guerilla warfare and deflect blame from the rest of the nation. He became a *shofet* over the Jewish nation before he married a Plishti woman named Delilah.[264] Delilah

---

263 *Shoftim* 14:1–4.
264 *Shoftim*, chapter 16.

managed to trick Shimshon into revealing the source of his incredible strength and victories in battle: his hair. She cut his hair so he could be captured and tortured. In his final act of rebellion, Shimshon destroyed a temple used for idolatry in which thousands of Plishtim were celebrating, killing himself and the many Plishtim in it.

Shimshon's mother watched her son as his life unfolded, and she participated in the outcome by maintaining his status as a *nazir*. She knew that her son was destined to fight a harsh battle, and she chose to support him in his efforts for the sake of the Jewish nation. By following the rules laid out by the angel, she lost all chances of being able to see her son lead a "normal" life. Then, despite her sincere efforts, her son veered from the path she had set for him.

> Shimshon's mother knew that her son was destined to fight a harsh battle, and she chose to support his efforts for the sake of the Jewish nation.

Think about it. This woman waited years for a son, and as soon as she became pregnant, she learned that she would never have a normal child. Shimshon's mission endangered him and robbed his mother of a close, loving son. Tzalphonis knew by following the laws of *nazir* that she may never have a son to care for her in her old age or see Jewish grandchildren. Yet Shimshon's mother listened to the angel. She raised a child and expended all her energy to help him become the best he could be. She stuck to his restrictive diet and made him look different from all his friends by not cutting his hair. She did this for no reason other than that it was good for the Jewish People. Her neighbors, relatives, and friends probably questioned her parenting all the time, talked about her behind her back, and wondered why her son was the one who intermarried. She sacrificed having a warm maternal relationship for the good of the Jewish People.

Getting Practical: Self-Sacrifice in Marriage

The lessons of the *eishes chayil* and Shimshon's mother are easy to understand but hard to implement. They both ask us to sacrifice something precious for the sake of others.

The *eishes chayil* sacrifices her work and time for the community. We can ask ourself if there is some way we can sacrifice some of ourself for others. This sacrifice does not need to be terribly taxing for it to impact our personality and our spiritual growth.

Rebbetzin Batsheva Kanievsky, *a"h*, was a young mother when she noticed that a neighbor was coming home from yeshiva to watch his children while his wife worked.[265] Rebbetzin Kanievsky volunteered to babysit the children at no charge for forty-five minutes each afternoon so that the father could continue learning, and the family could save money by not having to pay a babysitter. This arrangement continued for years. Only years later, once the children had already grown, did Rebbetzin Kanievsky admit that this "favor" had indeed been challenging for her at the time. Yet though it was inconvenient and her life would have been easier without it, she stretched herself to do a *chessed* for another.

Our ability to sacrifice when we are young lays the groundwork for greatness when we get older.

Later in her life, Rebbetzin Kanievsky was well-known for acts of kindness and service that far exceeded free babysitting. The homeless used her bed for naps, and emotionally unstable individuals routinely emptied her refrigerator, taking the food for themselves. These extraordinary acts stemmed from her efforts to push herself more when she was younger. Her ability to sacrifice when she was young laid the groundwork for her greatness when she got older.

Helping Our Children Grow

Shimshon's mother sacrificed something far more precious than her time and effort. She sacrificed her relationship with her child to help her nation become better. At first glance, her sacrifice seems so much larger than anything most of us confront. Still, when we look deeper, this sacrifice is something that mothers must be prepared to face.

---

265 Naftali and Naomi Weinberger, *Rebbetzin Kanievsky*, p. 117.

Our child is attending a Jewish day school to learn about his heritage, improve his spiritual life, and to learn to help his community. As a result, we have a carpool for him, thus limiting our job opportunities. We need to work to pay the tuition, and our child has long hours in school that leave our family with little vacation time to spend together. Are we not sacrificing time with our children for a greater good?

We can choose how we make that sacrifice. We can complain about the inconvenient vacation days, kvetch about the tediousness of carpool, or become irate about paying tuition. Alternatively, we can continually focus on how much good our child and the Jewish community as a whole are receiving because of our efforts.

> If the complaints about carpool and tuition outweigh our expressions of pride in their learning, how will they feel about these years and the hours they spend in school?

Many women would never think that there is an alternative to sending their children to Jewish schools. The question then is not whether we will make this sacrifice but how we choose to do it. No child wants to cause his parents pain. How will our children relate to the investments we have made for their schooling if they are bombarded with how much sacrifice it has taken? If the complaints about carpool and tuition outweigh our expressions of pride and excitement for their learning, how will they respond to the hours and years they spend in school? Will our children feel like it is too big a challenge and question doing this for their children, or will they value a Torah education as a primary goal for all Jewish children? Part of the commitment of Shimshon's mother was being supportive and positive despite the burden it placed on her.

The sacrifice of our time and our relationship with our children continues from there. There are mothers whose children are learning and/or living in Israel, others whose children serve in the IDF, and others whose children have sacrificed lucrative job opportunities that would let them live nearby in order to learn, teach, or live in a community with idealized Torah values. Each mother whose child pursues spiritual goals as an adult will be sacrificing her time with them, and she will often have valid reasons to worry about her children who are far away and facing challenges as a result of their choices.

How do we share in our children's journey when we miss them and worry for them? It does not tell us in the *Navi* how Shimshon's mother dealt with the emotional pain of the lost opportunities that she faced. It does not tell us how she reconciled her loss with the poor choices that Shimshon made that ultimately led to his punishment and death.

The Midrash chooses her as a role model because she did what was right at the time she was asked. She could not control her son's ultimate choices, but she could raise him with a desire to do what was right. She provided him with the foundation, values, and support in the best way she could.

> As mothers, we can provide our children with emotional support so they can fulfill their life's mission.

We cannot control the choices our children make. We can, however, prepare them to make the right choices even though those choices may not be easy for us. When our children make elevated but challenging choices, we can strive to communicate our pride in their decisions to better the Jewish nation with their service. We can provide them with emotional support so that they have the fortitude to fulfill their mission.

Both the *pasuk* and the Midrash are necessary to teach us what we can contribute to our community. The *eishes chayil* teaches us how to sacrifice something personally meaningful to us for the sake of others. Shimshon's mother teaches us how to support our children so that they will have the ability to sacrifice on behalf of others as well.

This kind of sacrifice requires a vision and a sense of belonging to something far greater than ourselves. It requires that we view ourselves as responsible for the community and the greater good. If we only think about our own needs and how we will benefit, we will never have the ability to reach for true greatness. If we realize that all of our gifts are opportunities to create something long-lasting, we will find that our life is enriched and that we receive so much more than we ever give away.

Summary

"She makes linen garments and sells them." סָדִין עָשְׂתָה וַתִּמְכֹּר
Mother of Shimshon אִמּוֹ שֶׁל שִׁמְשׁוֹן

From the Pasuk We Learn

The *eishes chayil* uses her leisure time to raise money for *tzedakah* and help others become self-sufficient, using her talents and creativity.

From the Midrash We Learn

Shimshon's mother, Tzalphonis, raised her son, who was born after many years of infertility, to be a *nazir*. She did so knowing that, as a result, her son would never be able to have a normal relationship with her. She sacrificed having a warm maternal relationship for the good of the Jewish People. From Tzalphonis we learn that the *eishes chayil* not only contributes her own talents to help others but also encourages her children to contribute to the greater community even as it impacts her children's time with her.

Practical Steps

1. Each day, try to help others in a way that is only slightly outside our comfort zone.
2. Think about which of our skills or talents would be beneficial to others or the community.
3. Once we have enough money for our needs, find a way to contribute our time and skills to others.
4. Look for ways to increase another Jew's business.
5. Help others network with people who can benefit them professionally.
6. Take pride in our children's spiritual accomplishments and explicitly let our children know of our pride even as we must sacrifice for their growth. Minimize our complaints about the

burden these choices have placed on us if we have chosen to invest in this area.
7. Recognize that we cannot control the outcome of our children's choices as adults. Provide our children with the foundation, values, and support as best we can and then let go of the results and of our children's ultimate decisions. Remember that outcomes are determined by Hashem, even if we don't understand the reasons.
8. Provide our children with emotional support so that they have the fortitude to fulfill their mission.

Questions

Self-Growth

1. What are my gifts, and how can I direct some of them to help the greater community?
2. How can I balance providing for our family financially so that we are self-sufficient and contributing my gifts to the community to benefit everyone?
3. How can I support people who are involved in helping others emotionally, physically, and financially?
4. Are there any people whom I can introduce to each other to help them in their professional lives?
5. How do I spend my leisure time? Is there a way to use my hobbies and things that relax me to benefit others or the community?
6. What *chessed* can I add to my day that is slightly outside of my comfort zone?

As Wives and Mothers

7. How do I balance contributing to the community and my responsibilities to my family?
8. How do I deal with the sacrifices I am making on behalf of my children so they and the community have a strong religious future?
9. How can I let my children know of my pride in them even as we must sacrifice for their growth?
10. How can I accept my children's choices, even if I disagree with them, after I have invested so much in raising them?
11. How can I give my children emotional support when they are working hard for Torah and *chessed*?

Teaching Our Daughters

12. How can I help my daughter learn to notice and respond to the needs of the community?
13. Are there any roles that I can encourage my daughter to fill now to help others and the community?

CHAPTER 18

As a G-d-Fearing Woman (Priorities)

עוֹז וְהָדָר לְבוּשָׁהּ וַתִּשְׂחַק לְיוֹם אַחֲרוֹן.

Strength and dignity are her clothing, and she laughs at the last day.

Peshat

The previous *pesukim* were far easier to understand than this one. The previous *pesukim* spoke of the *eishes chayil*'s achievements and her work on behalf of others. At first glance, this *pasuk* seems disjointed and unnecessarily abstract. The *pasuk* says that the *eishes chayil* wears strength and dignity and laughs at the last day.

What are strength and dignity, and why is she laughing?

Furthermore, we already know that the *eishes chayil* wears clothes of purple and linen that are dignified; why do we need to learn that she wears strength and dignity? What do these attributes about her clothing have to do with her humor about her last day?

This *pasuk* has a powerful lesson hidden in these abstract words. To understand its message, we must examine the meaning and seeming contradiction in this description of the *eishes chayil*.

Paradoxes

First, the *eishes chayil* is described as being clothed in *ohz*, strength. *Ohz* is a word that has multiple connotations. In *Pirkei Avos*, the *mishnah* says:

> הֱוֵי עַז כַּנָּמֵר, וְקַל כַּנֶּשֶׁר...לַעֲשׂוֹת רְצוֹן אָבִיךְ שֶׁבַּשָּׁמַיִם.[266]
> Be **strong** as a leopard and swift as an eagle
> to do the will of your Father in Heaven.

This *mishnah* continues:

> עַז פָּנִים לְגֵיהִנֹּם, וּבֹשֶׁת פָּנִים לְגַן עֵדֶן.[267]
> Those who have az panim go to Gehinnom
> and those who have boshes panim go to Gan Eden.

In the same *mishnah*, we are encouraged to have *ohz*, determination, while being warned that having the wrong type of *ohz* will lead us to eternal damnation. There is a paradox inherent in *ohz*: When it comes to the service of G-d, *ohz* is necessary. Otherwise, it is dangerous.

> We are encouraged to have *ohz*, determination, and warned that *ohz* will lead us to sin.

Ohz is strength and conviction. It is the ability to stand up to social norms and act independently. To do Hashem's will in the face of social pressures, one needs tremendous confidence (*ohz*). However, in other areas, being unconcerned about societal expectations will lead a person to the worst sins, as there are no

---

266 *Mishneh Avos* 5:20.
267 Ibid.

> *Ohz is the strength and conviction to stand up to social norms and act independently based on Hashem's will.*

constraints to a person's morality — even external pressure. If I am unconcerned about what others think and feel, I will bully them, criticize them, and offend them with impunity. My *azus panim*, my chutzpah, will lead me to sin and cause suffering to all those around me.

What distinguishes *ohz* from *azus panim*? The difference in how *ohz* manifests itself in people is based on its root. The Torah is called *ohz*, as it says in *Tehillim*:

ה׳ עֹז לְעַמּוֹ יִתֵּן.[268]

*Hashem gives His nation **ohz**.*

When our determination is rooted in the guidelines of the Torah, our morality and boundaries are held in check. When we act based on our own opinions and compulsions, we lead a life that is degraded, offensive, and damaging to others. In the case of the *eishes chayil*, she has *ohz* rather than *azus panim* because she is motivated to serve Hashem to the best of her ability.

The *eishes chayil* is also clothed in *hadar*, beauty. The Malbim explains that *hadar* is an external beauty that is noticeable to others.[269] Hashem is described as having:

כָּבוֹד וְהָדָר.[270]

Honor and Glory.

But *Mishlei* warns us:

אַל תִּתְהַדַּר לִפְנֵי מֶלֶךְ.[271]

Do not beautify yourself before the King.

---

268 *Tehillim* 29:11.
269 *Mishlei* 31:25.
270 *Yeshayah* 35:2.
271 *Mishlei* 25:6.

With respect to the laws of being happy on Sukkos, the Rambam warns that our service of Hashem must be motivated by a desire to serve Him.²⁷² If we do it for our own honor and self-aggrandizement, we are being תִּתְהַדָּר, beautifying ourselves, which is sinful and foolish.

The *eishes chayil* then has two traits — beauty and determination — that can be wonderful but are also spiritually dangerous if used incorrectly.

> The *eishes chayil* has two traits — beauty and determination — that can be wonderful but are also spiritually dangerous if used incorrectly.

The *pasuk* continues by telling us that the *eishes chayil* laughs. It uses the word וַתִּשְׂחַק, from the root שחק. *Schok* is yet another morally fraught behavior. In *Tehillim*, it describes how we will act with *schok* during the times of Mashiach:

>²⁷³ אָז יִמָּלֵא שְׂחוֹק פִּינוּ.
> Then our lips will be filled with laughter.

In contrast, the *mishnah* in *Pirkei Avos* states:

> שְׂחוֹק וְקַלּוּת רֹאשׁ, מַרְגִּילִין לְעֶרְוָה.²⁷⁴
> Laughter and frivolity habituates [a person] to promiscuity.

Laughter and frivolity, like *ohz* and *hadar*, determination and beauty, can ruin a person's eternal reward. They can lead to suffering and sin.

A Future Focus

How can the *eishes chayil* laugh, וַתִּשְׂחַק, have determination and beauty, and still be the ideal spiritual woman? How the *eishes chayil* navigates this balance is instructive.

There is a twofold answer to this paradox.

The *pasuk* describes the *ohz* and *hadar*, the strength and beauty, of

---

272   Rambam, *Mishneh Torah, Hilchos Lulav* 8:14.
273   *Tehillim* 126:2.
274   *Mishneh Avos* 3:13.

the *eishes chayil* as her *levush*, her clothing. When one looks at the *eishes chayil*, she seems beautiful and confident, self-assured and graceful. Externally, these are the qualities she projects, but they are only her externals. These qualities allow her to make important decisions even when they are not popular in her society. However, these qualities are not goals and priorities in and of themselves. Her strength and beauty function to allow her to serve Hashem.

The answer also lies in how the *eishes chayil* laughs and uses her character traits of beauty and determination. The Meiri explains that the *eishes chayil* does not get her enjoyment from the good of this world.[275] Instead, she focuses on her final days, the days in which she will receive her ultimate reward. This focus on her future allows her to have the necessary strength and conviction to do what is right. It allows her to find humor in difficult situations because she knows that a brighter future awaits her. It allows her to remain humble even though she is talented and beautiful and to prioritize what is important instead of focusing on superficialities.

Rebbetzin Chaya Shaina was the wife of Rav Elyashiv and the mother of ten children. For their first child's wedding, she bought herself a new dress to wear to walk her daughter down the aisle.[276] For each subsequent wedding, and then to the wedding of all of her grandchildren, she wore the same dress. She was the matriarch of a family devoted to Torah. One of her grandchildren recommended that it was well within her right to buy herself a new dress. Her response was that she saw no need to do so. Rebbetzin Elyashiv was more concerned about her spiritual goals than about what people would think.

> We can make our determination and beauty our clothing rather than our essence.

We are not expected to be Rebbetzin Elyashiv, but there is a point from the story to consider. We all have events at which we want to impress others. We may not be satisfied with having only one wedding

---

275   Meiri, *Mishlei* 31:25.
276   Naftali and Naomi Weinberger, *Rebbetzin Kanievsky*, p. 69.

outfit. However, we can all think about how much of a perfectionist we need to be when finding the dress or the sofa that we want. Every hour we spend on our *hadar*, our beauty, comes at the cost of doing something else. If we keep this value in mind and make decisions based on what is eternally important, we are making our determination and beauty our clothing rather than our essence.

The Midrash discusses a woman whose value system not only allowed her to make good choices about her future but also allowed her to survive tragedy and loss with her sense of self and her priorities intact.

Midrash – Elisheva

"Strength and dignity are her clothing."	עֹז וְהָדָר לְבוּשָׁהּ
This is Elisheva, daughter of Aminadav,	זוֹ אֱלִישֶׁבַע בַּת עַמִּינָדָב
who saw four celebrations	שֶׁרָאֲתָה אַרְבַּע שְׂמָחוֹת
[in one day]:	[בְּיוֹם אֶחָד]
her brother was the prince,	אָחִיהָ נָשִׂיא
her husband the high priest,	וּבַעְלָהּ כֹּהֵן גָּדוֹל
her husband's brother the king,	וַאֲחִי בַעְלָהּ מֶלֶךְ
and two of her sons were young priests.	וּשְׁנֵי בָנֶיהָ פִּרְחֵי כְהֻנָּה

Chazal point to one woman in *Tanach* who knew better than anyone else that the grandeur of this world is fleeting and superficial and that her focus should be on what is truly *ohz* and *hadar*, strong and beautiful: Elisheva, the wife of Aharon the High Priest.

The most glorious day of Elisheva's life should have come while the Jews were in the desert and had just finished erecting the Mishkan, the Tabernacle, on the first day of Nissan. No woman could have been happier than she on that day. Her husband, Aharon, was appointed as the High Priest who would perform the most elevated service in the Holy of Holies. He was dressed in the finest clothes made from gold thread and bedecked with precious stones. On that very same day, her brother,

Nachshon ben Aminadav, became the leader of the most powerful Jewish tribe, the tribe of Yehudah. Her brother-in-law, Moshe, was firmly established as the leader and teacher of the nation. Finally, according to the Midrash in *Mishlei*, she saw two of her sons become *Kohanim*, priests. Everyone in the nation would need her sons to celebrate births and atone for sins. She knew that her grandchildren and great-grandchildren would be accorded the honor of the *Kohanim* forever. On the first of Nissan, no woman had as much reason to celebrate as Elisheva did.

Midrash Mishlei is inconsistent with the account in the Torah. According to the Torah, on the first of Nissan, four — not two — of Elisheva's sons became *Kohanim*.[277] Also not mentioned in the Midrash is that during the festivities, tragedy struck her family. Two of her sons entered the Mishkan with *ketores*, incense, and were immediately burned by a divine fire.[278] Neither the distinguished clothing of her husband, nor the power of her brother-in-law, nor the royalty of her brother could save her two sons. This day of tremendous joy became a day of profound grief.

> Elisheva remained focused on what would make her happy in the final day. She continued to think about what mitzvos she could do in that moment.

Why the Midrash chooses Elisheva to represent this *pasuk* must be understood so that we can truly appreciate what it means for us. The Torah teaches us about Aharon HaKohen's reaction to this tragedy.

וַיִּדֹּם אַהֲרֹן.[279]

Aharon was silent.

He did not protest or celebrate. He accepted Hashem's judgment and continued the job that he had been assigned to do without wavering from his responsibilities.

---

277 *Vayikra* 8.
278 *Vayikra* 9.
279 *Vayikra* 10:3.

Elisheva had a different task. She was a passive observer to the events occurring. As an observer, she was getting joy from all her relatives. For any woman, this joy would have brought her to the greatest heights. At this moment of intense celebration, her world came crashing down. Any woman who would go from such great joy to such tragedy could be traumatized and shocked. It could take her years to recover — if she would ever recover at all. Somehow, Elisheva survived the trauma. How she did so is the lesson she is teaching us here.

The Midrash tells us that Elisheva saw the four celebrations. It does not tell us that she was swept away in their excitement or felt they changed her in any way. While her family's power and prestige changed her "status," these honors remained her *levush*, her clothing. Despite the external markers of success, Elisheva remained focused on what would make her happy in the final day. She continued to think about what mitzvos she could do, right then at that moment. Thus, when her sons died, she did not feel intense shame that her sons were publicly held up as sinners nor did she collapse from her loss. Instead, she continued to ask herself what Hashem wanted from her in that moment. She continued to have *ohz*, strength, to do what was right. Just as the nation learned from Aharon HaKohen's silence, they learned from Elisheva's way of bearing her pain and surviving it. She taught the nation that power and prestige were meaningless when faced with death.

Elisheva taught the nation how to bear pain and survive it.

Elisheva's strength of character was not lost with her. From then on, her children, the *Kohanim*, learned what it meant to have the character trait of *ohz*. According to the Maharal, the *Kohanim* became synonymous with the trait of *ohz*.[280] The Shem Mi'Shmuel elaborates that in the times of the Hellenist Greeks, it was the *Kohanim* who had the ability to fight them.[281] They had the character trait of *ohz* and could stand up to a nation that knew no boundaries and cared only

---

280 Maharal, *Chiddushei Aggados, Kiddushin* 70.
281 Shem MiShmuel, *Miketz* 678.

about themselves and their desires. The strength that Elisheva displayed was passed down as a family inheritance to help all the nation.

Where did Elisheva get this trait from? The *Zohar* tells us that her great-grandmother Tamar also had *ohz* when she went to meet Yehudah and bear his children.[282] Elisheva gained from her and then bequeathed her strength to her children.

Getting Practical: Priorities in Marriage

The *eishes chayil* and Elisheva taught Jewish women what is valued in this world and what is valued in the next. Most women don't mind getting a nice piece of jewelry or a nice outfit every now and then. Most of us would love to have our Shabbos table be as perfect as the one on the cover of a magazine. There are the right shoes, the right purses, the right belts for us, our kids, and our grandchildren. It takes a lot of shopping and planning to get it all right.

Aside from just what we own, what we eat, and what we wear, there is also the consideration of who knows us. Are we connected? Are we the woman people call to arrange meals for friends? Are we the president of our PTA? Are we famous or powerful? Is our life extraordinary in some way? What do people think of us? Do we feel inferior if we lead a quiet life of anonymity?

Do we feel inferior if we lead a quiet life of anonymity?

Clothing, jewelry, power, and fame are very tempting. They make us feel connected and important. They draw our attention and trap us into thinking that our lives will be miserable if we do not have "that one more thing" that is right over…over…over…there.

Elisheva comes and reminds us that the Italian shoes and the Coach bag are really just not worth it. Elisheva teaches us that possessions, power, and fame are not priorities that will ultimately bring us joy.

Joy will only come through a life well-lived. The *eishes chayil* lives this kind of life. She prioritizes how she uses her time not based on trivial

---

282 *Zohar, Acharei Mos* 278.

goals and what others will think of her but on what will ultimately give her the most happiness in the World to Come.

As wives and mothers, we are often confronted by the same challenge. What is true and what is false? How much time should I invest in decorating my house, buying clothes, or having influence on a school board or in my community? Where should I invest my energy even though everyone I know is doing something different?

The answer is to do a reality check and look at Elisheva; see what is important and what is not. We can ask ourselves if any given activity is worth our time or not. If this were the last day on earth, would I want to spend time on this activity?

When we have the strength to stand with our convictions, we learn from Elisheva that it is not only our world that is changed for the better. We give our children, grandchildren, and all future descendants the ability to withstand their own trials in their own lives.

> If this were the last day on earth, would I want to spend time on this activity?

The key to making enlightened choices is to develop our trait of *ohz* to help keep our spiritual priorities as our top goals. To do so we must tap into one thing that is called *ohz*: the Torah. The Torah is our anchor; it helps us remember what is important

and what is not. A woman cannot survive the daily challenges of life without reinforcing her spiritual supports. What these spiritual supports look like will differ for each person, but they must be there. Every woman needs to gain *ohz* from learning something new every day. We must ask Hashem for help and guidance in this endeavor every day. It is only through the *ohz* of the Torah that we can have true *ohz* and choose substance over style and thus face our future with a sense of joy and anticipation.

Summary

"Strength and dignity are her clothing." עוֹז וְהָדָר לְבוּשָׁהּ
Elisheva, the daughter of Aminadav אֱלִישֶׁבַע בַּת עַמִּינָדָב

From the Pasuk We Learn

The *eishes chayil*'s main priorities are the World to Come and doing Hashem's will. She projects strength and beauty so that she can make difficult decisions that may be unpopular but are the right ones. In this way, her last day will be one of joy as she accepts her eternal reward.

From the Midrash We Learn

In one day, Elisheva went from ultimate celebration to profound grief and loss. She survived this dramatic change by focusing on doing what was right in the moment. From her we learn that the *eishes chayil* makes choices by focusing on what is the next right thing to do. In this way, she makes spiritually motivated decisions rather than decisions intended to please bystanders.

Practical Steps

1. Set our day's schedule based on our priorities.
2. Consider our necessary shopping and budget our time to shop calmly so that we are neither stressed nor obsessive about finding the the right item.
3. At times of celebration, sadness, or grief ask what Hashem wants from us in that moment.
4. Make sure we have daily spiritual supports so that we keep our priorities in mind.

Questions

Self-Growth

1. What are my top three spiritual priorities? How can I set my daily schedule to reflect these priorities?
2. How can I minimize *azus panim?* How can I express my opinion and get my needs met without imposing my opinions and will on others? How should I respond when others disagree?
3. How can I increase my *ohz* and act based on my higher values even when others disagree?
4. How can I set a realistic time budget for shopping for *simchas*, the home, etc.?
5. How can I separate my externals (job, looks, family) from my self-perception?
6. When I am challenged, how do I focus on staying in the moment and doing the next right thing rather than living in the past or future?
7. Is there any way to bring more spirituality into my life to help me cope with life's challenges?

As Wives and Mothers

8. How can a future focus help me cope with the challenges of being a wife and mother?
9. How can I introduce spirituality to my children as a tool to help them get through challenges?

Teaching Our Daughters

10. How can I model good choices and help my daughter develop a spiritual focus in her life?
11. How can I help my daughter learn to focus on the next right choice rather than worry about the future?

CHAPTER 19

As a Woman of Intelligence (Communication)

פִּיהָ פָּתְחָה בְחָכְמָה וְתוֹרַת חֶסֶד עַל לְשׁוֹנָהּ.

*She opens her mouth with wisdom,
and the law of kindness is on her tongue.*

Peshat

So far, most of the focus on the *eishes chayil* has been about her work on behalf of her family and community. We have read about her self-focused work toward character development as well as her professional and personal accomplishments. We have read little about her relationships with those who are significant in her life. We know she is a talented woman who is devoted to her

As a Woman of Intelligence (Communication)   287

family and community. Still, how does the *eishes chayil* impact others in her life?

This *pasuk* gives us the formula for how to make a difference and influence others. It discusses how, when, and why the *eishes chayil* communicates and how that changes the world in which she lives. Each word in this *pasuk* is integral to understand this important skill of how to communicate with those we love.

The *pasuk* begins with the words:

פִּיהָ פָּתְחָה בְחָכְמָה.
She opens her mouth with wisdom.

The word פָּתְחָה, whose root means open, focuses our attention on the beginning of the *eishes chayil's* communication. It means both how she begins her speech each day when she awakens, and how she initiates conversation with others.

When a Jewish woman wakes up, she should say:

מוֹדָה אֲנִי לְפָנֶיךָ מֶלֶךְ חַי וְקַיָּם, שֶׁהֶחֱזַרְתָּ בִּי נִשְׁמָתִי בְּחֶמְלָה,
רַבָּה אֱמוּנָתֶךָ.[283]
*I am thankful before You, Living and Eternal King,
that You returned my soul with kindness, great is
Your faithfulness.*

Modeh Ani is an expression of thanks to G-d, recited upon awakening, for being alive.

This *tefillah* of *Modeh Ani* is what the *eishes chayil* has on her lips as she starts the day. Why is it considered intelligent to recite *Modeh Ani*? How is her recital different from someone else's? How is it wise?

The *pasuk* is telling us that the *eishes chayil* says this phrase purposefully, mindfully, and thoughtfully.[284] Most of us awaken with the same disturbing thought: "I did not get enough sleep last night." Our next thought is, "I do not have enough time to get everything done

---

283   *Siddur*, Morning Prayers.
284   *Meam Loez, Mishlei* 31:26.

today." We mumble *Modeh Ani* and rush into our day. This sense of lack and need carries into our day as we count all the things we are missing and what we will never accomplish. We fall asleep with the same litany on our lips as we review all that we did not do or get in our time awake. Our day is spent disconnected and in stress.

> Most of us awaken with the same disturbing thought: "I did not get enough sleep last night," followed by, "I do not have enough time to get everything done today."

Saying *Modeh Ani* with feeling takes a different approach. It recognizes that the day and all we have is a gift from Hashem. With Him in charge, there are no needs unfilled. When we wake up, we have everything we need; we are already blessed. Our day can only continue to receive more blessings. By opening her day with words of gratitude, the *eishes chayil* sets up her day so she will notice the good she receives and will be accompanied by a sense of gratitude all day long. Opening her day in this manner is a choice that is wise and made with *chochmah*.

Intelligent Speech

The words פִּיהָ פָּתְחָה בְחָכְמָה, she opens her mouth with wisdom, not only refer to the first words of the day but how and when the *eishes chayil* initiates conversation.[285] Some people chat to fill in the quiet space and awkwardness with others. If you have ever been around teenage girls, you might notice that there is a hum around them — many talk, hoping to be liked, and do not really listen to what the others are saying. Old friends can sit next to each other in amiable silence and enjoy the company with not a word exchanged. The *eishes chayil* thinks before she speaks so that what she says is said with intelligence rather than driven by insecurity. In these conversations, she tries to speak about ideas rather than people. Her conversations elevate others and stem from her wisdom rather than from a need to be seen and acknowledged.

---

285 *Metzudas Dovid, Mishlei* 31:26.

The *eishes chayil* is also thoughtful about the initial tone of a conversation.²⁸⁶ Sometimes, we need to communicate difficult information. We need to tell our daughter that we cannot afford for her to go to summer camp. We want to find out where our son is going with his friends. We were offended by an offhand comment our husband made. We need to communicate, and we do not know how the other person will respond. Starting a conversation that is meaningful requires *chochmah*, intelligence.

The conversations of the *eishes chayil* stem from her wisdom rather than from a need to be seen and acknowledged.

Our daughter just returned home. Do we call over to her in front of the whole family and tell her that the budget isn't there for camp? Do we tell our son that we do not like his friends and then ask him where he is going? Do we shame our husband when we are hurt and tell him he is an awful person? These reactions are reactive, not intelligent.

Eishes Chayil is asking us to have a different awareness. Nothing will happen if I do not have the conversation NOW. I can choose to start the conversation later, when my senses and propriety are not being overwhelmed by my emotions. How we choose to start conversations can impact how they will end. If the conversation begins with blaming and contempt, then it will continue that way. Both sides will wound each other, and the small problems will soon be insurmountable. If the other person is not in the right frame of mind, it can wait. We can wait for a private moment after the other person has calmed down to engage him in conversation.

My husband and I once had to have a difficult conversation with one of our children. We knew that in our house, we would never be able to have a calm and reasonable talk. We invited the then-eight-year-old out to lunch with us. After a leisurely lunch, and frequent affirmations that we understood his concerns, we were able to address a thorny issue that was causing him problems.

---

286 Ibid.

When a conversation starts with confrontation, it is very hard to get the conversation to skip back to neutral tones. A conversation that starts confrontationally will only escalate. We may not get what we want if we begin a conversation with thoughtfulness, but we are more likely to at least end the conversation with our integrity intact.

The *chochmah*, the intelligence, mentioned in the first phrase is referring to more than just the techniques for communication. The *eishes chayil*'s speech is full of common sense and the spiritual wisdom of the Torah.[287] Every person, the *eishes chayil* included, spends most of the day engaged in mundane activities, whether in a professional or personal capacity. The *eishes chayil* elevates her speech in all areas by connecting what she does with a Torah thought even if she does not explain to others the source of her comments. In this way, even her ordinary activities allow her to connect to Hashem as she actively discusses and thinks about spiritual topics throughout her day.

Toras Chessed

The second half of the *pasuk* states that the *eishes chayil* has:

תּוֹרַת חֶסֶד עַל לְשׁוֹנָהּ.

A law of kindness is on her tongue.

What is a *Toras chessed*? What is a law of kindness? Could there be a Torah that is not kind?[288]

The *eishes chayil* understands that her main purpose in life is to serve Hashem. One of the pillars of Hashem's service is the performance of *chessed*. Doing kindness for others is her passion. Her day is devoted to elevating herself through her acts of service, and she lives, breathes, and thinks *chessed*. This all-consuming focus is her essence and becomes the

---

287 *Ohr HaChochmah*, Rav Uri Shraga Feivel Dubienka, quoted in *Sefer Eishes Chayil*, 233.
288 *Talmud Bavli, Sukkah* 49b.

topic of her conversations.²⁸⁹ Through her love of *chessed*, she teaches others to do *chessed* and encourages them in their righteous activities.

The *eishes chayil*'s communication with others is also a *chessed*. When the *eishes chayil* awakens, she starts her day with words of gratitude. She does not keep this philosophy to herself; rather, she shares this perspective with her family and encourages them to also find reasons to thank Hashem.²⁹⁰ This education to see life in a more spiritual way is her *Toras chessed* — her Torah of kindness — because through her teaching of spiritual ideas, she elevates others.

> The *eishes chayil* lives, breathes, and thinks *chessed*. This all-consuming focus is her essence and becomes the topic of her conversations.

A friend of mine once showed me a box that she kept on her dining room table. Whenever anyone in the family got something that he really appreciated, he wrote a thank-you note to Hashem. The box was full of reminders of Hashem's care for them. Another friend encouraged her family to keep a gratitude journal in which they recorded good things that happened to them. Another went around the table at dinner and asked each child to share a positive event from their day for which they could be grateful. These exercises that developed their family's joy were *Toras chessed*.

The *eishes chayil* also uses her speech to further her mission of *chessed* and *tzedakah*.²⁹¹ She calls a widow to wish her a good Shabbos, she finds out how she can do *bikur cholim*, she inquires about a family's needs in order to give *tzedakah*. While other women may like to chat about meaningless subjects, she uses her speech to do *chessed*.

This *pasuk* teaches us how to use our speech. The impact of our speech and what we can accomplish with it can be learned from the heroine of the Midrash, Serach bas Asher.

---

289   *Meam Loez, Mishlei* 31:26.
290   Ibid.
291   Ibid.

Midrash – Serach bas Asher

"She opens her mouth with wisdom."	פִּיהָ פָּתְחָה בְחָכְמָה
This is the woman of intelligence	זוֹ אִשָּׁה חֲכָמָה
who said, "Listen, listen,	שֶׁאָמְרָה "שִׁמְעוּ שִׁמְעוּ
please say to Yoav,	אִמְרוּ נָא אֶל יוֹאָב
come here and I will speak to you"	קְרַב עַד הֵנָּה וַאֲדַבְּרָה אֵלֶיךָ"
(Shmuel II 20:16).	(ש״ב כ:טז)
She saved the city with her intelligence.	שֶׁהִצִּילָה אֶת הָעִיר בְּחָכְמָתָהּ
This was Serach the daughter of Asher.	וְזוֹ הָיְתָה שֶׂרַח בַּת אָשֵׁר

The Midrash recounts a fascinating story about this extraordinary woman to illustrate the power of speech.

The story comes from the end of the Book of Shmuel that teaches about the reign of Dovid HaMelech. Toward the end of Dovid's life, his charismatic son Avshalom launched a full-fledged coup to overtake his kingdom.[292] The insurrection was put down by Dovid and his general Yoav in a tragic military campaign. On his return from battle, Dovid was confronted by a man named Sheva ben Bichri who cursed him and his dynastic kingdom. Sheva ben Bichri fled to the city of Avel to gather supporters and further undermine the fragile monarchy of Dovid.[293]

Dovid recognized that Sheva ben Bichri was a threat who could not be ignored.[294] He sent his general, Yoav, to arrest and kill Sheva ben Bichri for treason. Yoav besieged the city where Sheva had barricaded himself. Indeed, Yoav was ready to annihilate the city for harboring a traitor.

Saving a City

It is at this moment the Midrash recalls the brave words of the smart woman, who the Midrash identifies as Serach bas Asher, who saved both her city and the legacy of Dovid.

---

292 *Shmuel II*, chapters 16–19.
293 *Shmuel II*, chapter 20.
294 *Shmuel II* 20:6, Radak.

Serach came to the city walls and began her speech in a manner that diffused the tensions.

She asked, "Are you Yoav?" She did not ask his name because she forgot it. She was asking, "Aren't you Yoav who has a reputation for being a Torah scholar?"

She continued with humility, "Will you listen to the words of your maid?"

Yoav, who was now acknowledged to be a Torah scholar, agreed to engage in conversation with a humble woman.

Serach asked, "Does it not say in the Torah that before an army conquers a city, the army must first make overtures of peace? I represent the people of Avel who are faithful to Dovid and to the Torah."

> Serach maintained her composure and negotiated her safety with forethought. She communicated so that her audience would be available to listen.

Yoav, hearing Serach's argument, replied in the same dispassionate and considerate manner. He explained that Sheva ben Bichri, who was taking refuge in the city, was a traitor. As a result, Sheva ben Bichri and anyone who helped him were deserving of death.

Serach told Yoav that she would arrange for Sheva's head to be tossed over the wall to resolve the conflict.

Now Serach had to work through another piece of delicate negotiations. The residents of the city of Avel were from Binyamin; they were kinsmen with Sheva and were also from the tribe of Shaul, the king whom Dovid replaced as monarch. Their loyalty should lie with their tribe of Binyamin and not with Dovid. How would she convince them to go against their instinct and kill their relative rather than defend him and his honor? The *Navi* reports:

וַתָּבוֹא הָאִשָּׁה אֶל כָּל הָעָם בְּחָכְמָתָהּ. [295]
And the woman came to all the nation in her wisdom.

Serach marshalled effective halachic arguments to convince the population to comply with the request of the sieging army. In fact,

---

[295] *Shmuel II* 20:22.

this episode is the basis for other *halachos* derived from it regarding when it is permissible to sacrifice one named person to protect a group.[296] The city agreed to kill Sheva and throw his head to Yoav and his army, at which point Yoav returned to Yerushalayim and left the city of Avel in peace.

In this story, despite grave odds, Serach maintained her composure and negotiated her safety by entering negotiations with both Yoav and the city of Avel with forethought. She checked that both were ready to listen and marshalled ideas routed in Torah to convince the other party to agree to her demands. She used logic and clear thinking to communicate in a manner that would make her audience available for listening.

A Gentle Touch

This story was the last of a series in which Serach was involved where she used her communication skills to help others.

The first time the Midrash includes Serach in a story in Tanach is during her early life as a granddaughter of Yaakov. Then too, she used both questioning to dissipate tension and her awareness of the listeners' needs to communicate in a way that accomplished her goals.[297]

Yosef was sold as a slave by his ten older brothers. He eventually ended up in Egypt where, after a series of miracles, he became the viceroy. After twenty-two years, Yosef revealed to his brothers who he was. During this intervening period, Yaakov had mourned for Yosef and could not be consoled from his loss. He had no inkling that his beloved son was alive so he spent his days in mourning for him.

The brothers, after learning of Yosef's survival and rise to power, needed to tell Yaakov of this wonderful news. They feared that the shock of the news, even if it was good, would be so powerful that it would kill him. They asked Serach the daughter of Asher, the granddaughter of Yaakov, to break the news to him. The Midrash relates

---

296 *Talmud Bavli, Sanhedrin* 72b.
297 *Bereishis Rabbah* 94:9.

that while Yaakov was standing in prayer, Serach came over to him and gently asked, "Is Yosef in Mitzrayim? Are his children Menashe and Ephraim?"[298] By using a gentle question, Serach gave Yaakov the time to process the information so he was not overwhelmed by it. Yaakov's joy and gratitude was so intense that he blessed Serach that she should enter Gan Eden alive. For this reason, she was alive hundreds of years later and used a similar tactic of questioning to help save a whole city.

> By using a gentle question, Serach gave Yaakov the time to process the information so he was not overwhelmed by it.

Revealing Secrets

The Midrash also lists two other episodes where Serach used her wisdom to help her people. Serach lived in Egypt during the time of slavery there.

After having fled to Midyan at the age of twenty, Moshe returned as an eighty-year-old and declared to the nation that he would redeem them from slavery.[299] The Jews did not know whether to believe him or not. Thirty years before, men from the tribe of Ephraim, the son of Yosef, had declared it was time to ascend to Eretz Yisroel and had been killed. The nation knew that Yaakov had given a sign to his children to indicate who the savior would be, but they did not know what it was. There were few alive who would have heard Yaakov's sign. Most of the survivors who had heard from Yaakov were descendants of Yosef, and the nation did not trust them since the tribe had miscalculated leaving Egypt thirty years earlier and had been met with destruction. The nation came to Serach bas Asher, who inquired what the new savior had said. She confirmed that the phrase Moshe used was indeed the words that Yaakov had promised would be spoken by the legitimate savior.

A year later, the Jews were preparing to leave Egypt. That night, the Jews requested gold, silver, and clothing from their Egyptian

---

298 *Midrash Gadol, Bereishis* 48:26.
299 *Pirkei D'Rabi Eliezer, Bereishis* 49.

neighbors. Only Moshe searched for his own treasure: Yosef had made his family swear that his bones would be brought for burial to the Land of Israel from their burial spot in Egypt.[300] The only problem was that nobody knew where those bones were. After much searching, Moshe sought help from Serach, who had proven to be so trustworthy and knowledgeable when he had arrived. She told him where to find Yosef's bones so that the Jews could fulfill their promise.

While these stories are not mentioned in the Midrash on *Eishes Chayil*, they give us a fuller picture of Serach's life. While in Egypt, Serach had knowledge entrusted to her by her family. She did not share that knowledge until the right time. Then she exemplified פָּתְחָה בְחָכְמָה — she opened her mouth intelligently, at the right time when it was appropriate. With Yaakov and with Yoav, she also initiated the conversation intelligently. She spoke with *Toras chessed* — in a manner that recognized the other's needs — and communicated her care and respect.

Getting Practical: Communication in Marriage

Communication is one of the most fundamental aspects of a peaceful and positive relationship. What is said and how it is said can build or destroy a relationship. So much has been written about good communication that it could — and does — fill bookshelves in the library. This *pasuk* contains much of that wisdom, encapsulated in a few words.

Starting a Conversation

The *eishes chayil* and Serach taught us that how we begin a conversation is just as important as what we have to say. A famous researcher found he could predict the outcome of a discussion between a husband and a wife by watching its first three minutes. Those conversations that

---

300   *Talmud Bavli, Sotah* 13a.

began with criticism or sarcasm ended poorly. Those that began with respect ended with the couple feeling closer.

- "I was upset today, is now a good time to talk?" This would be an example of a softer start to a conversation.
- "What's the matter with you, how could you do that?" This would be an opening to a conversation that would go downhill quickly.

One of the differences between a soft start and a harsh start is the difference between stating our needs and criticizing.

We need to train ourselves to state our needs rather than criticize. When we state our needs, we are explaining what we need simply and nonjudgmentally. When we criticize, we are attacking the other in a personal way.

- "I asked that you call when you would be late." This states the issue at hand without judgment.
- "You are always so inconsiderate and my whole evening was ruined because of you." This is a criticism.

> Criticism and its evil brother, sarcasm, can destroy even the best relationships.

Criticism and its evil brother, sarcasm, can destroy even the best relationships. The other person gets defensive and feels unsafe, and this undermines the goal of the conversation.

When our emotions run high, it helps to communicate using a simple four-part formula to keep the beginning of the communication positive and productive and to avoid blaming and criticizing. The four parts are:

1. Observation
2. Feeling
3. Need
4. Request

Observation

First, we state what we see or have experienced without embellishing or judging.

"I'm noticing you are not looking at me when I talk." This is an observation.

Compare this to, "How could you look away from me? That is so rude." This is judgmental.

Feeling

Next, we state either our feelings or make a guess about what the other person is feeling to get feedback and determine if we are correct.

"I'm feeling disconnected." This lets the other person know how his behavior is impacting us.

"Are you feeling bored?" This gives us the chance to understand our partner and what he is experiencing.

Need

Next, we state what we need at the moment. Stating a need allows us to let the other person know what we feel we are missing.

"I need companionship now. I need to feel connected."

The need is presented as a truth that is independent of the other person. We are not making him responsible for the fact that we have needs but are acknowledging that our needs exist.

Request

The fourth step, the request, allows us to ask the other person to help us with our need but also gives him a chance to say no without being manipulated or coerced.

"Can you look at me while we talk now and not look at your text messages?"

Our husband may say "no" because he is in the middle of work, or he may say "yes" and turn his attention to us.

No matter the other person's response, we have done the best we could and have been assertive without damaging the other person or diminishing ourselves. This kind of conversation is carried out with the intelligence that the *eishes chayil* and Serach have taught us.

Tone

Serach also taught us that the tone of a conversation makes a big difference. A slight change in intonation can communicate volumes. A harsh tone, a grimace, or a raised voice conveys as much negativity as a nasty word. It is kinder and gentler to come closer, speak gently, and use a pleasant tone.

The Content of Our Speech

There are a number of other lessons contained in this *pasuk*.

Our speech reflects who we are. The *eishes chayil* and Serach held the trust of their family and friends during crucial moments because of how they talked. If we want to be trusted and valued, we must do the same. We need to think of enlightened ideas to share and keep our focus on spiritual and intellectual ideas rather than on people or things.

Is talking about a friend helpful or gossip? As a general rule, if we need to talk about another person, we should talk to her directly.

Sometimes, we might think we need to talk about people and their lives to help them. Often times, these conversations are, in effect, just gossip without the guilt. Serach taught us that just because we know information does not mean we need to share it with others.

Gossip vs. Concern

Sometimes, it is very hard to make this call. We know a young woman who is looking to get married. Is talking about her with a friend helpful or gossip? Another friend seems stressed and harsh with her children. Should I talk to another friend about it? As a general rule, if we need to talk about a person, we should talk to her directly. If we need to talk to a third party, these conversations should not be spur-of-the-moment but should be planned and thought through.

I was once at a dinner where I saw a woman flitting from table to table chatting about a tragedy in the community asking people for advice and help. Watching the interactions, I felt like a mirror had been shone on my own behavior. How often had I done the same? The dinner was a public affair and was not the appropriate time or place. It cheapened the help she was trying to organize. If we need to find out more information, we need to schedule a meeting in a private place so that we are not tempted to gossip and abuse the situation to make ourself feel important.

Flattery vs. Praise

How did the *eishes chayil* encourage others to do *chessed*? How did Serach convince Yoav and her townspeople to follow her plan? They both used their speech to praise the other person, which influenced the decisions that were made. This recognition is different from flattery.

> Instead of saying, "You are such a good daughter; I love you," describe what is prompting the compliment.

Flattery has an ulterior motive that, while it may make the other person feel good about himself, does not help make him a better person. In contrast, sincere, concrete praise helps the other person see his strengths and enables him to be able to use them in the future. The goal of flattery is a focus on "me" and may be exaggerated, while praise is true and is focused on the other person.

People improve when their good qualities are genuinely noticed. To be sincere and impactful, praise must be specific and outline the good results. Instead of saying, "You are such a good daughter; I love you," we can describe what is prompting the compliment.

"You helped me prepare for Shabbos, and I got to go to sleep before two in the morning! I was well rested today. Thank you!"

Specific praise helps the recipient know exactly what she can keep doing, and it encourages her when her efforts are noticed. This is the *Toras chessed* of the *eishes chayil* and Serach that helps promote peace, mitzvos, and *chessed*.

The *eishes chayil* and Serach taught Jewish women the power of communication. When we communicate with wisdom rather than emotion, we change worlds. In the case of Serach, she saved her city from death and helped herald the Jewish nation to freedom. Communication requires that we be in the right frame of mind with a spiritual awareness that comes from using our speech to thank Hashem and to discuss His Torah. Like Serach, we need to be sensitive to how the recipient will hear our words so that what we say can be heard. When we do so, we are guided to speak in ways that can change the world.

Summary

"She opens her mouth with wisdom."   פִּיהָ פָּתְחָה בְחָכְמָה
Serach, the daughter of Asher   סֶרַח בַּת אָשֵׁר

From the Pasuk We Learn

The *eishes chayil* uses her speech to elevate her life and the lives of others. She begins her day with gratitude and begins her conversations purposefully, with meaningful conversation. She tries to save difficult conversations for when she is calm and the other person is receptive, and she speaks with a gentle tone. Her speech helps others, and she teaches others to do *chessed* using her speech.

From the Midrash We Learn

Serach bas Asher used her speech to help save herself and others. She negotiated peace between her city and Yoav by being humble, logical, and respectful. She broke emotionally charged news to Yaakov Avinu using gentle communication. She also only shared confidential information at the right time with the right people to help the Jewish People recognize their salvation. From Serach, we learn how to navigate difficult and potentially confrontational conversations, how to communicate difficult news, and how to be trustworthy and discreet with confidential information.

Practical Steps

1. Say *Modeh Ani* mindfully, recognizing that no matter how much we accomplish during the day, everything we have is a gift from Hashem. When we wake up, we have everything we need; we are already blessed. Our day can only continue to receive more blessings.
2. Notice the good that comes our way all day long and express gratitude for it.
3. Be comfortable with amiable silence. Initiate conversation to communicate ideas rather than to speak about people.

4. When we need to communicate difficult information, check that we are emotionally calm, that the setting is appropriately private, and that the listener is available and receptive to listening. Use nonconfrontational language to increase the chances of a successful conversation and to diffuse tension.
5. Base our ideas and conversations on the spiritual wisdom of the Torah even when we don't explicitly share the source.
6. Share our passion for *chessed* or another mitzvah with others to involve them. Keep a family journal, a box with notes, or just share our experiences at the dinner table.
7. Use our speech to uplift and help others.
8. When having to share difficult news, do so gently and with sensitivity to minimize shock and to help the listener process the information rather than be overwhelmed by it.
9. State our needs rather than criticizing, catastrophizing, or attacking the other person's personality. State the issue without judgment.
10. To communicate our needs:

    A. State observations.
    B. Describe our own feelings or try to verify the other person's feelings.
    C. Describe our needs.
    D. Make a request that allows the other person to say no.

11. Check our body language and tone during a conversation. It is kinder and gentler to come closer to the other person, speak gently, and use a pleasant tone.
12. Be trustworthy with confidences. Unless we are told we can share information, we should not pass along information or news to others.
13. Schedule conversations that are about other people so that we are less likely to gossip, and the conversation will be productive and goal driven.
14. Use speech to build others' confidence in themselves. Use concrete praise that is specific and outlines the positive results.

Questions

Self-Growth

1. How do I develop my sense of gratitude during the day for my life and everything I have, as described in *Modeh Ani*?
2. How do I make my conversations with others meaningful?
3. How would a real conversation sound — using positive communication techniques — with coworkers and family members about a sensitive or conflictual topic? (Ideas to include: gentle starters, complaints not criticism, stating needs, feelings, requests)
4. What are the emotional, physical, and spiritual cues that I am ready to communicate successfully?
5. What would a conversation sound like that is infused with more Torah-based ideas but is not stilted and preachy?
6. How can I teach and encourage others to do *chessed*?
7. What are some ways to use speech to do *chessed*?
8. How do I safeguard my communication used to do *chessed* from turning into gossip?
9. What would praise versus flattery sound like with friends, colleagues, or family?
10. How can I remind myself not to spread news about other people when I am sharing about my day with friends?

As Wives and Mothers

11. What would quality communication (gentle starters, complaints not criticism, stating needs, feelings, requests) sound like in my conversations with my husband?
12. Think of a scenario that could lead to harsh conversations, and practice the conversation with a gentle start and then with a harsh start.

13. Taking both my husband's schedule and my schedule into account, what timing would work well for a difficult conversation?
14. Practice giving my husband and children sincere and concrete praise that encourages future growth.
15. How do I communicate with my children when I am frustrated and tired? What are some strategies to lower the volume and soften the tone of my parenting?
16. How do I respond to my children when they are highly critical and they are communicating in a difficult and challenging way?
17. How can I preserve the confidentiality of my conversations with individual children, or my husband, within the family? What information can I share about my family with other family members? With others?

Teaching Our Daughters

18. How do I help my daughter learn positive communication strategies? How and when should I respond when the communication is negative?
19. How can I help my daughter want to do *chessed,* and how do I encourage her to do so?
20. How can I help my daughter feel more gratitude, and less entitlement and resentment, during her day?
21. How can I help my daughter learn to maintain the confidentiality of others without discouraging her from sharing openly about her day?

CHAPTER 20

As a Mother (Involvement)

צוֹפִיָּה הֲלִיכוֹת בֵּיתָהּ וְלֶחֶם עַצְלוּת לֹא תֹאכֵל.

She monitors the ways of her household and does not eat the bread of laziness.

Peshat

This *pasuk* ends the section of the poem that talks about the many roles of the *eishes chayil*: she is a mother, a homemaker, a wife, a professional, and a woman with relationships with her friends and community. The *pasuk* adds an important dimension to her role as a mother and a wife. The *Meam Loez* points out that there comes a time for every woman when she can no longer participate in the physical activities that were the staple of her life as a young woman.[301] Eventually,

---

301 *Meam Loez, Mishlei* 31:27.

a woman grows older, tires, and becomes limited in what she can physically do for others. This *pasuk* teaches us how the *eishes chayil* remains involved in directing and nurturing her family even when her hands-on contributions are more limited. It is the transformation of a mother into a matriarch.

The *pasuk* begins that the *eishes chayil* is *tzophiah* — she monitors — the ways of her house. The word *tzophiah* has two different implications: It is related to the word מִצְפֶּה, an overlook. To be מִצְפֶּה is to oversee. The *eishes chayil* oversees the ways of her household. This is a different role than we have seen before.

This *pasuk* discusses the transformation of a mother into a matriarch.

In the earlier *pasuk*, וַתִּתֵּן טֶרֶף לְבֵיתָהּ — *She gives food to her home*, we are told that the *eishes chayil* made lunches. In לֹא תִירָא לְבֵיתָהּ מִשָּׁלֶג — *She is not afraid of snow for her house*, the *pasuk* is telling us that she bought clothing.

The previous *pesukim* described a woman who was very active and busy. In contrast, in this *pasuk*, the *eishes chayil* is passive. She is keeping track of what her family is doing and monitoring their *halichos*, their comings and goings, their priorities, and their behavior.[302]

The root of *tzophia*, from the root צפה, is also used in connection with prophecy. Prophecy, or, better defined, communication with G-d, happens when an individual is spiritually connected and has a deep and meaningful relationship with Hashem. By overseeing her family, the *eishes chayil* is creating an environment where her household is spiritually elevated and will be worthy of prophecy.[303]

The role described in this *pasuk* begins with marriage and never ends, no matter how old one's children are. A wife and mother can always provide input and guidance for her family. For this reason, this role is the last one mentioned and includes all the other roles listed.

---

302 Ralbag, *Mishlei* 31:27.
303 Rabbi Eliyahu HaKohen of Izmir, *Midrash Eliyahu*, quoted in *Sefer Eishes Chayil*, p. 249.

Involvement vs. Enmeshment

The *eishes chayil* is encouraged to oversee her household, but this involvement must be well defined. No one appreciates the mother-in-law who is always watching and notices every mistake we make and points it out. A busybody is unpleasant to be around; a busybody is not a matriarch.

The *eishes chayil* is monitoring very specific attributes in her children; she does not become nosy and overinvolved. Rashi explains that the *eishes chayil* focuses on the traits of *tznius* and *emes*, modesty and truth.[304] Modesty means that she watches to see that her children's goals are privacy and spirituality rather than publicity and honor. *Emes*, truth, means that she wants to make sure that her children are authentic and that what they do and what they say reflect who they truly are. Without honesty and modesty, a person's spiritual life becomes empty, people-driven, and superficial. Modesty and honesty lead to greatness and allow for sincerity and an authentic connection to Hashem.

> Without honesty and modesty, a person's spiritual life becomes empty, people-driven, and superficial.

Being *tzophiah*, being involved with growing children and adult children, requires perseverance and wisdom. One cannot retire from the role of being a mother. The second half of the *pasuk* teaches how a woman can stay involved in a positive and energetic way without becoming resentful and anxious.

The Bread of Laziness

The *pasuk* ends with the phrase:

לֶחֶם עַצְלוּת לֹא תֹאכֵל.

She does not eat the bread of laziness.

---

304 Rashi, *Mishlei* 31:27.

As a Mother (Involvement)

This implies that eating the bread of laziness would inhibit a woman from being a proper observer of her family's direction. לֶחֶם עַצְלוּת, bread of laziness, can have multiple meanings and applications to this role:

- "Bread of laziness" can be defined as bread that is attained through laziness.[305] The *eishes chayil* is averse to receiving pleasure from the work of others when she could have done the work herself. Eating another's bread is lazy if a woman could have made the bread herself. The *eishes chayil*, on principle, will not use the work of others unnecessarily so as not to become lazy. Doing for herself rather than accepting unnecessary help keeps her young and active.

> The *eishes chayil* does for herself rather than accepting unnecessary help from others.

- Another implication of the "bread of laziness" is that the meal is eaten with laziness.[306] At this point in her life, the *eishes chayil* has many options as to how to spend her free time. She could indulge her time eating elaborate meals, shopping, or preparing luxurious food. She chooses not to do either so that she can use that time in a more worthwhile manner.

This attitude to the meal, according to the *Midrash Eliyahu*, leads to a healthy woman.[307] The Rambam writes:

אֲכִילָה גַּסָּה לְגוּף כָּל אָדָם כְּמוֹ סַם הַמָּוֶת
וְהוּא עִקָּר לְכָל הַחוֹלָאִים.[308]

Overeating is like poison to anyone's body.
It is the main source of all illness.

---

305 Rav Moshe Dovid Vally, *Mishlei* 31:26.
306 *Metzudas Dovid*, ibid.
307 Rabbi Eliyahu HaKohen of Izmir, *Midrash Eliyahu*, quoted in *Sefer Eishes Chayil*, p. 253.
308 Rambam, *Mishneh Torah, Hilchos Deos* 4:15.

Eating and a preoccupation with food have a steep price, both physically and spiritually. The *eishes chayil* avoids falling into this trap by keeping herself productive and helping others whenever the need arises.

Staying Energetic

As I mentioned in the dedication at the start of this book, my grandmother exemplified this trait. When she was in her nineties, she told me that a woman should reinvent herself every decade. She was sixty-seven years old when my grandfather died, and she had never driven a car. She took driving lessons, learned to drive, and got her license for the first time at the age of sixty-nine. In her seventies, she traveled to Israel to volunteer. In her eighties and into her nineties, she became the president of her sisterhood chapter and became a Hebrew tutor. She kept learning and traveling as long as she could. Her desire to do for herself and to remain vital gave her the energy to learn and do more in her eighties than most women do in their fifties.

The character trait that is being highlighted at the end of all the descriptions of the *eishes chayil*'s numerous positive qualities is her intellectual and emotional engagement with her family. She uses her resources to help shepherd her family at a time when she could relax and enjoy herself. She chooses not to be lazy; she focuses on qualities such as modesty and honesty and encourages their growth in herself and in her family.

Spiritual greatness depends on the two ideas highlighted in this *pasuk*.

The first is vigilance. Growth and spiritual connection are not something that are achieved like a degree from school. They need to be constantly nurtured and monitored.

There is a famous *mashal*, a parable, that compares life to a descending escalator. Whoever stands on that escalator continually needs to be walking up to get closer to the higher floor. In life, we are either actively connecting to Hashem, or we are choosing to disconnect from Him. The *eishes chayil* monitors the spirituality of herself and her family to avoid entropy and its ensuing problems.

The second trait needed for spiritual greatness is persistence. Every day is a new opportunity with new choices and new challenges. At times, we may get tired of the constant work, and we may want to give up. The key is to value the hard work for its own sake and to choose to always do for ourselves what we can. This will help us maintain our energy and enthusiasm to continue even when it is hard or when others offer us a break.

Growth and spiritual connection are not things that are achieved like a earning a degree in school. They need to be constantly nurtured and monitored.

Midrash – Ovadiah's Wife

"She monitors the ways of her house."	צוֹפִיָּה הֲלִיכוֹת בֵּיתָהּ
This is the wife of Ovadiah	זוֹ אִשְׁתּוֹ שֶׁל עוֹבַדְיָה
who saved her sons	שֶׁהִצִּילָה בָּנֶיהָ
and they did not serve idols with Achav	וְלֹא עָבְדוּ ע"ז עִם אַחְאָב

The Midrash discusses one woman whose efforts and advocacy for her children saved them physically and spiritually.

Ovadiah, whose wife is the focus of this Midrash, was a wealthy, righteous man who lived during the reign of King Achav and Queen Izevel, the rulers of the Kingdom of Yisroel a number of generations after it had split from the Kingdom of Yehudah. Passionate and sadistic, both Achav and his wife Izevel tormented those who disagreed with their corrupt ways. Ovadiah worked for this evil couple while still maintaining his own spiritual greatness as a prophet of Hashem.[309]

Izevel hated all who clung to a monotheistic faith and was hunting one hundred righteous prophets who lived in her kingdom. In an act of self-sacrifice, Ovadiah gathered these beleaguered souls into a cave and

---

309   *Melachim I* 18:3, *Talmud Bavli, Sanhedrin* 39b.

provided them with food and shelter.[310] His vast funds soon ran out, and he was forced to accept a loan from a corrupt businessman named Yehoram, the son of Achav, at an exorbitant interest rate.[311] Ovadiah agreed to the terms but died unable to pay back the loan, leaving behind two sons and a wife. With no compassion for a heartbroken widow, Yehoram demanded that Ovadiah's two sons become his slaves to pay off his debt.[312]

The *Navi* recounts how Ovadiah's righteous wife turned to Elisha, a famous prophet, for help.[313] Elisha informed her that he would perform a miracle with a small jug of oil that was the only item of value left in the home and instructed her to borrow vessels that could hold oil. The vessels were borrowed, and they closed the door to her home so the miracle would remain private. Ovadiah's wife began to pour oil, filling one vessel and then another. Her sons ran to her with all the empty vessels in the home, and soon every jug became filled with valuable oil. Ovadiah's wife received permission to sell this miraculous oil to pay off her debts. She and her children continued to live righteous lives free from the threat of Yehoram and his evil family.

Ovadiah's wife, as portrayed by the *Navi*, was the epitome of this *pasuk*. Clearly, she protected her children, advocated for them, and saved them from a life of slavery. The Midrash, though, adds a few explanatory words to the *pasuk* that seem extraneous to our story and were not mentioned in the text of the story. The Midrash adds that had Ovadiah's wife not intervened, her children would have worshiped idols.

The Midrash is emphasizing that Ovadiah's wife also saved her children spiritually. Ovadiah's wife did not want her children to live with idolaters and be influenced by them. The Midrash is pointing out that without their mother's intervention, Ovadiah's G-d-fearing sons would

---

310   *Melachim I*, 18:4.
311   *Shemos Rabbah* 31:3.
312   Rashi, *Melachim II*, 4:1.
313   *Melachim II*, 4:1–7.

have begun to serve idols because they could not have helped but be influenced by their surroundings. Through her involvement and supervision, Ovadiah's wife helped her children remain true to their heritage and continue the legacy of her husband who sacrificed his time and energy in the service of Hashem.

> Without their mother's intervention, Ovadiah's G-d-fearing sons would surely have been influenced by their surroundings.

Getting Practical: Involvement in Marriage

The *pasuk* and the Midrash are emphasizing that a mother must be concerned with her children's physical, emotional, and spiritual safety. Physically, we must check on our children's diets, sleep patterns, and exercise. Emotionally, we need to concern ourselves with how our children are feeling and how they connect with others. If we limit our concerns to these areas, however, we are robbing our children of help in the area that we can best help them.

Rashi says that our primary concern should be to look after our children's spiritual health, namely their modesty and honesty. Similarly, the Midrash teaches us that we must be concerned about our children's spiritual worlds.

How do we monitor an internal state such as spirituality? How do we guide our children to a life devoted to truth and marked by modesty?

The Midrash informs us that our role in monitoring our children's spirituality is to monitor our children's influences. Ensuring that our children are in a positive environment is the main area in which we can advocate for them. Who they learn from will shape their worldview; what they hear will shape what they believe. We may not be able to protect them from all problems, but when we know what they are experiencing, we can help support them in overcoming their challenges.

Of course, there is a boundary between overseeing and hovering. We must be careful how we intervene and advocate so that we don't handicap our children's growth and independence.

Helpful Supervision

As mothers, we are always looking to put ourselves out of business. We want our children to begin to function independently without needing our involvement. We cringe at the image of the twenty-five-year-old living in the basement with his mother still doing the laundry, asking him where he is going, and helping him make all his decisions.

Rashi on this *pasuk*, as well as the Midrash, give us helpful guidelines for our involvement. Rashi tells us that a mother should look at *how* a child is acting with honesty and modesty. He does not say that a mother can force her child to act with modesty and honesty. Rather, she should notice what is going on in her home regarding these specific characteristics. The Midrash does not tell us that Ovadiah's wife intervened for every episode in her children's lives or that she limited their interactions with everyone. When they were clearly in spiritual and physical danger, she became fully involved.

A mother should notice what is going on, not force it to go the ways she wants.

Other *meforshim* explain that a mother should be mindful and aware of where she may be needed. The focus is on being aware of — not to micromanage — our children's lives. This awareness is an intellectual activity. It means noting who our children's friends are, what they enjoy, and how their days are spent so we can choose the best course of action to help them. If something concerns us and we react mindlessly, then we are responding from our own anxiety and not for our child's benefit. Once we notice an issue and sit with it, we can then plan how we can best influence a situation, and we have a chance of shepherding a better outcome.

There is another caveat that must be mentioned. Our goal is to help guide our children and give them the best chance we can at healthy influences. We want them to be spiritually focused and to fear and love Hashem. We cannot engage in activities that go against Hashem's will to ensure our children's spirituality. If we have concerns, we need to act only within the bounds of halachah. If we gossip about other families or are nasty to others because we want to protect our children, we are undermining the very value system we are trying to protect. Only through acting with Hashem's will in mind will we merit the help that Ovadiah's wife had in saving her children.

Staying Active

The end of the *pasuk* is also important in this regard. It says that the *eishes chayil* does not eat from the bread of laziness. She does not have others do for her what she can do for herself; she does not become indulgent but remains productive. By maintaining her independence and vitality, the *eishes chayil* can become proactive when necessary. Her attitude is confident, and she is solution-oriented rather than acting like a victim or a bystander as the drama of life plays out. Ovadiah's wife was able to approach the *navi* of Hashem, the leader of the generation, because she valued her role as an advocate for her children. She would not leave any stone unturned or give up and become despondent. She eschewed the bread of laziness when she approached Elisha to save her children.

> The *eishes chayil* is solution-oriented, not a bystander as the drama of life plays out.

Shlomo HaMelech is leaving us with this final appeal to value ourselves. He is reminding us that our children and husband need us. They will not be as successful without us there to help them. We need to value our hard work as a goal. We need to recognize that if we do not continue to grow as people, we are harming ourselves and our families. If we continually try to progress and look for areas of improvement in ourselves and in our family life, we create the legacy that will be the subject of the next four *pesukim*.

Summary

"She monitors the ways of her household." — צוֹפִיָּה הֲלִיכוֹת בֵּיתָהּ
The wife of Ovadiah — אִשְׁתּוֹ שֶׁל עוֹבַדְיָה

From the Pasuk We Learn

The *eishes chayil* is aware of what her children are doing and experiencing. She is particularly mindful of her children's modesty and honesty. This role takes energy. The *eishes chayil* stays active and independent; she values hard work so that she can continue influencing her family as she ages.

From the Midrash We Learn

The wife of Ovadiah went to the *navi* to beg him to save her sons from being forced into slavery to repay debts. She did so because she realized that her sons would be influenced by their new master to serve idols. We learn from her actions that we must advocate for our children spiritually — in addition to physically and emotionally. Part of our role is monitoring which people will influence our children.

Practical Steps

1. Be aware of children's spiritual, physical, and emotional health.

    A. Spiritually: Notice the areas of modesty and honesty and those that influence our children.
    B. Physically: Monitor diet, sleep, and exercise.
    C. Emotionally: Check in with how they are feeling and how they connect with others.

2. Don't critique all behavior or respond in the heat of the moment. Be mindful to what is happening and plan how and when to get involved.

3. Don't allow others to do for us what we can do for ourselves (unless it is a kindness or necessary, for any reason, to accept the help).
4. Limit the quantity of food and length of our meals so we remain healthy and have time and energy to be active.
5. Try to learn and practice new skills and to have new experiences every year.
6. Express appreciation for the ability to work hard at a task.
7. If we have concerns, we need to act only within the bounds of halachah. No gossip or aggressive, entitled behavior will help our children.
8. Stay solution-oriented: What can I do that will improve this situation?
9. Value ourselves. Our children and husbands need us and will not be successful without us.

Questions

Self-Growth

1. How do I incorporate the values of honesty and modesty into my life? How do these qualities empower me in my spiritual growth?
2. What things can I do for myself that I ask others to do for me?
3. What is my attitude to mealtime? What healthy eating habits do I want to incorporate into my routine?
4. What is the balance between self-care and overindulgence?
5. What new skill can I learn in the next five years? In what way can I impact my community in that time?
6. What are some spiritual goals I can work toward that require me to go outside my comfort zone?
7. How do I support daily growth without burnout?

As Wives and Mothers

8. When do I ask my husband to do things that I am capable of doing myself because of laziness?
9. Are these things helpful to the relationship with my husband because they are appreciated acts of service that increase our love for one another?
10. How do I provide guidance to my children that will be accepted?
11. When should I get involved, and when should I allow my children to work things out on their own?
12. How do I make honesty and modesty traits that are valued by all the children in my family?
13. Who and what influences my children? Do I need to provide them with any support because of these circumstances?

Teaching Our Daughters

14. How can I help my daughter appreciate modesty in today's world, when there is so much freedom and judgment regarding the issue?

CHAPTER 21

Results: Recognition

קָמוּ בָנֶיהָ וַיְאַשְּׁרוּהָ בַּעְלָהּ וַיְהַלְלָהּ.

*Her children rise up and praise her;
her husband also, and he extols her.*

Peshat

This *pasuk* begins the last section of the *Eishes Chayil* poem. Let's review:

- In the first section of the poem, we were introduced to the *eishes chayil* and the three foundations of her greatness: partnership, trust, and kindness.
- In the second section, we discovered the activities in which she participates.
- In the third section, we learned about her different roles and the quality of her relationships.

In this fourth and final section, we focus on the results of her lifetime of service. We look at the praise and acknowledgment that she receives from her children and her husband.

The *pasuk* begins with the praise of her children. The *pasuk* says *her children rise up*, and *they* praise her. While it is clear that the children are rising, it is unclear who is praising the *eishes chayil*. Is it the children themselves or is it others observing the children?

Both explanations are correct.

There are many people who are famous and are highly praised in popular venues. A person may be called renowned or famous by a newspaper, but that does not make the praise accurate; the praise may be self-promotional or have been written in exchange for advertising dollars. It is hard to judge whether a person is truly great because so much can be faked or changed for popular consumption.[314] The *pasuk* tells us:

קָמוּ בָנֶיהָ וַיְאַשְּׁרוּהָ.

A woman's children rise up and they praise her.

When the *eishes chayil*'s children rise as great people themselves, people can legitimately praise her.

> It is rare for a child to succeed without a mother's encouragement, support, and education.

Every person has free will. A child with a great mother may make bad choices and defy his mother's upbringing. However, it is very rare for a child to succeed in a world that goes against moral values without a mother encouraging, supporting, and clarifying the correct priorities.

Rabbi Yehoshua ben Chanania was a scholar in Mishnaic times who was a student of the great Rabbi Yochanan ben Zakai. Rabbi Yochanan ben Zakai praise him by saying:

אַשְׁרֵי יוֹלַדְתּוֹ.[315]

Praised is the one who gave birth to him.

Rabbi Yochanan ben Zakai attributes Rabbi Yehoshua ben Chanania's greatness in Torah learning to his mother. When Rabbi Yehoshua ben

---

314 Rabbi Shlomo Sofer, *Introduction to Ksav Sofer on the Torah*, quoted in *Sefer Eishes Chayil*, p. 267.
315 *Avos* 2:8.

Chanania was still a baby, his mother wanted him to grow up to be a Torah scholar.[316] She brought his bassinet to the house of learning so that he would be immersed in the sounds and sights of Torah from a young age. Later, when Rabbi Yehoshua ben Chanania achieved greatness, his teachers understood that his accomplishments stemmed from the actions of his mother.

A Child's Praise

Children themselves know whom to thank when they see their own accomplishments. For this reason, the *pasuk* can also be interpreted to mean that the children rise up to praise their mother.[317] The children realize that their mother is the one responsible for helping them become who they are. The children, and the children alone, can praise their mother because they know how much work she invested and how much this was her deepest desire for them. They also know that as a woman who valued modesty, their mother would never have bragged about her efforts to her neighbors. Her children now must rise to praise her.

Our matriarch Leah expressed what every mother feels when she has children. Leah named Zilpah's second son and was responsible for his upbringing. She called this second son Asher because, in her words:

אִשְּׁרוּנִי בָּנוֹת.[318]

Girls will praise me [that I'm happy].

Leah was expressing that a mother's greatest joy is to watch her children succeed. Children know that. When children rise spiritually and "get up," they know they are making their mother happy, and they tell others that this was what she wanted for them.

וַיְאַשְּׁרוּהָ.

They praise her [they deemed her happy].

---

316 *Talmud Yerushalmi, Yevamos* 8b.
317 Malbim, *Mishlei* 31:28.
318 *Bereishis* 30:13.

The children's praise of their mother in the first half of the *pasuk* precedes the praise of her husband, which is described in the second half of the *pasuk*. A woman's children reflect her greatness, as she is the primary person who has influenced their development.[319] By the time he marries, a man has already matured and has had numerous people who impacted his life, including his own mother. While his wife is an integral support in his quest for his spiritual greatness, all of his accomplishments cannot be laid at his wife's feet. For this reason, the children's praise precedes the husband's words.

A Husband's Thanks

While the children recognize that their mother is happy and feels blessed by what they do, only a husband can truly praise her, וַיְהַלְלָהּ, for what she has done. Only a husband knows about his wife's sleepless nights, how she turned down the promotion so she could be home when their kids got off the bus, or how much she hated playing Candy Land but did so anyway. He knows how much she invested, the tears she cried, and the hours she spent trying to help her children. The children may appreciate a mother, but only a husband really knows what went into making her dreams for them a reality.

> Only a husband knows about his wife's sleepless nights or how she turned down the promotion so she could be home when their kids got off the bus.

Midrash – The Shunamis

"Her sons rise up and praised her."	קָמוּ בָנֶיהָ וַיְאַשְּׁרוּהָ
This is the Shunamis	זוֹ שׁוּנַמִּית
Who is called a great woman.	שֶׁנִּקְרֵאת אִשָּׁה גְדוֹלָה

---

319 Rabbi Shlomo Sofer, Introduction to *Ksav Sofer* on the Torah, quoted in *Sefer Eishes Chayil*, p. 267.

And for what reason?	וּמִפְּנֵי מָה
Because she supported Elisha	מִפְּנֵי שֶׁהֶחֱזִיקָה בֶּאֱלִישָׁע
with food.	לֶאֱכֹל

The Midrash illustrates with a story from the *Navi* how a woman can merit having children who rise to praise her.

During the reign of the kings of Yisroel and Yehudah, Elisha was the prominent *navi* who would travel around Eretz Yisroel to inspire the nation. There was an older childless couple who lived comfortably in Shunam.[320] The wife in this prestigious couple recognized Elisha's stature and wanted to host him in a way that was befitting a man of his caliber. She had a room built separate from their own living quarters so that Elisha could relax comfortably and modestly, as was appropriate for a man of G-d. She wanted to honor this great man and his Torah.

Elisha was touched by her thoughtfulness and asked what she needed. She told him that she had no needs. Elisha's servant informed his master that the couple was childless so that Elisha could bless them with a son. A child was indeed born, and he worked alongside his father on their farm. One day, the child was helping his father in the field and fell ill with a headache. The father quickly brought him home, whereupon he died.

The boy's poor mother rushed to Elisha and begged him to do something, anything, to give her back her son. Elisha came to the house, performed a great miracle, and the child came back to life.

Values and Rewards

This story, when read literally, is described by the *pasuk* being discussed. A child who had died arose, and his mother could be called happy. How blessed she was that her child was alive! Her husband could praise her because he went from being childless to being a father and then when he thought he lost his child, the child was revived.

---

320 *Melachim II*, 4:8–31.

However, the Midrash has never been superficial in its connection to the *pasuk,* and it is not in this instance either. We must examine the deeper implications of the story to clarify our understanding of the *pasuk.*

What prompted Elisha to bless the woman? Why did she and her husband merit a miracle to have a child, and then another to have that child be revived?

The woman from Shunam merited these miracles because of her value system. She wanted to honor Torah and have its presence in her home. She did not invite Elisha into her home as a charm for having children. In fact, she denied having any needs when Elisha explicitly asked her what she wanted, and it was only through the intervention of Elisha's servant that the blessing was given. This woman truly valued Torah study and wanted to honor the Torah and those who learned it in the best way possible without any ulterior motive. Because of her desire to give honor to the Torah, she merited miracles to have a child who could carry on these values.

It was only because of the values of the Shunamite woman and the sacrifices she made as a result of her ideals that she merited happiness and miracles. This same message applies to all mothers. Every woman has values for which she sacrifices. When a woman extends herself for something greater than herself, she merits having children who will extend her legacy. Her efforts will give her children the strength and conviction to become great and will save them from both physical and spiritual danger. A mother's aspirations for her children ultimately create the people they become.

> A mother's aspirations for her children ultimately create the people they later become.

Getting Practical: Communicating Values

The *pasuk* and the Midrash are teaching us that our children's achievements will occur, in part, because of our purposeful efforts. Specifically, what we value and how we communicate what we value mold what our children cherish. If we value Torah, or if we make kindness a priority, our children will learn that from us. If we value careers, clothing, or money, that message will be clear to them as well. Our children pick up on our value system, and it shapes who they become.

Talking the Talk

Meriting having children who understand what we value and having our husband praise us for our efforts requires planning and thought. At times, we may have conflicting values. We want our children to be kind but we also want them not to be taken advantage of. We may value *tzedakah*, yet we are also frugal with our money. If we want to make sure that our children know our priorities and our values, we must be intentional with how we communicate them and pass them on.

What are our family's bumper stickers?

At a parenting workshop I attended, the presenter asked each of us to think about our core values using a technique called "family bumper stickers." Every family, she explained, needs to be able to articulate their family's most important values in clear language. With slogans and direct communication, it is more likely that children will remember and absorb the values being taught. No two families should be alike. Bumper stickers help children embrace their individuality and recognize their membership in their family as important. It helps the family set joint goals and set their principles as more important than the personality of any individual member.

Walking the Walk

Equally important, the values we espouse must match our behavior. The woman from Shunam was so excited about Torah and honoring scholars that she remodeled her house to make it happen. Had she spoken about Torah but not taken any action, she would never have merited a child who shared her values.

Our children will glean what we believe from what we do more than from what we say. They will notice when we get excited, when we sacrifice, when we make a party, and what we talk about at dinner as gauges for what should be important to them. If we want our children to make our spiritual ideals their own, we have to walk the walk as well as talk the talk. Unless we use our time and resources for the values we hold dearest to our hearts — the values of Torah, *yiras Shamayim*, and mitzvos — our children will not take these values seriously and be willing to make choices based on them.

> If we want our children to make our spiritual ideals their own, we have to walk the walk as well as talk the talk.

Of course, our children have free will and will ultimately make their own choices in their relationship with Hashem. We cannot take responsibility for another person's decisions. However, we play a large role in giving our children the opportunity to love Torah and mitzvos by providing guidance, purposeful teaching of our values, and living according to our ideals. When we communicate our beliefs and live in accordance with what those ideals demand, we can look forward to our children recognizing what makes us happy and anticipate the appreciation our spouse will feel for helping to create this reality.

Summary

"Her children rise up and praise her."   קָמוּ בָנֶיהָ וַיְאַשְּׁרוּהָ
The Shunamis   שׁוּנַמִּית

From the Pasuk We Learn

The children of the *eishes chayil* become great. The children themselves and other people acknowledge that the children's achievements are because of the influence of their mother and her pride in their accomplishments. The *eishes chayil*'s husband, who is the only one who knows what sacrifices his wife has made, praises her commitment and lets others know what she did for them.

From the Midrash We Learn

The woman from Shunam extended herself to host and honor Elisha because he was a Torah scholar. As a result, when her son was stricken with illness, he was brought back to life by Elisha. From her we learn that our value system creates a legacy for our children. When we live in accordance with our values and make them a part of our everyday life, they become a source of strength to our children.

Practical Steps

1. Acknowledge to ourselves and others what our mothers have contributed to our development.
2. Be intentional with how we communicate to our children what choices and values of theirs would give us pride (preferably before they are faced with decisions).
3. Find ways to demonstrate our value system in our choices and behaviors.
4. Act in accordance with the values we preach or minimize our preaching of those values.
5. Create a list of agreed upon "family bumper stickers" with our family.

Questions

Self-Growth

1. What are my top five values? Are they generic or do they represent my unique qualities?
2. What are my three favorite slogans that represent my values?
3. How do I demonstrate these values in my actions and choices?
4. Are there any inconsistencies between my values and my behavior?

As Wives and Mothers

5. What are the top two values of my marriage? Are they generic or do they represent my unique qualities?
6. What are four slogans that represent my family's values?
7. How do I, and my family as a whole, demonstrate these values in our actions and choices?
8. Is there flexibility in my family values to allow for differences in personality and temperament?
9. Do I articulate my family values to my children?
10. Do my children see that our family values are consistent with my behavior?
11. How do I let my children know what would make me proud?
12. How am I helping my children learn to make these values their own?

Teaching Our Daughters

13. How can I help my daughter develop as an individual within our family and make the family values her own?

CHAPTER 22

Results: Excellence

רַבּוֹת בָּנוֹת עָשׂוּ חָיִל וְאַתְּ עָלִית עַל כֻּלָּנָה.

*Many girls have done valiantly,
but you excelled above them all.*

Peshat

This *pasuk* contains the praise that the *eishes chayil*'s husband and children share directly with her. In it, the family lauds their mother's greatness, compare her to other righteous women, and then proclaim that her superior qualities surpass those of all other women.

This comparison seems out of place.

In a spiritual journey, a woman cannot compete with anyone but herself. Every woman has her own unique qualities, challenges, and gifts; no two women can be compared to one another. Rather than elevating the *eishes chayil*, this comparison seems to debase her achievements by

> In a spiritual journey, a woman cannot compete with anyone except herself.

turning them into a contest of sorts that can be judged by people, not G-d.

To address this issue, the *Midrash Eliyahu* explains that this *pasuk* is putting the greatness of the *eishes chayil* in context so that her achievements can be better appreciated.[321] People are often judged by the people around them. When a person is surrounded by mediocrity, it is easy to be viewed as exceptional. As an example, the Torah says about Noach:

תָּמִים הָיָה בְּדֹרֹתָיו.[322]
He was perfect in his generation.

Rashi explains that there can be two ways to interpret this verse.[323] Either Noach was great despite the evil of those around him, or Noach was objectively average but was only considered great because of the people with whom he was being compared. Similarly, many women may seem spiritual and enlightened but only because they are being compared to obviously flawed individuals. When an *eishes chayil* is present, it is obvious that she is inarguably great, while all other women are recognized for who they truly are in comparison.

Comparing the Eishes Chayil

In this *pasuk*, the family is also praising another aspect of the *eishes chayil*:

רַבּוֹת בָּנוֹת עָשׂוּ חָיִל.
Many girls [collectively] have achieved chayil.

There are many women who have one or two exceptional qualities.[324] One woman may be kind, another wise, while another may be industrious. To achieve *chayil* and to embody all of the praiseworthy attributes mentioned in the poem, women need to band together with

---

321 *Midrash Eliyahu*, quoted in *Sefer Eishes Chayil*, p. 273.
322 *Bereishis* 6:9.
323 Rashi, ibid.
324 Vilna Gaon, *Barak HaShachar* quoted in *Sefer Eishes Chayil*, p. 274.

other women who have different strengths so that every important characteristic is represented. In contrast, the *eishes chayil* is exceptional in her own right and has all of the qualities mentioned herself.

There is a final message contained in this *pasuk*. The family of the *eishes chayil* recognizes that many women can become great because they have the time and energy to focus on themselves and their own growth. Without whining children and an imperfect husband, it is easy to stay calm and pleasant. The *eishes chayil* chose to live deeply involved with others, with her family and her community. As a result of her constant interactions with others, she had many more opportunities to be challenged and to make mistakes. What made the *eishes chayil* great was that she became great while helping others to become great as well.

> Without whining children and an imperfect husband, it is easy to stay calm and pleasant.

This *pasuk* seems to be describing the objective quality of the *eishes chayil* but does not appear to contain lessons that can help women in their own growth. To understand what we can learn from this *pasuk*, we need to turn to the Midrash.

Midrash – Rus

"Many girls have done valiantly,	רַבּוֹת בָּנוֹת עָשׂוּ חָיִל
but you excelled above them all."	וְאַתְּ עָלִית עַל כֻּלָּנָה
This is Rus the Moabite,	זוֹ רוּת הַמּוֹאֲבִיָּה
who entered under the wings of the Shechinah.	שֶׁנִּכְנְסָה תַּחַת כַּנְפֵי הַשְּׁכִינָה

The Midrash on the next three *pesukim* describes one woman — Rus — who was the great-grandmother of Dovid and the great-great-grandmother of Shlomo, the author of *Eishes Chayil*. Rus was not merely a woman who Shlomo learned about as part of his family lore. He grew up with his great-great grandmother and was impacted by her greatness.[325] He devotes the

---

325 *Midrash Zuta, Rus* 1:1.

last three *pesukim* of *Eishes Chayil*, where children praise their mother, to praise the matriarch of his family.

The Midrash seems to imply that Rus is greater than all the other women who have been described by the Midrash so far.[326] It would follow that Rus is better than Sarah, who was a greater prophet than Avrohom; greater than Rivka, who partnered with Yitzchok in creating a home reminiscent of Sarah; and greater than Rochel and Leah, who mothered the twelve tribes.

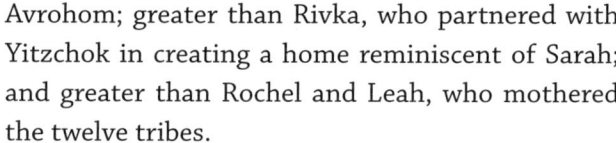
It seems unlikely that Shlomo HaMelech is judging Rus to be more perfect than the *Imahos*.

It seems unlikely that Shlomo HaMelech is judging Rus to be more perfect than the *Imahos*.

The Midrash answers this question by giving a reason for this distinction. The Midrash says that Rus entered under the wings of the *Shechinah*. In Talmudic language, this phrase means that Rus did a complete *teshuvah* that was accepted by Hashem. According to this logic, Rus did a more complete *teshuvah* than any of the other matriarchs because she converted. However, there was another woman mentioned by the Midrash who also converted: Basya, the adoptive mother of Moshe, was also a convert who repented for her past misdeeds and, according to our Midrash, entered Gan Eden alive! Why is Rus better than her?

The Greatness of Rus

If we look at the life story of Rus, it is far different from that of any other woman who preceded her in the Midrash. Rus was born a princess in the very wealthy and powerful kingdom of Moav. When she was a young woman, a family from Judea moved to her area, and she and her sister Orpah were courted by a pair of wealthy brothers. Rus married Machlon, and Orpah married Kilyon, Machlon's brother. They lived happily for a few short years until both husbands died, leaving the two widows childless and penniless.

---

326   Rav Chaim Palagi, *Chaim Tovim*, quoted in *Sefer Eishes Chayil*, p. 275.

Despite the tragedy, the young women did not return to their father's home and way of life. They chose to live with their mother-in-law, Naomi, who herself had been widowed, to help her survive in the foreign land. Naomi, poor and bereft of her family, decided instead to return to her ancestral homeland of Eretz Yisroel. She had planned to return alone, but her daughters-in-law insisted on accompanying her on her journey to Eretz Yisroel.

On the journey, Naomi exhorted the young widows to remain in Moav because she knew that their lives would be filled with suffering were they to come with her. Her daughters-in-law were young women and could marry again in the land of Moav. This would not be the case for them were they to live in Eretz Yisroel. There is a *pasuk* in the Torah that states:

לֹא יָבֹא עַמּוֹנִי וּמוֹאָבִי בִּקְהַל ה'.[327]
A converted Moabite or Ammonite may not marry anyone Jewish.

At the time, the halachah regarding to whom this statement referred had not yet been definitively decided. The masculine term used in the *pasuk* for the Moavi is ambiguous in the Hebrew language. It could mean that only Jewish women could not marry Moavi men, or it could mean that both Jewish men and Jewish women were prohibited from marrying individuals from the land of Moav.

One of the widows, Orpah, heeded Naomi's advice and returned to her father's home. Rus chose to continue the journey with her mother-in-law. Eretz Yisroel was an agricultural society; property was transferred through inheritance. Being a single woman in this society was a recipe for poverty and loneliness. Despite Naomi's warning, Rus not only chose to accompany Naomi to Eretz Yisroel, she also chose to convert and accept upon herself the consequences of that decision. She acknowledged that if she violated Torah law, she could be punished or killed.

Life for Rus and her mother-in-law Naomi was as difficult as Naomi predicted. The pair returned to Eretz Yisroel without any means of financial support. However, Eretz Yisroel was ruled by Torah laws that

---

327 *Devarim* 23:4.

provided food for the poor. The poor could gather in the fields and pick whatever gleanings had been left on the ground by the harvesters. They could harvest food for themselves from a corner of the field set aside by the property owner. Rus, a former princess, offered to do the work on behalf of Naomi and herself. Rus happened upon a field owned by Boaz, Naomi's cousin, and began her harvest.

Initially, her reception was harsh. When Boaz, the owner, inquired about her, his foreman's response was unwelcoming:

נַעֲרָה מוֹאֲבִיָּה הִיא הַשָּׁבָה עִם נָעֳמִי מִשְּׂדֵה מוֹאָב.[328]

She is a Moabite girl who returned with Naomi from the fields of Moav.

The foreman saw Rus not as a convert or as a kind woman, but merely as a stranger and a Moabite woman.

Boaz saw past the label and recognized Rus's sacrifice and greatness. He invited her to return to his field on subsequent days so that Rus would feel comfortable and accepted on his land and would not feel compelled to search for a new field from which to collect. Boaz also offered Rus a hot meal from the rations he provided his workers. Rus questioned Boaz's offer and kindness. Until then, she had been rejected and isolated from others in the community.

Boaz explained to Rus what made her unique. Boaz noted that Rus devoted herself to her mother-in-law after Rus's husband died; he recognized that she abandoned her family and her homeland and traveled to a foreign country. Boaz understood the depths of Rus's kindness and blessed her that Hashem should repay her for her good deeds since, as is quoted in the Midrash, she came to rest under the protection of Hashem.

This phrase that Boaz used is quoted by the Midrash, and it means that Rus converted with no ulterior motives. She had sacrificed everything she had to become close to Hashem. Only Hashem could repay this monumental sacrifice, since Rus had made herself completely reliant on Him with no hope of help from any person and no visible means of support.

---

328 *Rus* 2:6.

It is for this reason that Rus is greater than all other women.[329] To the casual observer, Rus was merely a Moabite woman of low status. People did not respect her nor what she did. In truth, Rus surpassed everyone else. She consciously sacrificed everything she had and chose a life of poverty to connect to Hashem. She chose to live as an outcast and be close to Hashem rather than to be popular but far from Him. While the other women mentioned in the Midrash had been willing to sacrifice for Hashem, only Rus truly had to abandon everything she had to live the life she felt was right.

> While the other women mentioned in the Midrash had been willing to sacrifice for Hashem, only Rus abandoned everything to live the life she felt was right.

Getting Practical: Excellence in Marriage

At first glance, the *pasuk* seems to be encouraging competition, but, on further reflection we understand that this is not the case. The *pasuk* is describing the objective greatness of the *eishes chayil* and how she embodies all the positive attributes written about her. The Midrash helps us focus on how to become objectively great in the eyes of Hashem.

What makes a woman great according to the Midrash? Rus was exalted above other women even though there were many in Eretz Yisroel who would not accept her as a Jew. It was not important how others judged her; her main priority was to do what was right. Rus did not need to convert. It was not a sin for her to remain in Moav and marry a Moavi man. She chose to sacrifice what she had to become close to Hashem, and she did so even though her choice made her a social outcast.

To become great, we must be able to make choices based on our relationship with Hashem rather than out of concern for what others think. We must be willing to give up our money and prestige for a chance to bring Hashem into our lives.

> To become great, we must be able to make choices based on our relationship with Hashem rather than out of concern for what others think.

---

329 Rav Chaim Palagi, *Chaim Tovim*, quoted in *Sefer Eishes Chayil*, p. 275.

At times, sacrificing for Hashem and having communal esteem are one and the same. Learning in yeshiva or teaching Torah requires sacrifice and commitment and is considered a virtuous religious calling. That extra support helps in the tough times.

Sometimes the choice is not easy. Sometimes doing the right thing will make our friends think less of us. The challenge is to do the right thing anyway.

There was a man with a long beard and big black yarmulke who had a reputation of being an outstanding Torah scholar. He had a teenage daughter who was rejecting the lifestyle with which she had been raised. The child was in desperate need of love and acceptance but was also flouting the boundaries her father set. One day, she came downstairs dressed in an outfit that clearly showed she was rebelling against the standards of other girls her age in the neighborhood. It was not vulgar, but it was not acceptable in the culture of her community. She looked at her father to see his reaction. Would he reject her or accept who she was in this new identity? With other children, or on other days, this father may have sent his child back to her room to change. He recognized that she was testing his love to see if he could accept her without reservations. He walked over to his daughter and invited her to go for a stroll with him around the block.

In the community's eyes, the father was allowing his child to reject Hashem and His Torah. He was not being a strong parent who stood up for the values in which he believed. Only he knew why he made his choices. He could not share his reasoning with others. His act of love was a sacrifice to do what Hashem wanted, even though his neighbors would judge him poorly.

Greatness comes from doing Hashem's will rather than ours or our neighbors. If we make choices so that we are popular with others, we will never be able to accomplish what Rus did. If we make choices guided only by what Hashem wants, even when it is hard, then we can truly become exceptional. We will be guaranteed, like Boaz promised Rus, to be cared for directly by Hashem and be brought under His protection.

Summary

"Many daughters have done valiantly, but you excelled above them all."
Rus the Moabite

רַבּוֹת בָּנוֹת עָשׂוּ חָיִל
וְאַתְּ עָלִית עַל כֻּלָּנָה
רוּת הַמּוֹאֲבִיָּה

From the Pasuk We Learn

The *eishes chayil* is objectively great in all the areas that have been listed thus far. She is not dependent on others to supplement her strengths, nor does she rely on being compared to those who are weaker so she can seem strong in comparison.

From the Midrash We Learn

Rus was described as the ultimate *eishes chayil* by Shlomo, her direct descendant, because of what she sacrificed to reach her spiritual heights. She was willing to leave a life of luxury for a life of poverty, a life of power for a life of loneliness. From her we learn that true greatness will only come if we focus on leading a life based on what Hashem wants rather than trying to be popular.

Practical Steps

1. If we are not yet an *eishes chayil* and have not yet perfected each aspect of our character, we can join with others whose strengths complement ours so together we can become greater.
2. Make choices based on our relationship with Hashem rather than out of concern about what others think.

Questions

Self-Growth

1. How do I resist the urge to compare myself to other women?
2. How do I resist judging the behavior of others?
3. What are the characteristics of my friends who help me do the right thing based on what I know is right?
4. How do I determine when and how I should make choices that are at odds with my community?

As Wives and Mothers

5. How do I define what is correct for me to do as a mother and wife?
6. Are there any communal expectations that are healthy for my role as mother and wife? Are there any unhealthy expectations?

Teaching Our Daughters

7. How do I help my daughter recognize when she is feeling peer pressure and then make choices based on her own internal compass as to what is right?

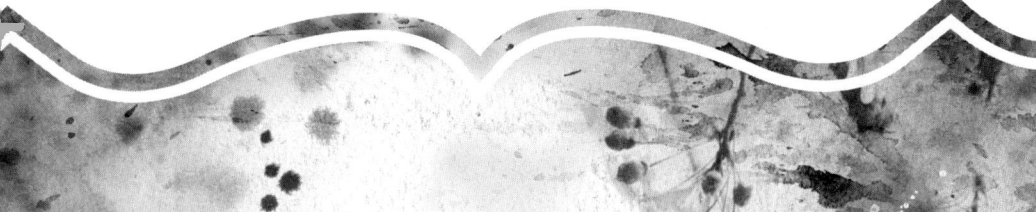

CHAPTER 23

Results: True Beauty and True Rewards

שֶׁקֶר הַחֵן וְהֶבֶל הַיּוֹפִי אִשָּׁה יִרְאַת ה׳ הִיא תִתְהַלָּל.

Grace is deceitful, and beauty is vain, but a woman who fears Hashem, she shall be praised.

תְּנוּ לָהּ מִפְּרִי יָדֶיהָ וִיהַלְלוּהָ בַשְּׁעָרִים מַעֲשֶׂיהָ.

Give her of the fruit of her hands, and let her be praised in the gates by her deeds.

Peshat

The last two *pesukim* of *Eishes Chayil* are joined in the same phrase in the Midrash and are also thematically related to each other. For these reasons, we will learn them as one unit. These *pesukim* outline for what the *eishes chayil* should be praised and what her reward should be.

שֶׁקֶר הַחֵן וְהֶבֶל הַיֹּפִי אִשָּׁה יִרְאַת ה' הִיא תִתְהַלָּל.
Grace is deceitful, and beauty is vain,
but a woman who fears G-d, she shall be praised.

The first *pasuk* describes why a woman should be praised and why she should not be praised. *Chein* — a woman's charm, and *yofi* — her appearance, are superficial and meaningless. Praising a woman for those qualities is insulting. Praising her character, on the other hand, is complementary and thoughtful.

Charm and Beauty

Charm and beauty have a number of things in common. Both depend on another person to judge them.³³⁰ In different cultures, different features are considered beautiful. A woman who is considered obese in one society is called beautiful in another, while a thin western model would be considered emaciated in another culture.

> Charm and beauty both depend on another person to judge them.

Not only are beauty and charm in the eyes of the beholder, but they also are completely a gift from Hashem.³³¹ Yirmiyahu the prophet said:

אַל יִתְהַלֵּל חָכָם בְּחָכְמָתוֹ וְאַל יִתְהַלֵּל הַגִּבּוֹר בִּגְבוּרָתוֹ.³³²
A wise man shouldn't praise himself for his wisdom, a
strong person shouldn't praise himself for his strength.

Charm and beauty, like wisdom and strength, are genetically determined conditions. Hashem chooses who is beautiful and who is charming. A person can try to manipulate her beauty and charm to conform to what other people want, but, aside from plastic surgery, her basic looks are hers from birth. Praising a woman for her looks is as meaningless as praising her for her shoe size. It is effectively

---

330   *Midrash Eliyahu,* quoted in *Sefer Eishes Chayil,* p. 279.
331   Rav Chaim Vital, *Etz Hadaas HaTov,* quoted in *Sefer Eishes Chayil,* p. 282.
332   *Yirmiyahu* 9:22.

noticing something about her that does not reflect her efforts and/or personality.

Finally, beauty and charm fade with time. A woman is at the height of her good looks early in life, after which the body naturally begins to lose its physical strength and attractiveness. It is foolish to make beauty a goal for which to aspire; it is irrational to praise something that is a given in youth by virtue of one's existence and then lost, despite any reasonable efforts.

> It is foolish to praise something that is a given in youth and then lost, despite reasonable efforts.

Instead, the *pasuk* encourages us to praise a woman who fears Hashem. Chazal tell us:

הַכֹּל בִּידֵי שָׁמַיִם חוּץ מִיִּרְאַת שָׁמַיִם.[333]
Everything is in the hands of G-d, excluding fear of G-d.

Hashem determines a person's station in life — whether he will be rich or poor, smart or stupid, beautiful or ugly; all circumstances of one's life are predestined. The only thing a woman controls is her choice between good and bad, given her conditions. No matter what her lot in life is, there are always choices a woman can make that can either stem from her fear of G-d or from her lack of concern for Him. Of all the things that a woman has in life, only her choices can be praised because they are the only things that can be considered her own.

This raises an important question. Rivkah was mentioned in the Torah as being beautiful.[334] Rochel was also described as being attractive.[335] Yerushalayim is said to have nine out of the ten measures of beauty in the world.[336] In addition, it is written in the Torah:

וַנֹּחַ מָצָא חֵן בְּעֵינֵי ה׳.[337]
And Noach found grace in the eyes of Hashem.

---

333 *Talmud Bavli, Berachos* 33b.
334 *Bereishis* 24:16.
335 *Bereishis* 29:17.
336 *Talmud Bavli, Kiddushin* 49b.
337 *Bereishis* 6:8.

If the Torah views beauty and grace as positive attributes, why is Shlomo calling them false and vain?

Rabbi Chaim Mordechai Katz, *zt"l*, the *rosh yeshiva* of Telz-Cleveland, interprets this *pasuk* in a novel way.[338] He notes that every character trait can be used for bad and good. If a woman has fear of G-d, then even her beauty and grace can be praised, for she will use them in Hashem's service rather than as a goal unto themselves. Without fear of G-d, beauty and grace are meaningless. With them, they can be praiseworthy.

The *Meam Loez* explains that the Torah is not praising grace and beauty as positive qualities with no qualification; it is praising these traits because of what they represent.[339] Every woman who is described as beautiful in the Torah had challenges because of her beauty; Sarah was put in Pharaoh's harem, and Dinah had to be concealed in a box to be protected from Esav's eyes. Beauty is a challenge that forces a woman to make choices. Will she use it to attract attention, or will she use it appropriately in her Divine service? The women in the Torah chose, because of their fear of G-d, to maintain their modesty and act according to Hashem's will. They are praised as possessing beauty not because beauty was a goal for them but because they were forced to make challenging choices because of it.

> When we die after 120 years, our children won't say, "Mommy had the nicest shades of lip gloss."

In modern society, beauty and charm are considered very important in both secular and religious societies. This *pasuk* is asking us to realize that our overinvestment of time and money in our looks to be beautiful and charming as an end goal is strange. When we die after 120 years, our children won't say, "Mommy had the nicest shades of lip gloss." Our husband won't comment at our funeral about the highlights in our *sheitel*. He will mention what

---

338   Rav Chaim Mordechai Katz, *Beer M'Chokek* quoted in *Sefer Eishes Chayil*, p. 298.
339   *Meam Loez*, Mishlei 31:31.

kind of character we had: were we patient, kind, or thoughtful? That's what will be praised, and we should therefore make these things our priority.

A Mother's Care

The last *pasuk* in the poem continues this theme.

תְּנוּ לָהּ מִפְּרִי יָדֶיהָ.
Give her of the fruit of her hands.

According to the Ibn Ezra, the husband of the *eishes chayil* is saying to his children, "Acknowledge to your mother what she has done! It's all because of her! She has spent her life doing so much for you and for others. Her choices and hard work should be celebrated."[340]

The selfless devotion of a wife and mother bears fruit and shows results in the lives of everyone and everything she touches. A mother does not have the same opportunity to do mitzvos and learn the Torah as her children. A wife who encourages her husband to become a Torah scholar by providing a warm, nurturing home and supporting his endeavors is somewhat limited in what she can accomplish. Sending her children to yeshiva to learn Torah takes dedication and sacrifice. Chazal ask:

נָשִׁים בְּמַאי זָכְיָן?[341]
Women — with what do they merit [the World to Come]?

How can a woman who has devoted herself to advancing her children and her husband's Torah study and not her own ever hope to merit *Olam Haba* — her eternal reward? Men are obligated in learning Torah with no time limitations. Women do not have this obligation; to support that burden, they give up their own opportunities for prayer in quiet concentration and for learning Torah.

---

340   Ibn Ezra, *Mishlei* 31:31.
341   *Talmud Bavli, Berachos* 17a.

The answer Chazal give is that their reward comes from bringing their children to learn Torah, sending their husbands out to the *batei midrash* (the study halls) to learn, and by waiting up for them to get home.

Everything that men or children accomplish is laid at the feet of the *eishes chayil*. She gets the rewards for every mitzvah performed and for every word of Torah learned.

One of the foremost scholars in the Mishnah was Rabbi Akiva. As was mentioned earlier, when he was forty, he was still an ignorant shepherd tending flock at the home of Kalba Savua. Rochel, the daughter of Kalba Savua, noticed his potential and married him even though it meant being disowned by her wealthy father and beginning a life of poverty. She encouraged Akiva to leave their home for twelve years — and then for another twelve years — so he could learn from the greatest scholars of their generation. In the meantime, Rochel lived a life of privation to allow her husband to learn. After twenty-four years of intense study, Rabbi Akiva returned home accompanied by thousands of his students.

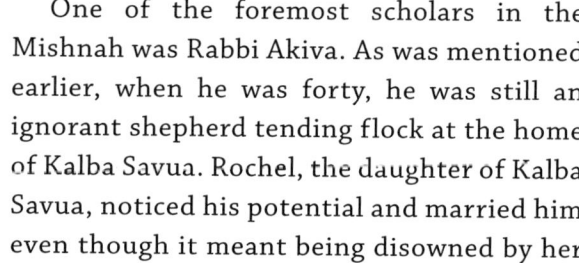

How can a woman who has devoted herself to advancing the Torah learning and spiritual pursuits of her husband and children, at the expense of her own, ever hope to merit *Olam Haba* — an eternal reward?

Dressed in her rags, Rochel went to meet him. She pushed through the crowd and fell at her husband's feet. Rabbi Akiva's students tried to push Rochel away from their prominent master. Rabbi Akiva stopped his students and told them:

שֶׁלִּי וְשֶׁלָּכֶם שֶׁלָּה הוּא.342

What is mine and what is yours is all hers.

Rabbi Akiva was informing his students (and all husbands and children for all time) that their accomplishments are the fruits of the *eishes chayil's* hands.

---

342 *Talmud Bavli, Nedarim* 50a.

RESULTS: TRUE BEAUTY AND TRUE REWARDS 345

The *pasuk* ends:

וִיהַלְלוּהָ בַשְּׁעָרִים מַעֲשֶׂיהָ.
And let her be praised in the gates by her deeds.

A woman might be concerned that the praise and acknowledgement that she receives from her children will lessen her eternal reward. This is not the case. Each of her many positive actions will come to the gates of Heaven and demand that she receive her due reward. Every one of our actions in this world will be remembered; all of our work for ourselves and our families accompanies us to the World to Come and serves as our advocate during our final judgment.

The Midrash powerfully describes what a meaningful impact a woman can have on generations when she abandons false priorities and makes Hashem and his Torah the centerpiece of her life. It describes Rus, the great-great grandmother of Shlomo HaMelech, the author of *Eishes Chayil*.

"Grace is deceitful, and beauty is vain."	שֶׁקֶר הַחֵן וְהֶבֶל הַיֹּפִי
Who left her mother,	שֶׁהִנִּיחָה אִמָּהּ
her ancestors, and her affluence,	וַאֲבוֹתֶיהָ וְעָשְׁרָהּ
and came with her mother-in-law	וּבָאָה עִם חֲמוֹתָהּ
and accepted all of the mitzvos:	וְקִבְּלָה כָּל הַמִּצְוֹת
the boundaries of Shabbos, as it says,	תְּחוּם שַׁבָּת
"Where you go I will go"	"אֶל-אֲשֶׁר תֵּלְכִי אֵלֵךְ"
(Rus 1:16);	(רות א:טז)
the prohibition of being alone with a man,	אִסּוּר יִחוּד עִם אִישׁ
"And where you lodge, I will lodge";	"וּבַאֲשֶׁר תָּלִינִי אָלִין" (שם)
the 613 mitzvos,	תרי"ג מִצְוֹת
"Your people shall be my people";	"עַמֵּךְ עַמִּי" (שם)

עֲבוֹדָה זָרָה	idolatry,
"וֵאלֹהַיִךְ אֱלֹהָי" (שם)	"And your G-d is my G-d";
אַרְבַּע מִיתוֹת בֵּית דִּין	the four deaths of the Jewish court,
"בַּאֲשֶׁר תָּמוּתִי אָמוּת" (שם)	"Wherever you shall die, I will die."
לְפִיכָךְ זָכְתָה	Accordingly, she merited
וְיָצָא מִמֶּנָּה דָּוִד	that Dovid came from her,
שֶׁרִוָּה לְהקב"ה	who pleased Hashem
בְּשִׁירוֹת וְתִשְׁבָּחוֹת	with songs and praises.
לְפִיכָךְ נֶאֱמַר	Therefore, it is written,
"תְּנוּ לָהּ, מִפְּרִי יָדֶיהָ	"Give her of the fruits of her hands,
וִיהַלְלוּהָ בַשְּׁעָרִים מַעֲשֶׂיהָ"	and let her be praised in the gates by her deeds."

The Midrash describes what Rus chose, the implications of her choice, and the reward for her decisions.

The Midrash begins by reminding us that Rus was a princess who abandoned a life of comfort, wealth, and security. She chose to accompany her mother-in-law, a poor, old, brokenhearted widow, in her move to the Land of Israel so that she could convert to Judaism. When Rus accepted the mitzvos, she did so with full awareness of the lifestyle she was choosing. She acknowledged that she was willing to keep Shabbos, abandon idolatry, and limit her interactions with men as was required by the Torah. She even accepted upon herself the punishments that would come if she violated the most serious commandments. She wanted a life where she could die because she believed in the truth of the One and Eternal G-d, and she rejected the futility of her former life.

> When Rus accepted the mitzvos, she did so with full awareness of the lifestyle she was choosing.

The Midrash tells us that her reward was repaid to her in this world as well as the next. Her reward in this world was a great-grandchild (Dovid HaMelech) who wrote the book of *Tehillim*.

The Link between Rus, Dovid, and Tehillim

The Midrash links Rus's singular devotion to Hashem and her great-grandchild's composition of *Tehillim*. What is the connection between these two things, and why does the Midrash not include more about the life of the great Dovid HaMelech, the author of *Tehillim*? Dovid was a great Torah scholar who was the head of the Sanhedrin, the king of a united nation, and the person who laid the foundation for the construction of the Holy Temple. Why are the fruits of Rus's choices only the book of poetry and prayers that Dovid wrote?

To understand the connection, we must explore why Dovid wrote *Tehillim* and the significance of *Tehillim* to the Jewish People.

Dovid was very much like his great-grandmother Rus. The *pasuk* tells us about him:

וַיִּשְׁאַל דָּוִד בַּה׳.[343]

Dovid asked G-d.

When Dovid had a difficult choice, he sought guidance from Hashem. Like Rus, Dovid was constantly trying to seek a connection with Hashem; like Rus, he was most concerned about fulfilling Hashem's will, even if the choice made his life more difficult; and, like Rus, he considered his wealth and his stature as vanities and instead tried to live his life according to Hashem's will.

Tehillim was Dovid's vehicle for connecting to Hashem, no matter his circumstance. In his psalms and songs, he begs for help and sings of Hashem's glory in the world. His words, according to the Malbim, encompass every experience of life.[344] The deepest emotions of the human heart: joy, sadness, confusion, satisfaction, sorrow, triumph, and failure, can be found in its words and pages. There is a chapter of *Tehillim* for every emotion and experience in Dovid HaMelech's life.

> *Tehillim* was Dovid's vehicle for connecting to Hashem, no matter his circumstance.

Connecting to Hashem

Rus sought an authentic connection to Hashem and had a great-grandson who could — and did — authentically

---

343 *Shmuel I* 23:2.
344 Malbim, introduction to *Tehillim*.

connect to Hashem through every emotion and event that he experienced. He expressed his connection in *Sefer Tehillim*, which he wrote, according to the *Midrash Tehillim*, with all Jews in mind for eternity.³⁴⁵ The book of *Tehillim*, which was inspired by Rus, became a source of connection and solace for the nation she joined. There is a chapter of *Tehillim* to help any Jew at any time, whenever he is in need. Dovid, through writing *Tehillim*, helped every Jew make choices like the ones Rus made, based on the truth of Torah and not on that which was הֶבֶל and שֶׁקֶר, false and fleeting things. When every Jew connects to Hashem, Hashem can be found in the midst of the Jewish People. Thus, it was Rus the convert — who so wanted to connect to Hashem — who helped lead an entire nation to do just that.

> The book of *Tehillim*, which was inspired by Rus, became a source of connection and solace for the nation she joined.

There is another link between the actions of Rus and how they led her great-grandson to compose the songs and praises that comprise *Tehillim*.

Rus was a convert. Converts introduce a unique perspective to the nation.³⁴⁶ We see the gift that converts bring from the story of Yisro, the father-in-law of Moshe, who was also a convert to Judaism.

Moshe said about him:

וְהָיִיתָ לָּנוּ לְעֵינָיִם.³⁴⁷

And you will be for us as eyes.

Yisro was not literally the eyes of the Jewish nation, nor was he responsible for charting their journey in the desert. The verse means that, as a convert, he changed the perspective of the Jewish people by helping the nation see G-d and His miracles in a different light. What the nation accepted as normal, Yisro viewed as special and unique. He

---

345 *Midrash Tehillim* 18.
346 Chaim Markowitz, my brother, quoting a *shiur* by Rav Dovid Feinstein, *shlita*. http://nefesh-chaim.blogspot.com/2006/06/uniqueness-of-geirim.html.
347 *Bamidbar* 10:31.

helped those around him realize that they, too, were witnessing the greatness of Hashem, and they should not accept their life as mundane.

Rus, as a convert, provided this gift of an enlightened perspective to her great-grandson. She helped him notice that what others assume to be happenstance is an abundance of miracles and gifts from Hashem. With this outlook, Dovid HaMelech was able to write *Sefer Tehillim* because he noticed Hashem's presence while others ignored the miracles of daily life. Rus taught Dovid HaMelech to appreciate all that Hashem had done for him and to seek His help whenever he felt lost. Although Dovid was the one who authored the *Tehillim*, Rus was the spirit behind the psalms.

Getting Practical: True Rewards and True Beauty in Marriage

As we conclude *Eishes Chayil*, we can leave with the wonderful perspective that Rus has provided.

There are things in life that are true, and there are things that are a waste of our precious time and energy. That which stems from our *yiras Hashem*, our fear of G-d, will be a source of pleasure in this world and the next. That which does not, is false and worthless.

> Living a life that is spiritually focused can be scary. While we can accept sacrifices for ourselves, how will our children react?

Living a life that is spiritually focused can be scary. While we can accept sacrifices for ourselves, how will our children react? Will they feel disadvantaged and disheartened by the life they are expected to lead?

The life of Rus was marked by struggle. Her choices were not easy ones, and her children saw how they impacted her. Her willingness to sacrifice everything in this world for a relationship with an all-powerful G-d did not lead to children who felt deprived and depressed. Quite the opposite. Rus's great-grandson Dovid was in touch with the full array of emotions and saw the beauty in this world with clarity and joy. He felt the nurturing care of Hashem through even the most challenging moments of life. Rus's resolve gave her great-grandson strength and hope.

A Gift for Our Children

We can give our children the gift of having a relationship with Hashem and teach them that it serves as a comfort and support during challenging times. To give our children this gift, we must choose what is everlasting instead of being drawn to what is temporary. As was stated in the *pasuk*, charm and beauty are false; they are merely tools to people-please. When we work with the mind-set that we need beauty and charm to be successful, we are always going to be hustling after someone's approval. We will always be one step away from not being connected enough, technologically advanced enough, or young enough to have worth in the eyes of those who are looking to judge.

Instead of descending into the world of competition and chaos, we can choose to make decisions based on what Hashem wants from us. This elevates us from constant stress to a life in which we can appreciate beauty and feel good about what we have done.

It is true that accepting the premise of a G-d-centered world comes with some sacrifices. We become responsible for our behaviors and cannot blame them on others. We cannot become absorbed in mindless activities and superficial thinking. We have to police ourselves and live within boundaries and limits. However, these responsibilities are far better than living in a world in which we are dependent on unreliable people and ideas for approval.

Teaching Connection

It is possible to live our lives connected to Hashem without our children having that strength themselves. As mothers, we need to introduce our children to Hashem's love when challenges arise in their lives. One day, my son came home from school angry and frustrated. He felt his teacher was unfair, the administration was ignoring the issue at hand, and he was stuck with an assignment that he could not do. We discussed the various options and realized that there really was no good solution to his dilemma. At that point, I asked him if we could daven to Hashem for help and calmness. He was shocked.

"What about doing our efforts, our *hishtadlus*? Maybe we should try more? You can't just daven to take away your problems!"

I asked him if there was anything he or I could do to change the situation. He realized that we had exhausted all possibilities. We said a *tefillah* together asking Hashem for help and insight into what we could do. My son's body relaxed, and we moved onto another topic. I cannot guarantee that my son will remember this lesson, but I planted a seed that will hopefully bear fruit in a more joyous and spiritually enriched life.

By living lives of meaning and worth, we give our children hope and strength.

When we live a life with Hashem as its driving force, we will have transformed it into a life filled with significance. When we communicate this message to our family, we will also have the satisfaction of knowing that our children, grandchildren, and even great-grandchildren can lead rich and meaningful lives.

Dovid, the great-grandson of Rus, never felt alone. He always knew that he could reach out to Hashem for help and that Hashem was with him in all circumstances. Similarly, when we live lives of meaning and worth and teach our children to do so also, our children will know G-d in a personal way, and they will trust Him. Their lives will be devoted to making their world a better place. Like Dovid HaMelech, they will always have Someone they can turn to, no matter what.

Seeing this joyous life that our children, with Hashem's help, will lead — that is the fruit of our labors. It will accompany us to the highest gates in the World to Come and continue to elevate our souls long after we leave this earth.

Summary

"Grace is deceitful, and beauty is vain." שֶׁקֶר הַחֵן וְהֶבֶל הַיֹּפִי
"Give her of the fruit of her hands, תְּנוּ לָהּ מִפְּרִי יָדֶיהָ
and let her be praised in the gates by her deeds. וִיהַלְלוּהָ בַשְּׁעָרִים מַעֲשֶׂיהָ
Rus the Moabite רוּת הַמּוֹאֲבִיָּה

From the Pasuk We Learn

The *eishes chayil* is praised for the choices she made rather than for the gifts with which she had been born. She invested her time and gave her family the wherewithal to grow spiritually. This commitment placed limits on what she individually could gain. Her children's accomplishments are counted as her merits for her eternal reward.

From the Midrash We Learn

Rus abandoned her false priorities to convert to Judaism and live by the Torah. She strove to have an authentic connection to Hashem throughout her life. In this merit, she had a great-grandson, Dovid, who connected to Hashem through all of his experiences, good and bad. He, in turn, helped the Jewish People connect to Hashem for all time using the songs and psalms he wrote in *Sefer Tehillim*.

Practical Steps

1. Choose to praise those things that require moral courage rather than things that a person is born with (intelligence, beauty, etc.).
2. Use *Tehillim* as a means to connect to Hashem during every experience and through every emotion: joy, sadness, confusion, satisfaction, sorrow, triumph, and failure.
3. Seek a fresh perspective from those who share our values but have different backgrounds.
4. For wives and mothers: encourage husbands and children to learn Torah and do mitzvos.

Results: True Beauty and True Rewards

5. Make decisions based on what Hashem wants from us rather than peer pressure.
6. Reinforce Hashem's love for us to ourselves and to our children when challenges arise in life.
7. Daven when a challenge arises over which we have no control and let go of the results knowing Hashem is caring for us.

Questions

Self-Growth

1. What is the difference between people-pleasing and being gracious and kind? How does it feel different, and what impact does it have on me?
2. How can I differentiate between self-care and appropriate grooming, and being overly involved in beauty and fashion?
3. How do I craft praise for behavior that reflects good choices rather than traits that are inborn?
4. How can I use *Tehillim* as a means to connect to Hashem during every experience of life and through every emotion: joy, sadness, confusion, satisfaction, sorrow, triumph, and failure?
5. How can I use the tools of prayer during challenges over which I have no control?
6. How can I appropriately seek a fresh perspective and broaden my awareness from those who share my values but have a different background?

As Wives and Mothers

7. How can I appreciate the importance of my sacrifices for the growth of my children and husband?
8. How can I encourage my husband and children to learn Torah and do mitzvos?
9. What individual spiritual growth do I need to maintain so that I can help others?
10. How can I achieve spiritual connection to Hashem through *Tehillim*?
11. How do I give my children an awareness that Hashem is caring for them?

Teaching Our Daughters

12. How do I teach my daughter of her inherent worth so she does not feel less important than friends or siblings who may have different talents?

13. Do I ever give the unwitting message that I consider my sons more important than my daughters and/or that I value their strengths more?

14. How do I instill a love and appreciation of *Tehillim* in my daughter?

Conclusion

This book has been a journey. I hope that through its pages you have come to know yourself and your strengths (and weaknesses) better. I hope that the journey has been a joyous one, full of acceptance and growth.

This journey can never end. Every day that we awaken we have the chance to make new choices that will make this new day the greatest we have had yet.

The words of *Eishes Chayil* — and the women who have taught us so much through the Midrash — can continue to serve as a beacon and guide to help us become the women we are meant to be.

May we all continue to grow *me'chayil el chayil*, from strength to strength.

Appendix A:
Glossary of Jewish Names and Terms

Achav: King Ahab from the kingdom of Israel.
Adoniah: King David's son.
Aharon HaKohen: Aaron the High Priest.
akeres ha-bayis: the matriarch of a home.
Aleph-Beis: the Hebrew alphabet.
Amram: Moses' father.
ani: a poor person.
Asher: one of Jacob and Leah's sons.
Avinu: lit., "our father"; a respectful title for the Patriarchs.
avodas Hashem: the service of G-d.
Avos: the Patriarchs: Abraham, Isaac, and Jacob; the Mishnah tractate of that name.
Avrohom: Abraham.
Avshalom: Absalom, King David's third son who rebelled.
azus panim: audacity; chutzpah.
baalas chessed: a doer of kind deeds.
Bais Yaakov: a genericized name for Orthodox Jewish elementary and secondary schools for girls.

Bamidbar: the Book of Numbers.

bas: the daughter of.

BasSheva: Bathsheba, King David's wife.

Basya/Bisya: Bithia, Moses' foster mother.

batei knesios: synagogues.

batei midrash: religious study halls.

beis din: rabbinical court.

Beis Hamikdash: the Holy Temple in Jerusalem.

beis midrash: lit., house of study; the study hall of a yeshiva or synagogue.

Betzalel: the chief craftsman and architect of the Tabernacle.

bikur cholim: the mitzvah of visiting the sick.

Bilhah: Jacob's wife.

Binyamin: Benjamin, Jacob's youngest son.

challah: a special braided bread eaten on Sabbath and holidays.

Channah: Hannah, Samuel's mother.

chayil: valor; strength.

Chazal: an acronym for the Hebrew phrase "*chachamim zichronam l'verachah*" ("Our Sages, may their memories be blessed"), referring to Jewish sages from the Mishnaic through the Talmudic time periods.

chein: grace.

chessed: acts of kindness.

chaburah: a learning group.

chevrah: a social group.

chochmah/chochmas: knowledge (of).

chametz: leavened bread.

Chumash: the Five Books of Moses.

Daf Yomi: a system of studying the entire Gemara during a cycle of seven-and-a-half years, at the rate of one page per day.

daven/davening: pray(ing).

derech eretz: manners and polite behavior.

Devarim: the Book of Deuteronomy.

Dinah: Jacob and Leah's daughter, who was kidnapped by Shechem.

Divrei HaYamim: the Book of Chronicles.

Glossary of Jewish Names and Terms

Dovid HaMelech: King David.

dvar Torah: a Torah thought.

Eichah: the Book of Lamentations.

Esav: Esau, Isaac and Rebecca's son; Jacob's twin.

eishes chayil: woman of valor.

Elisha: one of the prophets in the Bible.

Elisheva: Aaron's wife.

Eliyahu: Elijah the prophet.

emes: truth.

evyon: a desperately poor person.

Gan Eden: the Garden of Eden; paradise.

Gemara: commentary and discussion of the Mishnah (together they comprise the Talmud).

Hagar: the wife of Abraham, Sarah's handmaid.

HaKadosh Baruch Hu: the Holy One, Blessed be He.

halachah: Jewish law.

Har Sinai: Mt. Sinai.

Hashem: G-d.

haskamah: an approbation.

hishtadlus: effort.

Imahos: the Matriarchs: Sarah, Rebecca, Leah, Rachel.

Imeinu: lit., our mother; a respectful title for the Matriarchs.

Izevel: Jezebel, the wife of King Ahab.

Kiddush: the blessing recited over wine before Sabbath and holiday meals.

Koheles: the Book of Ecclesiastes.

Kohen/Kohanim: member(s) of the priestly tribe, descendant(s) of Aaron.

korbanos: sacrificial offerings in the Temple.

kumzitz(es): Informal choir(s).

kvetch: complain.

Lavan: Laban, the father of Leah and Rachel.

Leah: the wife of Jacob.

Levi: the third son of Jacob and Leah.

Levi/Leviim: descendants of Levi who served in the Holy Temple in a helping role.

Maariv: the evening prayer service.

malchus: kingdom.

mashal: parable.

Midrash: a compendium of rabbinic homiletic interpretations of phrases in *Tanach*.

meforshim: commentators on religious texts.

Menashe: the eldest son of Joseph.

middos: character traits (generally refer to positive character traits).

Minchah: the afternoon prayer service.

Mishkan: the Tabernacle in the desert.

Mishlei: Proverbs.

Mishnah: the codified Oral Law, redacted in the third century.

mishnah/mishnayos: specific paragraph(s) from the Mishnah.

Mitzrayim: Egypt.

mitzvah/mitzvos: Torah commandments, biblically or rabbinically based.

Mashiach: the Messiah.

Moav: the kingdom of Moab located east of the Jordan River.

Modeh Ani: the prayer recited upon awakening.

Moshe: Moses.

mussar: Jewish ethics and morals.

nachas: pride.

Navi/navi: one of the Books of the Prophets; a prophet.

nazir: a person who takes a Nazarite vow to abstain from grapes and grape derivatives, to avoid becoming ritually impure, and to refrain from cutting hair.

nevi'os: prophetesses.

Nissan: the first month of the Jewish year.

Noach: Noah.

Nosson: Nathan the Prophet, who lived during King David's time.

ohz: strength.

Orpah: Ruth's sister.

Ovadiah: a prophet in the kingdom of Israel.

Pesach: Passover.

peshat: the literal meaning of a text.

Glossary of Jewish Names and Terms   361

pesukim: Biblical verses.

Plishti: a Philistine.

Plishtim: the Philistines.

Rabbeinu: our teacher.

Rachav: Rahab from Jericho.

rav: a rabbi.

rebbe: a teacher.

rebbetzin: a rabbi's wife.

Rechavam: King Rehoboam, King Solomon's son.

rechilus: gossip.

Reuven: Reuben, Jacob and Leah's eldest son.

Rivkah: Rebecca, Isaac's wife.

Rochel: Rachel, Jacob's wife.

Rosh Hashanah: the Jewish New Year and Day of Judgment; the first and second days of the month of Tishrei.

Rus: Ruth, King David's great-grandmother.

Sanhedrin: the Jewish Supreme Court during the times of the Temple in Jerusalem.

sefer/sefarim: Jewish book(s).

semichah: rabbinic ordination.

Shabbos: the holy Sabbath; Friday night and Saturday.

Shacharis: the morning prayer service.

mishlo'ach manos: gifts of food sent on the holiday of Purim; colloquially termed "*shalach manos.*"

shalom bayis: domestic harmony.

Shas: an acronym for *Shishah Sedarim*, or six sections; the whole Talmud.

Shaul: King Saul, the first king of Israel.

Shavuos: a holiday celebrated on the sixth day of the month of Sivan commemorating the giving of the Torah at Mt. Sinai.

Shechinah: Divine spirit.

sheitel: a wig.

shevet/shevatim: tribe(s), sons of Jacob.

shidduch: a prospective suitor.

Shimon: Simon, Jacob and Leah's second son.
Shimshon: Samson, the leader who fought the Philistines.
shiur/shiurim: Torah class(es).
shivah: lit., seven; the week of mourning.
Shlomo HaMelech: King Solomon, King David and Bathsheba's son.
Shemos: the Book of Exodus.
Shmuel: Samuel, judge and prophet who anointed King Saul and King David.
shofet/shoftim: judge(s); leaders of Israel after the initial conquest of Canaan.
Talmud: the basic corpus of Jewish law (200 BCE–500 CE) consisting of the Mishnah and Gemara.
Tanach: the twenty-four books of the Jewish Bible.
techias hameisim: revival of the dead.
tefillah/tefillos: prayer(s).
tefillin: phylacteries.
Tehillim: Psalms, written by King David.
tzaddik/tzaddikim: righteous man/men.
tzaddekes: a righteous woman.
tzedakah: charity.
tznius: modesty.
Yaakov: Jacob, Isaac and Rebecca's son.
yarmulke: head covering for Jewish men.
yased: a tent peg.
Yehoram: Jehoram, King of Israel.
Yehoshua: Joshua, who led the Jewish People into Canaan.
Yehudah: Judah, Jacob and Leah's fourth son.
Yericho: Jericho.
Yerushalayim: Jerusalem.
Yeshayah: Isaiah the Prophet.
yiras Hashem: fear of G-d.
yiras Shamayim: fear of Heaven.
Yirmiyahu: Jeremiah, who was a prophet during the time of the destruction of the first Temple.
Yishmael: Ishmael, Abraham and Hagar's son.

Yisro: Jethro, Moses' father-in-law.

Yissachar: Issachar, Jacob and Leah's fifth son.

Yitzchok: Isaac, Abraham and Sarah's son.

Yoav: Joab, King David's general.

Yocheved: Jochebed, Moses' mother.

Yom Tov: a Jewish holiday.

Yonah: Jonah, who gave prophecy to the people of Nineveh.

Yosef HaTzaddik: Joseph the Righteous, Jacob and Rachel's eldest son.

zt"l: pronounced "zatsal"; an acronym for *"zecher tzaddik l'verachah"* ("May the memory of the righteous be a blessing").

zechus: merit.

zerizah: a woman who acts promptly and enthusiastically.

Zevulun: Jacob and Leah's sixth son.

Zilpah: Jacob's wife, Leah's handmaid.

Appendix B:
Personalities and Sources

Akeidas Yitzchok — Commentary written by Rabbi Yitzchok Arama (c. 1420–1494), one of the leading rabbis in fifteenth-century Spain

Avos — Tractate in Mishnah, *Seder Nezikin*

Baalei HaTosafos — Commentary on the Talmud by the Tosafists of the twelfth and thirteenth centuries (France/Germany)

Balanson, Rav Asher — *Rosh kollel/posek,* Yeshiva Ohr Yerushalayim

Bamidbar — Book of Numbers (Bible)

Bamidbar Rabbah — Midrash on the Book of Numbers

Barak HaShachar — Written by the Vilna Gaon, Rav Eliyahu ben Shlomo Zalman (1720–1797). He is often referred to by his acronym, the "Gra." He was the leader of the non-Chassidic community in Eastern Europe.

Be'er M'Chokek — Written by Rav Chaim Mordechai Katz (1894–1964), *rosh yeshiva* of Telz-Cleveland

Bereishis — Book of Genesis (Bible)

Bereishis Rabbah — Midrash on the Book of Genesis

Bigdei Mordechai — Written by Rav Mordechai Yafe Shlesinger of Chug Chasam Sofer

Chaim Tovim — Written by Rav Chaim Palagi (1788–1869), rabbi and author of *sefarim* in Turkey

Chanoch L'Naar — Written by Rabbi Shmuel Shaul Siriro, a sixteenth-century *chacham* from Morocco

PERSONALITIES AND SOURCES 365

Chiddushei Agados — Explanation of Aggadic portions of Talmud written by the Maharal, Rav Yehudah Loewe ben Bezalel (1526–1609), leader in Jewish thought and Chief Rabbi of Moravia, Posen, and Prague

Chovos Halevavos — *Duties of the Heart*, written by Rabbeinu Bachaya ben Yosef Ibn Pekudah in Arabic in 1080 and translated to Hebrew by Judah ibn Tibbon in 1160

Daas Mikra — Series of biblical commentary published by the Rav Kook Institute

Derech Hashem — Written by Rabbi Moshe Chaim Luzzato (1701–1746), rabbi, kabbalist, and philosopher from Italy and in later years, Eretz Yisroel

Devarim — Book of Deuteronomy (Bible)

Divrei HaYamim — Book of Chronicles

Eliyahu Rabbah — First section of Midrash in Tana Devei Eliyahu

Etz Hadaas HaTov — Written by Rav Chaim ben Yosef Vital (1542–1620), preeminent student of the Ari HaKadosh, kabbalist in Tzfas

Ha'amek Davar — Commentary on Torah written by the Netziv, Rav Naftali Tzvi Yehuda Berlin (1817–1893), *rosh yeshiva* in Volozhin, Lithuania

Hirsch, Rav Samson Raphael — Author of commentary on *Chumash* and leader of Frankfurt, Germany, community (1808–1888)

Ibn Ezra — Commentary on Torah written by Rav Avrohom Ibn Ezra (1089–1164); Spain

Imrei Meir — Rav Meir Tannenbaum

Introduction to Ksav Sofer — Written by Rabbi Shlomo Sofer. The Ksav Sofer was written by his father, Rav Avrohom Shmuel Binyomin Sofer of Pressburg (1815–1879). He was the grandson of the Chasam Sofer, Rav Moshe Sofer (1762–1839).

Kli Yakar — Classic commentary on the Torah, written by Rav Shlomo Ephraim Lunshitz (1550–1619), *rosh yeshiva* in Lemberg, rabbi of Prague

Kovetz Igaros — Compilation of correspondences and writings of Rav Avrohom Yeshaya Karelitz (1878–1953), also known as the Chazon Ish

Ksav V'Kabbalah — Written by Rabbi Yaakov Tzvi Mecklenburg (1785–1865), a German rabbi and scholar in the nineteenth century

Likutei Amarim — Written by Rav Tzadok HaKohen Rabinowitz of Lublin (1823–1900), a Chassidic scholar and philosopher

Likutei Sichos — Essays transcribed from public talks given by Rabbi Menachem Mendel Schneerson, the Lubavitcher Rebbe (1902–1994)

Malbim — Acronym for Rabbi Meir Leibush ben Yehiel Michel Wisser (1809–1879), and title of his commentaries on Tanach; Poland

Meam Loez — Twenty-three volume anthology of commentaries on books of *Tanach*, begun in Turkey in 1730 by Rabbi Yaakov Culi, originally written in Ladino; there were multiple authors over the years. The volumes were completed in Hebrew in Eretz Yisroel by Rav Shmuel Yerushalmi.

Midrash Eliyahu — Written by Rabbi Eliyahu Hakohen of Izmir (1650–1729)

Midrash Rabbah — Series of aggadic *midrashim* about the Torah

Midrash Tanchuma — Collection of *midrashim* on *Tanach* from teachings of the Talmudic sage, Rav Tanchuma bar Abba (fourth century)

Midrash Zuta — Collection of *midrashim*

Meiri — Commentary written by Menachem Meiri (1249–c. 1310), follower of the Rambam

Melachim I — Kings I (Prophets)

Melachim II — Kings II (Prophets)

Metzudas Dovid — Commentary on concepts in *Tanach* written by Rabbi Dovid Altschuler and completed by his son Rav Yechiel Hillel Altschuler in the seventeenth century

Metzudas Tzion — Commentary with the translations for difficult words in *Tanach* written by Rabbi Dovid Altschuler and completed by his son Rav Yechiel Hillel Altschuler in the seventeenth century

Mishlei — Book of Proverbs

Mishneh Torah — Code of Jewish Law, written by the Rambam, acronym for Rav Moshe ben Maimon (1135–1204)

Nebenzahl, HaRav Avigdor — Contemporary *rav* in the Old City of Yerushalayim

Nishmat Haim — Commentary written by Rabbi Haim Messas of Morocco (1843–1903). *Sefer Nishmat Haim* was published by his son in Eretz Yisroel

Ohr HaChaim — Commentary on the Torah by Rav Chaim ben Attar (1696–1743), a famous kabbalist and scholar in Italy and later in Eretz Yisroel

Ohr HaChochmah — Commentary written by Rav Uri Shraga Feivel Dubienka, student of the Maggid of Mezeritsch

Peirush HaGra Al Sefer Yonah — Commentary on the Book of Yonah by the Vilna

Personalities and Sources

Gaon, Rav Eliyahu ben Shlomo Zalman (1720–1797), often referred to by his acronym, the "Gra." He was the leader of the non-Chassidic community in Eastern Europe

Pirkei D'Rabi Eliezer — Midrash composed by the school of the *Tanna* Rabbi Eliezer ben Hyrcanus (c. 100)

Rabbeinu Bachaya — Commentary on *Chumash* written by Rabbeinu Bachaya ben Asher (1263–1340); Spain

Radak — Acronym for Rav Dovid Kimchi (1160–1235), author of commentary on *Tanach*

Ralbag — Acronym for Rabbi Levi ben Gershon (1288–1344), also known as Gersonides, who wrote a commentary on *Tanach*

Ramad — Acronym for Rav Moshe Dovid Vally, a student of Rav Moshe Chaim Luzzato

Ramban — Rav Moshe ben Nachman (1194–1270), wrote commentary on Torah, Talmud, and halachah; Girona, Spain; Eretz Yisroel

Rashi — Rav Shlomo Yitzchaki (1040–1105), wrote comprehensive commentary of Torah and Talmud; France

Rus — Book of Ruth

Revid Yosef — Rabbi Aharon Yosef Templer; Peitrikow, Poland

Seder Olam — Ancient historical work quoted by the Gemara, attributed to the *Tanna* Rav Yosi ben Chalafta

Seforno — Commentary on the Torah written by Rav Ovadiah Sforno (1470–1550) of Italy

Shem MiShmuel — Nine-volume work on Torah and Chassidus written by Rav Shmuel Bornsztain (1855–1926), second Rebbe of Sochatchov

Shemos — Book of Exodus (Bible)

Shemos Rabbah — Midrash on the Book of Exodus

Shmuel I — Book of Samuel I (Prophets)

Shmuel II — Book of Samuel I (Prophets)

Shoftim — Book of Judges (Prophets)

Sichos Mussar — Collection of sermons given by Rav Chaim Shmuelevitz (1902–1978), *rosh yeshiva* of Mir Jerusalem

Siriro, Rav Shaul — Sixteenth-century *chacham* from Morocco

Talmud Bavli — Further rabbinic discussion of the text in the Mishnah, compiled in Babylonia between the third and sixth centuries

Talmud Yerushalmi — Talmud compiled in Eretz Yisroel between the second and fourth centuries

Tehillim — Book of Psalms

Torah Shleimah — Multivolume encyclopedia of *midrashim*, scholarly explanations, and essays written by Rabbi Menachem Kasher (1895-1983)

Toras Bar Nash — Rav Kalev Feivel Shlezinger (1828-1911), student of the Ksav Sofer

Vayikra — Book of Leviticus (Bible)

Weinberg, Rav Shmuel Yaakov — *rosh yeshiva* of Ner Yisroel Rabbinical College, Baltimore (1923-1999)

Yefas Toar — Commentary on Midrash written by Rabbi Shmuel ben Yitzchok Yafa (1525-1595)

Yehoshua — Book of Joshua (Prophets)

Yeshayah — Book of Isaiah (Prophets)

Yirmiyahu — Book of Jeremiah (Prophets)

Zohar HaKadosh — Collection of kabbalistic teachings attributed to Rabbi Shimon bar Yochai; a commentary on the Torah

Appendix C:
The Eishes Chayil Chaburah

Over the years, I have been fortunate to have a group of friends who have genuinely propelled my growth and introspection. When I learn by myself, I can ignore uncomfortable truths, get stuck when I am overwhelmed, or miss important insights that could have helped me. When I learn with a group, I am always amazed by how much more I gain.

I have written this book with summaries and guide questions in the hope that the book can be used by groups of women to study together and to gain support from one another.

The questions included in the book are powerful. Listening to how others have solved common issues can help everyone. To allow a strong group to form, rules have to be made, and expectations should be set. This ensures that everyone feels comfortable enough with each other and that it is safe to share personal thoughts. If I know that what I say at a *chaburah* will be shared with your husband, sister, or friend, I can't really share and learn.

I cannot establish the norms that your group should have. Each group meeting has to discuss what works for them. Establishing this before the *chaburah* begins meeting regularly helps set expectations and maintain *shalom*.

I have been a part of a number of groups over the years. Some had the same leader each week; others rotated leadership. Some were by invitation only; others were open to anyone who wanted to join.

I would encourage that the guidelines and the intention for the group be read aloud at the beginning of each week. In one group, we read our intention and guidelines at each meeting. No matter how much learning took place at a given session, the guidelines refocused me on why I was there. Alternatively, everyone can have her own copy of the expectations. The norms can also be posted in a prominent place for all to see.

It is not enough to have norms of behavior. Each group needs to discuss what should be done if the norms are violated. We all at times may talk over others, get distracted by a side conversation, or speak more harshly than we would have hoped. The best way to deal with inevitable mistakes is to find a light, humorous way to steer conversation back in the right direction. The norms should also be revisited on a regular basis to make sure they are working as intended for the group.

Establishing the Norms

In order for the norms to determine how a group operates, all the members of the group need to accept them. If one person dictates the rules to everyone else, people will leave. One way to generate acceptance is to get a consensus as to what people want to experience. First, everyone has to contribute her ideas. This can be done in a brainstorming session — no idea can be wrong. All ideas are welcome and will be considered. It is more important to gather the ideas than to discuss whether an idea is practical. Once everyone's ideas have been included, you can come to a consensus as a group on which norms you can all agree to. No one person should dominate this process.[348]

---

348 Based on "Norms put the 'Golden Rule' into practice for groups," by Joan Richardson. Tools for School. August/September 1999, National Staff Development Council.

Questions to Consider

Following are some questions to consider when setting up guidelines for your group. Most are taken from a tool published by the National Staff Development Council. There are no right or wrong answers to these reflective questions.

Time
1. How often and when are meetings?
2. Will we set a beginning and ending time?
3. Will we start and end on time?

Listening
4. How will we encourage listening?
5. How will we discourage interrupting?

Confidentiality
6. Who is invited to our meeting?
7. What can be said after the meeting to each other? To those outside the meeting?

Decision-Making
8. How will we make decisions?
9. Will we reach decisions by consensus?
10. How will we deal with conflicts?

Participation
11. How will we encourage everyone's participation?
12. How can everyone get a chance to participate?
13. Will we have an attendance policy?

Expectations
14. What do we expect from members?
15. Are there requirements for participation?
16. Who will lead the meetings?
17. Who sets the agenda for the meeting?
18. What is our policy for electronic devices (texts/calls) during the meeting?

Sample Norms

Here are some norms that I have seen for study groups and at work that may help you to develop norms that reflect your needs:

- Start and end on time.
- Avoid interrupting others when they are speaking.
- Speak respectfully and don't talk down to each other.
- Have a different facilitator and recorder for each meeting.
- Express disagreement with ideas, not individuals.
- Feel responsible to express differing opinions within the meeting.
- Maintain confidentiality regarding anything expressed during the meeting.
- Listen respectfully to all ideas.
- Conduct group business in front of the group.
- Avoid checking for — or sending — text messages or email messages during meetings.

Sample Chaburah Guidelines

I am including some of the guidelines from one of my groups, with the permission of the participants. In addition to the guidelines, we included our intention to focus our group during our learning.

The following was the weekly program of the chaburah:

1. Read guidelines.
2. Read goals.
3. Read intention.
4. Read from a *sefer*.
5. Discuss what has been read.

Guidelines

- The focus is on ourselves and how we are growing and dealing with daily life. There is no room for gossip and negativity.

- Topics should be discussed with sensitivity to all members of the group.
- Everyone contributes equally to the running of the discussion and group. We will take turns leading the group.
- Whatever is said should be kept confidential.
- Please allow others to share without interrupting.
- Please share what has worked for you or what you have read about without telling another person what to do.
- Once a month, we will evaluate as a group if there needs to be any changes.

Goals

In this group, we are working on the following ideas:

- *Ein od milvado* — All is from Hashem
- Anything we have is for our good
- We accept all people for who they are (including ourselves) and will not judge them
- Achieving *simchas hachayim*
- Unconditional love of others; less resentment, anger, expectation, and disdain
- To be giving and positive people
- To develop tools to work with challenges that will always be present
- We are looking to improve, not to be perfect

Intention

This group is a positive way to deal with everyday challenges. There will never be a time in life when we have no challenges. We are not here to eradicate challenges. We are here to develop effective and positive tools to use our challenges to come closer to Hashem. This will help us in all areas of our lives: with ourselves, our family, and everyone else we meet.

At this point, we read part of the *sefer* and then followed it with discussions of how the ideas in the *sefer* were applicable to our circumstances.

Making It Your Own

These guidelines worked for another group; they may not fit yours. When you decide as a group how to work together so everyone can get what she needs, you have created a powerful tool that will help you to grow and learn. Together, you will be able to go *me'chayil el chayil*, from strength to strength.

About the Author

Shira Hochheimer has been educating woman and girls of all ages for over fifteen years. She is passionate about empowering women to find more fulfillment in their lives by learning Torah. She was a *rebbetzin* in Rochester, New York, and is now in a leadership role for girls' Jewish education in Baltimore, Maryland. Her proudest accomplishment is her role as a wife and mother of five.